UML FOR
DEVELOPING KNOWLEDGE
MANAGEMENT SYSTEMS

Agent-Based Manufacturing and Control Systems: New Agile Manufacturing Solutions for Achieving Peak Performance
Massimo Paolucci and Roberto Sacile
ISBN: 1574443364

Curing the Patch Management Headache
Felicia M. Nicastro
ISBN: 0849328543

Cyber Crime Investigator's Field Guide, Second Edition
Bruce Middleton
ISBN: 0849327687

Disassembly Modeling for Assembly, Maintenance, Reuse and Recycling
A. J. D. Lambert and Surendra M. Gupta
ISBN: 1574443348

The Ethical Hack: A Framework for Business Value Penetration Testing
James S. Tiller
ISBN: 084931609X

Fundamentals of DSL Technology
Philip Golden, Herve Dedieu,
and Krista Jacobsen
ISBN: 0849319137

The HIPAA Program Reference Handbook
Ross Leo
ISBN: 0849322111

Implementing the IT Balanced Scorecard: Aligning IT with Corporate Strategy
Jessica Keyes
ISBN: 0849326214

Information Security Fundamentals
Thomas R. Peltier, Justin Peltier,
and John A. Blackley
ISBN: 0849319579

Information Security Management Handbook, Fifth Edition, Volume 2
Harold F. Tipton and Micki Krause
ISBN: 0849332109

Introduction to Management of Reverse Logistics and Closed Loop Supply Chain Processes
Donald F. Blumberg
ISBN: 1574443607

Maximizing ROI on Software Development
Vijay Sikka
ISBN: 0849323126

Mobile Computing Handbook
Imad Mahgoub and Mohammad Ilyas
ISBN: 0849319714

MPLS for Metropolitan Area Networks
Nam-Kee Tan
ISBN: 084932212X

Multimedia Security Handbook
Borko Furht and Darko Kirovski
ISBN: 0849327733

Network Design: Management and Technical Perspectives, Second Edition
Teresa C. Piliouras
ISBN: 0849316081

Network Security Technologies, Second Edition
Kwok T. Fung
ISBN: 0849330270

Outsourcing Software Development Offshore: Making It Work
Tandy Gold
ISBN: 0849319439

Quality Management Systems: A Handbook for Product Development Organizations
Vivek Nanda
ISBN: 1574443526

A Practical Guide to Security Assessments
Sudhanshu Kairab
ISBN: 0849317061

The Real-Time Enterprise
Dimitris N. Chorafas
ISBN: 0849327776

Software Testing and Continuous Quality Improvement, Second Edition
William E. Lewis
ISBN: 0849325242

Supply Chain Architecture: A Blueprint for Networking the Flow of Material, Information, and Cash
William T. Walker
ISBN: 1574443577

The Windows Serial Port Programming Handbook
Ying Bai
ISBN: 0849322138

UML FOR
DEVELOPING KNOWLEDGE
MANAGEMENT SYSTEMS

ANTHONY J. RHEM

CRC Press
Taylor & Francis Group
Boca Raton London New York

CRC Press is an imprint of the
Taylor & Francis Group, an **informa** business
AN AUERBACH BOOK

CRC Press
Taylor & Francis Group
6000 Broken Sound Parkway NW, Suite 300
Boca Raton, FL 33487-2742

First issued in paperback 2019

ISBN-13: 978-0-8493-2723-0 (hbk)
ISBN-13: 978-0-367-39171-3 (pbk)
Library of Congress Card Number 2005049920

Library of Congress Cataloging-in-Publication Data

Rhem, Anthony J.
    UML for developing knowledge management systems / Anthony J. Rhem.
        p. cm.
    Includes bibliographical references and index.
    ISBN 0-8493-2723-7
    1. Knowledge management--Data processing. 2. UML (Computer science) I. Title.

HD30.2.R52 2005
658.4'038'0285--dc22   2005049920

Visit the Taylor & Francis Web site at
http://www.taylorandfrancis.com

and the CRC Press Web site at
http://www.crcpress.com

Table of Contents

Appendices

Preface

This book came from a need to establish a way to capture knowledge that can be easily translated into a computer program. To do this I wanted to establish a methodology or framework that would assist me. This framework must be a reusable method for getting this done. However, what should this framework contain? The first thing I wanted to be able to figure out was if the domain I was analyzing was suitable for development into an expert system.

I ascertained that there had to be concrete steps one can take to determine this. In 1991, I wrote an article called "Evaluating Potential Expert System Applications." In this article I examined information from several articles taken from the *AI Magazine*, where I came across the "Checklist Approach." This approach examined key areas of a system under discussion (i.e., task, payoff, customer management, system designer, domain expert, and user). I was intrigued by this approach, and I thought it was solid enough to adopt; therefore, this became my first step within the framework.

The next step and subsequent steps within the framework centered on building an expert system and how best to do this. In an expert system, the value of the system is related directly to the quality of knowledge that is discovered and constructed in its knowledge base. Therefore, once the domain was determined, I had to understand what the knowledge of the domain was and what types of knowledge were contained in the domain. This thinking led me to discover that the knowledge of a particular domain could be vast and that I must decompose this knowledge into smaller subtasks to understand it and understand it in a way that software could be developed for a computer program to interpret it. So, the next step became to "Decompose the Knowledge."

Whether this knowledge was tacit or explicit or wherever in the organization it came from, I knew at this point that it was all about the knowledge. I wanted to peel back the covers and really understand the aspects of the knowledge that would be discovered. These aspects included determining any interdependencies, recognizing any knowledge patterns, determining if the knowledge contained any judgmental aspects or "fuzziness," determining if there are any conflicts between experts when discussing similar aspects of the same domain and resolving them, and finally constructing the knowledge base.

Over the next several years I started to apply these techniques in my consulting practice developing expert (knowledge-based) systems. In doing so, the framework started to evolve and some best practices came to the forefront. In 1997, this led me to write an article titled "Capturing and Managing Intellectual Capital." In this article, building knowledge architecture and understanding the knowledge acquisition tasks were examined more closely.

In 1998, I became interested in knowledge management (KM) and knowledge management systems (KMSs). After attending and participating in several seminars in this area, I knew that the framework I constructed to build expert systems could be adopted for KMSs as well. Because both deal with knowledge and its acquisition, it is this synergy that led me to believe that this framework can be adopted. From this realization in 2001, I wrote the white paper "A Framework for Knowledge Acquisition." In this white paper, I formally developed a grid to describe and lay out the knowledge acquisition framework. This framework later became the Rhem-KAF (Rhem Knowledge Acquisition Framework).

I continued to work and study in the area of KM and KMSs. I also began to perform more knowledge modeling of the knowledge I discovered in the domains I worked with. I used several industry tools to perform knowledge modeling, but it was through my work with UML (Unified Modeling Language) that I thought I could apply this standard notation to build knowledge models.

My work with UML supplied the notation for the framework and addressed the final concept of the framework, which is constructing the knowledge base. Because the knowledge base is the hub of the KMS as it pertains to tacit and other types of knowledge, UML became an essential ingredient to the capturing and modeling of knowledge.

This book, *UML for Developing Knowledge Management Systems*, is a culmination of years of experience, study, and application of the various concepts mentioned earlier. This book was developed to give the knowledge engineer a framework in which to identify the types of knowledge and where this knowledge exists in the organization, as well as a way in which to use a standard recognized notation to capture (i.e., model) knowledge to be used in a KMS.

Goals

The goals of this publication are as follows:

- Provide a basic understanding of KM and KMSs.
- Provide an understanding of the various types of knowledge.
- Present the concept of knowledge modeling and the basics of knowledge modeling.
- Present a general overview of UML, particularly those artifacts that will be involved directly in constructing knowledge models.
- Explain how to apply UML to construct the various types of knowledge models and how to recognize the types of knowledge that are suitable for modeling.
- Present and apply a framework in which to qualify and capture knowledge and construct knowledge models that will be used in KMS.

Audience

The audience of this publication consists of knowledge engineers, systems analysts, designers, developers, and researchers interested in understanding and building KMSs.

How to Use this Book

This publication will serve as a reference book for understanding the various types of knowledge, the concept of knowledge modeling, and, in particular, knowledge modeling with UML. This book also serves as a guide to quantifying, qualifying, understanding, and modeling knowledge by providing a reusable framework that can be adopted for KMS implementation.

Organization of this Book

- Introduction — Gives the reader a brief history of KM.
- Knowledge Management — Gives the reader insight into KM and KMSs. This chapter will discuss the focal point of KMSs, which is knowledge acquisition. This chapter consists of the following topics:
  - Knowledge value.
  - Knowledge-value tree.

- – Knowledge management systems.
- – Knowledge acquisition.
- – Knowledge acquisition process.
- – What is knowledge?
■ Types of Knowledge — Explores the various types of knowledge that can be uncovered through the course of knowledge discovery within a domain. The following are the types of knowledge that will be addressed:
- – Declarative.
- – Procedural.
- – Tacit.
- – Explicit.
- – Process knowledge.
- – Concept knowledge.
- – Case-based reasoning.
■ Knowledge Modeling — Gives the reader an overview of knowledge modeling. This will include the various types of models that can be constructed and explains the concepts behind the construction of each of the knowledge models being presented.
■ Unified Modeling Language (UML) — Overview of UML. This chapter focuses on UML artifacts that will be used to construct knowledge models. This chapter is not a definitive reference for the UML notation.
■ Knowledge Modeling with UML — Focuses on giving the reader knowledge on applying UML to model knowledge.
■ Defining your Knowledge Acquisition Framework — Provides definitive information on defining and applying the Knowledge Acquisition Framework. This chapter explains the aspects of the framework in a practical manner and applies it to a real-world case study.

Acknowledgments

I would like to acknowledge Dr. Larry Medsker and Dr. Jeffrey Schwartz whose work assisted me and my organization on the National Science Foundation–sponsored project to automate the framework described in this book. Their contributions to that project led to the refinement of the framework and served as the basis for information gathered as part of Chapter 12 and Chapter 15.

I would like to dedicate this book to my good friend, colleague, and mentor Bruce Barker. Bruce always told me, "this sounds like a great concept, just get it down on paper and we can sell it!" My friend, you are truly missed.

Chapter 1

Introduction

The concept of knowledge management (KM) has been around since the mid-1970s. There is evidence of this through the work of Dorothy Leonard-Barton who authored the case study of Chaparral Steel, which has had an effective KM strategy in place since the mid-1970s. This case study led to her research titled "Wellsprings of Knowledge — Building and Sustaining Sources of Innovation" (Harvard Business School Press, 1995). During the late 1970s, Everett Rogers of Stanford, through his work in the diffusion of innovation, and Thomas Allen of MIT, through his work in information and technology transfer, both contributed to how knowledge is produced, used, and diffused within organizations.

In the late 1970s, computer technology started to contribute greatly to the amount of available knowledge being produced through computer products and processes. Doug Engelbart's Augment ("augmenting human intelligence") introduced in 1978 was an early groupware or hypertext application, which interfaced with other applications and systems. Rob Acksyn and Don McCracken's Knowledge Management System (KMS), an open distributed hypermedia tool, predates the Internet by a decade, were two such examples.

By the mid-1980s, the importance of knowledge as a competitive asset began to gain momentum, although from an economic perspective it had yet to recognize knowledge as an asset. However, at this time most organizations were still lacking the strategies, methods, and procedures to quantify and manage knowledge as an asset. During the late 1980s, there was an increase in the amount of knowledge available as well as products and processes, which produced a need for organizations to find a way to manage this knowledge.

The 1980s also brought the advent of work done in artificial intelligence (AI), specifically expert systems. This yielded knowledge acquisition, knowledge engineering, knowledge-based systems, and computer-based ontologies. As the 1980s continued, a consortium of U.S. companies started the Initiative for Managing Knowledge Assets (1989). This organization's mission was to provide a technological base for managing knowledge. This organization also introduced the term *knowledge management*.

By 1990, a number of management consulting firms in the United States, Europe, and Japan began KM practices and programs. KM was introduced in the popular press in 1991 through Tom Stewart's "Brainpower" in *Fortune* magazine. In 1995, Ikujiro Nonaka and Hirotaka Takeuchi authored, *The Knowledge-Creating Company: How Japanese Companies Create the Dynamics of Innovation*, which is considered the most widely read work to date on KM.

By the mid-1990s, KM initiatives began in earnest by incorporating the Internet. The International Knowledge Management Network (IKMN), which began in Europe in 1989, went to the Internet in 1994 and was followed by the U.S.-based Knowledge Management Forum and others. During this time many KM conferences, seminars, and organizations began growing. By 1995, the European community began offering funding for KM-related projects through their ESPRIT program. For the chronological listing of these events, see Figure 1.1 for a snapshot of the history of KM.

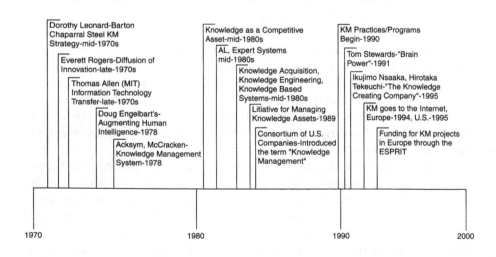

Figure 1.1   Knowledge Management Time Line

Some additional history of KM includes:

■ Late 1880s — Franz Boas, the founder of modern anthropology, studied knowledge production and diffusion within and between cultures, known as cultural cognition. Other anthropological studies in this area include those by Emile Durkheim, Ruth Benedict, and Margaret Mead. (See Stephen A. Tyler, ed., 1969.)[1]

■ Early 1900s — Joseph Schumpeter introduced the input of knowledge to the classical economic model, demonstrating that economic growth is dependent on technological change.

■ 1936–1960 — Though Karl Mannheim created the field of Sociology of Knowledge in 1936, Robert Merton expanded it into the form it is today. This field is best summarized in his 1945 paper, "Paradigm for the Sociology of Knowledge," in which he describes the forces in science and society that govern knowledge.

  – Social bases — social position, class, generation, occupational roles, mode of production, group structures: university, bureaucracy, academies, sects, political parties, society, ethnic affiliation, social mobility, power structure, social processes (competition, conflict, etc.).

  – Cultural bases — values, ethos, climate of opinion, type of culture, culture mentality.

  – Spheres of — moral beliefs, ideologies, ideas, the categories of thought, philosophy, religious beliefs, social norms, positive science, technology.

  – Reasons for — to maintain power, promote stability, orientation, exploitation, obscure actual social relationships, provide motivation, canalize behavior, divert criticisms, provide assurance, control nature, coordinate social relationships, etc.

  – (For more information on sociology of knowledge and social epistemology, see Steve Fuller, 1993.)[2]

■ 1957 — Herbert Simon coined the term *organizational learning*, and challenged the "rational man" concept in economics.

■ 1957 — Michael Polanyi introduced the importance of tacit knowledge.

■ 1960s — In a study about AT&T, Alvin Toffler discussed the need to shift from "handcraft" to "headcraft" to become an adaptive corporation and keep the procedural manuals fluid.

■ 1962 — Kenneth Arrow established the concept of "learning by doing" as a way for organizations to generate knowledge.

■ 1966 — Thomas Kuhn revealed how scientific knowledge evolves as a series of revolutions influenced by sociological forces.

- 1970s — Several cognitive scientists focused on social cognition vs. individual cognition. In 1997, the first RoboCup tournament was played in Japan to test social cognition theories.
- 1976 — John Holland introduced a mathematical framework that is used today as a model to measure the effectiveness of KM.
- 1978 — Nathan Rosenberg added to Kenneth Arrow's work "learning by using," generating knowledge by using a product.
- 1980s — The diffusion of information and communications technology forced the world into an information economy by reducing the cost of access to information.
- 1980s — Labs, hospitals, and businesses realized the benefits of computer-based knowledge systems. Expert systems, automated knowledge acquisition, and neural nets began to capture expert knowledge to help users of the system diagnose problems.
- 1982 — Nelson and Winter developed the Evolutionary Economic Theory that demonstrated how including knowledge as a factor in economics can improve the accuracy of an economic model.
- 1986 — Karl Wiig from Arthur D. Little coined the term *knowledge management* in an article about the use of AI in helping people manage knowledge.
- 1990s — Economist Paul Romer introduced New Growth Economics accounting for new knowledge and technological change.
- 1996 — Organization for Economic Cooperation and Development (OECD) issued a report called "The Knowledge-Based Economy."
- 1998 — United Nations sponsored a report called "Knowledge Societies: Information Technology for Sustainable Development."

Today KM continues to evolve. It has evolved to mean many things to the myriad organizations that institute this paradigm. However, we must realize that the practice of KM has its roots in a variety of disciplines, which include:

- *Cognitive science* — The study of the mind and intelligence, which comprises many disciplines including philosophy, psychology, and AI. Information learned from this discipline will improve tools and techniques in gathering and transferring knowledge.
- *Expert systems, AI, knowledge-based management systems* — Technologies, tools, and techniques from AI are directly applied to KM and KMSs.
- *Computer-supported collaborative work (groupware)* — In many parts of the world KM has become synonymous with groupware.

Sharing and collaboration have become vital to organizational KM and KMSs.

■ *Library and information science* — The art of classification and knowledge organization is at the core of library science; it will become vital as we gather more information. This science will most certainly contribute to tools for thesaurus and vocabulary management.

■ *Technical writing* — Technical writing, also called technical communications, is directly relevant to the effective representation and transfer of knowledge.

■ *Document management* — The managing of electronic images, document management has made content accessible and reusable. This has become an essential piece in KMSs and KM activities.

■ *Decision support systems* — Decision support systems have brought together several disciplines, which include cognitive science, management science, computer science, operations research, and systems engineering — all of which will assist the knowledge worker in the performance of their tasks. This primarily focuses on aiding managers organizationswith their decision-making process.

■ *Semantic networks* — Semantic networks are knowledge representation schemes that involve nodes and links between nodes. The nodes represent objects or concepts and the links represent relations between nodes. This discipline is now in use in mainstream professional applications, including medicine, to represent domain knowledge in an explicit way that can be shared. This is one of several ways that a knowledge engineer can represent knowledge.

■ *Relational and object databases* — Relational and object databases primarily contain structured and unstructured data, respectively. However, through data-mining techniques we have only begun to extract the explicit knowledge contained in these resources.

■ *Simulation* — Referred to as a component technology of KM (computer simulation) continues to contribute significantly to e-learning environments. E-learning is another key ingredient of the KMS.

■ *Organizational science* — Organizational science deals with the managing of organizations, understanding how people work and collaborate. Organizations contain many dispersed areas of knowledge where a KM policy and KMSs are essential. This discipline has led to many of the aspects involved in communities of practice and the development of communities of practice within a KMS.

■ *Economics* — Specifically knowledge economics, which is the study of the role of knowledge in creating value, is the next step for the evolution of KM. This will give KM a higher level of visibility because it will associate it with the valuation of the enterprise.

There have been many contributors to the field of KM. Four contributors warrant special mention:

Karl Wiig is considered by many to be the first to introduce the term *knowledge management*. He authored a three-volume series on KM in the mid-1990s, which represents landmark events in the field and has done much to establish the early legitimacy of KM as a new intellectual field of study.

Peter Drucker has been writing about management for 60 years. He has authored over 30 books on management strategy and policy, which have been translated into more than 20 languages. He is recognized worldwide as the thought leader in corporate management. He has consulted with many of the world's largest corporations as well as nonprofit organizations and government entities. He is considered to be the "arch-guru of capitalism" and the "father of modern management, social commentator, and preeminent business philosopher."

Paul Strassmann is an expert on information economics. He is an accomplished author, lecturer, and consultant. He has held many senior-level information officer positions and, through his work with the U.S. military, has pioneered the advancement of U.S. information superiority.

Peter Senge is a lecturer, author, and consultant who was named "Strategist of the Century" by the *Journal of Business Strategy* in 1999. His 1990 book *The Fifth Discipline* popularized the concept of the "learning organization." This publication in 1997 was identified by the *Harvard Business Review* as one of the seminal management books of the past 75 years.

Peter Drucker and Paul Strassmann have stressed the importance of explicit knowledge as an organizational resource. Peter Senge has focused on learning organizations as a cultural dimension of managing knowledge.

These individuals have significantly paved the way to understanding the importance of information and the learning and sharing of knowledge. This book, *UML for Developing Knowledge Management Systems,* will focus on what I believe to be at the core of KM and KMSs, *knowledge!* How do we capture and model this knowledge? We will use a standard notation for modeling the various types of knowledge that we need to capture. I will also show the different techniques that must be utilized to correctly articulate and verify the knowledge captured through the use of a case study. This will be essential to building "robust knowledge" structures within your KMS.

Notes

1. Tyler, S.A. *Cognitive Anthropology* (New York: Holt, Rinehart, and Winston, 1969).
2. Fuller, S. *Philosophy of Science and its Discontents* (New York: Guilford Press, 1993).

Notes

Chapter 2

Knowledge Management

Overview

Today there is a proliferation of information addressing the knowledge economy and the belief that the future of business success will be based on the ability to capture, manage, and leverage an organization's knowledge. What does this mean? How do you create an environment to capture and manage enterprise knowledge? More precisely, what is KM? Before we begin to construct a KM initiative, we must first agree on a definition. If you were to speak to ten different KM practitioners, you would probably receive ten different definitions. For us to move forward, we will use the following definition to set the framework for our continuing discussion about KM.

KM consists of methodology practices, new software systems, processes, and operating procedures that are developed to validate, evaluate, integrate, and disseminate information for users to make decisions and learn. Now that we have a definition of KM, what exactly are we managing? In other words, what is knowledge?

Let us start by distinguishing between data, information, and knowledge (see Figure 2.1). At the beginning of the spectrum, you have *data*. Data consists of random bits and pieces of something. This "something" can be numbers, text, video, or voice. On the other hand, information puts these random bits and pieces of "something" into a logical order that is meaningful to its user. The results of this logical order could be a report of some kind (e.g., a stock report for an investor, voice recording of a business meeting, a patient summary for a nurse, or a spreadsheet for an accountant).

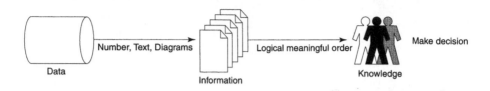

Figure 2.1   Data-Information-Knowledge

Furthermore, knowledge enables the user of information to make a decision or learn something from the information that has been presented. For instance, from a stock report, an investor can ascertain what stock she should buy or sell; a video may be delivering instructions about a procedure or process; and from a patient summary, a nurse may be able to determine when a certain medication should be administered to a patient.

Now that we have a clear picture of the evolution of knowledge, it is appropriate to continue with our understanding of KM. Remember our above-stated definition. With any definition, we must be aware that a narrow definition will tend to produce results that will lead to simple human resource policies and procedures leaving much of the value of KM unrealized. However, a definition that is too broad will be too abstract and lead to an unclear implementation of KM policies, practices, and procedures. Therefore, our definition reflects theories of KM that differentiate knowledge from information and integrate people with policies, practices, and procedures while allowing technology to aid in its implementation.

To give you a frame of reference, KM has connections with several established management strategies and practices. These practices include change management, risk management, and business process reengineering. There is a common thread between these practices, which recognizes that knowledge is a corporate asset and organizations need strategies, policies, practices, and tools to manage these assets. Discussions about KM always lead to discussions of intellectual capital both tacit and explicit. This has brought about the implementation of technology-driven methods for accessing, controlling, and delivering information that the corporate culture can transform into knowledge. This enables the corporate culture to create new knowledge value while leveraging existing knowledge. The concept of knowledge value will be discussed in further detail later in this chapter.

Intellectual capital consists of three major components:

1. Human resources — consist of the employee's collective experience, skills, and expertise of how the organization operates and the uniqueness of how it operates vs. its competitors.
2. Intellectual assets — consist of any piece of knowledge that becomes defined, usually by writing it down or inputting it into a

computer, such as inventions, design approaches, and computer programs. Intellectual assets represent the source of innovations, which firms commercialize.

3. Intellectual property — consists of intellectual assets, which can be legally protected. This includes patents, copyrights, trademarks, and trade secrets.

Intellectual capital takes two forms — explicit and tacit. Explicit knowledge is knowledge contained in documents, computer programs, databases, etc., and can be articulated easily; tacit knowledge resides in the minds of individuals. It is the tacit knowledge that never is quantified into a manual or other accessible form, but resides in the minds of the people who have worked with and developed that information. The problem is that when someone leaves the company or for a different assignment within the company, this intellectual capital leaves also. To capture this tacit knowledge, knowledge acquisition techniques must be utilized.

Knowledge Value

Historically, KM programs can take a considerable amount of time to show results or visible return on investment (ROI) for an organization. However, there is an approach in which to estimate the value of the intangible benefits of KM. The Knowledge Value Equation (KVE) simply states that the value created from managing knowledge is a function of the costs, benefits, and risks of the KM initiative. Thus, mathematically stated:

KM value = F (cost, benefit, risk), which equals total discounted cash flow (DCF) created over the life of the KM investment.[1]

This formula attempts to quantify the intangible impacts of KM, relating it back to cash flow. This includes improved problem solving, enhanced creativity, and improved relationships with customers.

KM projects produce a stream of benefits over time. This is why we use the KM Value Model. This will enable KM projects to be evaluated based on a series or stream of cash flows. In doing this, we must understand the concepts of time value of money and DCF. To take the intangible aspects of KM and turn them into a series of cash flows that can be discounted over time, we must first start with ways to increase DCF. The following list represents several ways in which to do this:

■ Increase revenue by selling more products or by introducing new products and services
■ Lower expenses by decreasing quality, transactional, administrative, production, and other costs

- Improve margins by increasing operational and economic efficiency to improve profit
- Lower taxes through smart strategies that minimize the tax liabilities of the firm
- Lower capital requirements by decreasing the amount of capital needed by regulation to run the business
- Lower costs of capital by decreasing the cost of loans, equity, and other forms of financing[2]

To model the benefits of KM as cash flows we must tie them back to one or more of the ways to increase DCF as mentioned above. We must also be aware of how KM projects transform business processes and practices to improve operations and generate DCF.

Knowledge-Value Tree

The knowledge-value tree is a treelike graphical representation that is used to make the connection between knowledge and value more visible. The mapping is as follows:

KM functionality → business transformation → DCF → value[3]

To depict this connection we have constructed the knowledge-value tree of XYZ Shipping Company (see Figure 2.2).

There is a connection between new KM functionality and business processes and individual practices:

KM functionality → processes and practices → change in business metrics

For example, review the knowledge-value tree of our fictitious XYZ Shipping Company below.

There is a link between the change in business metrics and one or more aspects of DCF. A change in business metrics will have an effect on one or more of the drivers of DCF. The presentation of knowledge-value trees has to be convincing to business stakeholders and senior management. This has to be positioned in order to show how we would achieve a ROI on the intangible benefits of a KM investment (i.e., KM functionality → processes and practices → business metrics → DCF drivers → value).

Building knowledge-value trees tends to get complex, and they are difficult to read. However, a robust theory of business knowledge provides the necessary drivers to demonstrate the relationship between KM

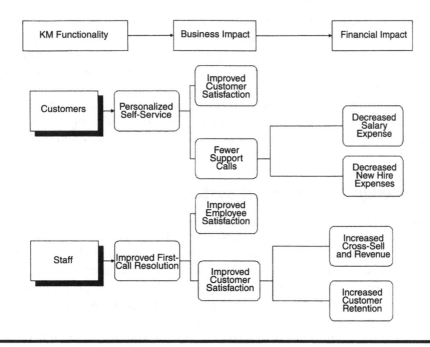

Figure 2.2   XYZ Shipping Company — Knowledge-Value Tree

functionality, business practices, and the creation of value for an organization. Knowledge-value trees also provide a mechanism for determining where and how economic value is being created. Discovering these knowledge-value drivers is one of the central tasks of KM.

Knowledge-value trees and the calculations associated with them involve some assumptions. To reduce the risks associated with these assumptions we must consider the following:

- Use financial reports and other summary documents to make informed judgments.
- Review all assumptions with the appropriate business experts.
- Quantify risks associated with your assumptions by determining how a change in the assumption influences the total DCF.
- Use computations, rather than absolute evaluation by developing a set of scenarios that look at a range of assumptions.
- Use models to frame assumptions whenever possible. The assumptions that go into knowledge-value trees should be based on the best business data and experience available.

Developing a knowledge-value tree provides a way to see and quantify key risks and refine theories to drive KM initiatives.

Why manage knowledge? We manage knowledge because organizations compete based on what they know. We manage knowledge because the products and services that are produced are increasingly complex, commanding a significant investment in information and knowledge. Finally, we manage knowledge because there is a need to facilitate corporate learning through knowledge sharing. The result of managing knowledge has presented the opportunity for achieving significant improvements in human performance and competitive advantage.

Knowledge Management Systems

A knowledge management system addresses the needs of an organization that desires not to reinvent knowledge and not to spend excess time locating difficult-to-find knowledge; an organization that desires to successfully absorb and use the growing volumes of new knowledge flowing into and out of that organization every day. All of which cost millions of dollars annually. KM also combines cultural and process changes along with enabling technology to achieve bottom-line results.

KMS components consist of customer relationship management (CRM), document management, knowledge acquisition, collaboration, workflow, and E-learning (see Figure 2.3).

Knowledge Acquisition

Knowledge acquisition is a key component of the KMS architecture as shown in Figure 2.3. Knowledge acquisition includes the elicitation, collection,

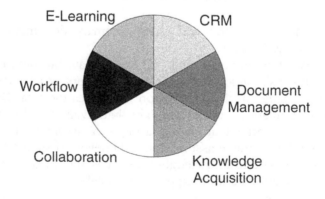

Figure 2.3 Knowledge Management System Components

analysis, modeling, and validation of knowledge for knowledge engineering and KM initiatives.[4]

Any application constructed will depend directly on the quality of the knowledge acquired. During this process, it is vital to determine where in the organization the knowledge exists, how to capture it, and how to disseminate this knowledge throughout the enterprise. The approach to knowledge capture may take on many forms. Developing a framework for knowledge acquisition will allow for a consistent method for capturing the knowledge of a particular enterprise, organization, or human (domain) expert.

Knowledge acquisition is the most expensive task in building and maintaining knowledge in a KMS. Although there are many techniques and methodologies to help the knowledge engineer elicit knowledge, none of these techniques incorporates the use of UML as a construct. UML provides a direct modeling medium that will give this framework a standard notation in which many readers are familiar.

The use of knowledge-based systems has expanded enormously in recent years with applications ranging from medicine to engineering and aerospace. Knowledge-based systems are software systems that apply advanced technical knowledge, or expertise, to problem solving. Applications of knowledge-based systems typically replicate some form of human expertise to support the solution of problems in a target domain. Knowledge-based systems are being called on to provide automation in increasingly complex domains. As domain complexity increases, so does the complexity and difficulty of building a knowledge-based system.

Knowledge acquisition is the process of acquiring, organizing, and studying knowledge about a certain domain. The object of knowledge acquisition is to identify the rules, policies, procedures, and practices that are reflective about the domain under development. This is an identification of requirements, which provides an in-depth understanding of the domain area.

To elicit or acquire knowledge about a domain, the knowledge engineer interviews the domain experts or subject matter experts (SMEs). A knowledge engineer is a "software development professional who applies engineering methodologies to the analysis of human knowledge."[4] A domain expert is a professional within an industry who has a core competence in the policies, procedures, and practices followed to solve problems or to perform a task within the domain. The objectives of the interviews are to uncover concepts and problem-solving methods used by the domain expert. Each session will progressively drill deeper and deeper into the problem area and explore increasingly more detailed information.

This should come as no surprise to any software professional — knowledge acquisition is a form of requirements analysis, which has long been known to play a critical role in building quality software. Like other forms of requirement analysis, knowledge acquisition is one of the most difficult and error-prone tasks encountered when implementing a system. The cost and performance of the application depends directly on the quality of the knowledge acquired.

To elicit knowledge from an expert, the traditional approach to knowledge acquisition is that, regardless of the variation used, it is costly because at least two (typically) expensive people are involved, i.e., the domain expert and the knowledge engineer.

The second thing to note is that the methods are error prone. Surprisingly, people cannot easily say what it is that they do in a manner that can be understood by others. This is mostly because skills are usually learned through apprentice-style learning, and the small, faltering steps required by the expert during initial learning have long since become embedded in longer phases of automated behavior, and the constituent steps are no longer readily accessible. Therefore, interpretations of what experts do are often faulty and incomplete and sometimes based on rationalizations by the experts of what they think they are doing rather than what they actually are doing. These misinterpretations are often easily committed by well-trained knowledge engineers, let alone less well-trained practitioners.

The third thing to note about the traditional approach to knowledge acquisition is that it is time consuming because errors, gaps, and inconsistencies may be difficult to discover, requiring many interactions between the domain (subject matter) experts and knowledge engineers to debug a field-ready application.

Clearly, costs must be reduced, errors eliminated, and development time shortened. An approach to solving these issues is to augment the knowledge engineer with a framework for knowledge elicitation that will provide a guide for consistent method in which to capture the knowledge of a particular enterprise, organization, or human (domain) expert. Use of a framework will have a significant effect on the quality and cost of these applications.

Incorporating UML as a direct modeling medium from which the domain expert can verify the representation of knowledge will ensure that the expert system reflects the domain expert's view of the domain instead of the intermediary's view.

The use of UML has an ancillary benefit in training knowledge engineers. There are many techniques and methodologies to help the knowledge engineers — but related to each of them there are various sets of skills that are required by the knowledge engineer. These may include exhibiting the skills of a cognitive psychologist, a communication expert, a programmer, and a domain expert. There could be situations in which the knowledge engineer may be required to play more than one role. Because this publication will present standard representations, we can eliminate much of the special training required by the knowledge engineer.

Knowledge Acquisition Process

Acquiring knowledge about a certain domain is inherently an exploratory effort. Many in management lack the understanding of the tasks and problems to be solved by capturing knowledge about the domain and automating this knowledge in the form of a knowledge base (expert) system. These systems serve as the cornerstone of the KMS (see Figure 2.3). Therefore, a general understanding or framework has to be established and then used as a guide for further probing for additional information.

An important part of the process concerning knowledge acquisition is identifying the sources of where to uncover and identify the rules, policies, procedures, and practices applied to the domain. Such sources include SMEs where tacit knowledge is uncovered, and literature, application code, and database-stored procedures where explicit knowledge is uncovered. These sources and others will be examined in later chapters. However, it is important to look at the role SMEs have in the knowledge acquisition process.

Subject Matter Experts

The SME can take on many forms. These individuals range from the business analyst, end user, or business manager to an experienced professional with several years working in the specific domain under development. Analysts will often view a problem from a low-level detail-oriented perspective. The end user will often view the problem from a high-level, considering the major issues. Working with the end user early in the development effort is of particular value when the knowledge engineer lacks an initial general understanding of the problem area. The end user is also valuable later in the development cycle for identifying shortcomings or oversights in the gathering of knowledge about the domain area.

One effective technique is to involve multiple SMEs, even though this approach tends to lengthen the acquisition process. It offers several distinct advantages. No one person has a perfect comprehensive competency in any problem area. Using multiple SMEs combined with several analysts and end users allows the knowledge engineer to identify conflicting information, errors, contradictions, etc., more readily. These multiple sources also allow the knowledge engineer to resolve issues by consensus.

Most development efforts that choose to use multiple SMEs will identify one to be the primary resource. This approach helps to reduce confusion and resolve conflicts caused when SMEs provide conflicting information. More often, multiple SMEs exhibit expertise in separate areas within the domain; in such cases, expanding the number of SMEs is a way of distributing the sources of information within the domain.

Knowledge Acquisition Tasks

The tasks involved in acquiring knowledge begin with identifying a suitable domain area for a knowledge-based system or KMS implementation. The next step involves collecting information about the domain area, which is regarded as the most difficult task of the knowledge engineer.

Collection tasks in the early cycles of the acquisition process focus on attaining a basic understanding of the problem area. As the cycles progress, increasingly more detailed information about the specifics of the domain area is obtained. This is an iterative style of collecting information and is in line with the latest and more efficient ways of software and process engineering.

The task of interpretation follows collection. This task involves a review of the collected information and the identification of key policies, procedures, practices, and processes. Because the knowledge gathered early on is general, it is the job of the knowledge engineer to focus on defining the specification of the overall domain area. This involves informal review of all the materials collected. This review is to establish the domain's goals, constraints, and scope. During further iterations, more formal methods (e.g., frameworks) should be used to interpret, model, and construct the knowledge base or bases of the domain area.

From tasks performed during interpretation, key pieces of identified information will provide insight into forming theories on the organization and classification of the knowledge. During early iterations, the knowledge engineer identifies the important concepts and forms a general understanding of the policies, procedures, practices, and processes as well as how they are used to solve issues within the domain area.

Following the completion of the collection, interpretation, and analysis tasks, the knowledge engineer will have formulated an understanding of the domain area that can aid in further investigations. Thus far, the knowledge engineer has been exposed to new concepts and problem-solving strategies that will need further exploration. This information will contribute to guiding the design and establishing the goals and agenda for collecting additional information during future sessions.

An Iterative Approach

As mentioned earlier, the tasks of collection, interpretation, and analysis are done in an iterative fashion. This is done because the knowledge acquisition process is repeated a number of times, each time building on knowledge gained from the previous session. The collection task of the acquisition cycle requires only a short time to complete relative to the timeframe of the entire cycle. Most interview sessions with SMEs will last more than a few hours in length. However, the other phases of the cycle are more time-consuming efforts.

Roles of Knowledge Acquisition Team Members

Forming a team of both talented and cooperative individuals is an important initial step in the knowledge-gathering process. Each of the team members plays an important role in the process and provides specific and necessary contributions. In most cases, the acquisition process involves at least two key individuals or skill sets:

1. SME — Knowledge of business, customers, and domain
2. Knowledge engineer — Knowledge of acquisition methods, practices, and frameworks

Larger projects will require the participation of additional personnel. Teams may be broken along lines of functional system components or specialization within certain aspects of a complex domain.

Role of the Subject Matter Expert

It is recommended that the SME be involved in the project throughout the project's life cycle. This is not only a characteristic of building knowledge-based systems or KMSs, but also a characteristic of any software application development. Knowledge engineers recognize the importance of this teaming with the SMEs and encourage this partnership, incorporating joint application development (JAD) and joint application requirements (JAR) sessions as an essential aspect of a successful system development effort.

SMEs can help the process extensively during acquisition by providing an initial high-level insight into the domain area. They can help to define the system's operational requirements as well as provide useful feedback throughout the development effort. Some of the other roles that the SMEs can fulfill are the following:

- Provide an overview of expected functionality
- Define system input and output requirements
- Define explanation facility requirements
- Define operational requirements
- Assist in testing and evaluation
- Provide feedback on the validity of the knowledge captured
- Assist in the interpretation and analysis of policies, practices, procedures, and processes

Role of the Knowledge Engineer

Knowledge engineering is an interdisciplinary effort. The knowledge engineer must perform a range of tasks, beginning with the introduction of knowledge-based system or KMS technology to all individuals involved and ending with the integration of the knowledge components into the application under development.

The major tasks of the knowledge engineer are the following:

- Collecting information about the domain area
- Interpreting the information about the domain area
- Analyzing the information about the domain area
- Coordinating efforts of the team members
- Assigning specific tasks
- Arranging JAD and JAR sessions with the SMEs

This iterative process is repeated with each new knowledge acquisition session, because the issues to be pursued in any one session depend on what was learned in prior sessions. The tasks performed by the knowledge engineer during the knowledge-gathering process require both technical and personal skills. The knowledge engineer must have the technical skills for interpreting and analyzing the collected body of domain knowledge. On the personal side, the knowledge engineer must have excellent communication skills, sensitivity to the interest and politics of the customer's working environment, and general project management skills.

Issues in Knowledge Acquisition

Some of the most important issues in knowledge acquisition center on the following issues:

- Most knowledge is in the heads of experts (tacit knowledge).
- The experts have vast amounts of knowledge and do not realize all that they know, which makes it difficult to describe and capture.
- The experts are usually too busy to enable someone to gain from their knowledge.
- There are usually multiple experts in a particular domain, which makes it difficult to validate the knowledge captured.
- Knowledge has an expiration date: knowledge about a certain domain may become obsolete over time as new techniques are discovered or technology is developed.

Knowledge Acquisition Techniques

Many techniques have been developed to help elicit knowledge from an expert. These are referred to as knowledge elicitation or knowledge acquisition (KA) techniques. The term *KA techniques* is commonly used.

The following list gives a brief introduction to the types of techniques used for acquiring, analyzing, and modeling knowledge:

- Protocol-generation techniques — Include various types of interviews (unstructured, semistructured, and structured), reporting techniques (such as self-report and shadowing), and observational techniques.
- Protocol-analysis techniques — Used with transcripts of interviews or other text-based information to identify various types of knowledge, such as goals, decisions, relationships, and attributes. This acts as a bridge between the use of protocol-based techniques and knowledge modeling techniques.
- Hierarchy-generation techniques — Techniques such as laddering are used to build taxonomies or other hierarchical structures such as goal trees and decision networks. Laddering lends itself well to UML notation, a technique we explore further in Chapter 9 and Chapter 10.
- Matrix-based techniques — Involve the construction of grids indicating such things as problems encountered against possible solutions. Important types include the use of frames for representing the properties of concepts and the repertory grid techniques used to elicit, rate, analyze, and categorize the properties of concepts.
- Sorting techniques — Used for capturing the way people compare and order concepts. Sorting techniques can lead to the revelation of knowledge about classes, properties, and priorities.
- Limited-information and constraint-processing tasks — Limit the time or information available to the expert when performing tasks.

For instance, the 20-questions technique provides an efficient way of accessing a domain's key information in a prioritized order.

■ Diagram-based techniques — Include the generation and use of concept maps, state transition networks, event diagrams, and process maps. The use of these is particularly important in capturing the "what, how, when, who, and why" of tasks and events. The diagram-based techniques are most amendable to the use of UML in its implementation, which we explore further in Chapter 9 and Chapter 10.

Differential Access Hypothesis

Why have so many techniques? The answer lies in the fact that there are many different types of knowledge possessed by experts, and different techniques are required to access the different types of knowledge. This is referred to as the Differential Access Hypothesis and has been shown experimentally to have supporting evidence.

Comparison of Knowledge Acquisition Techniques

Figure 2.4 — Knowledge Acquisition Techniques presents the various techniques described above and shows the types of knowledge they mainly are aimed at eliciting. The vertical axis of the figure represents the dimension from object knowledge to process knowledge; the horizontal axis represents the dimension from explicit knowledge to tacit knowledge.

Typical Use of Knowledge Acquisition Techniques

How and when should the techniques described above be used in a knowledge acquisition project? To illustrate the general process, a simple method will be described. This method starts with the use of natural techniques and then moves to using more contrived techniques. It is summarized as follows.

Conduct an initial interview with the expert to (a) scope what knowledge is to be acquired, (b) determine to what purpose the knowledge is to be put, (c) gain some understanding of key terminology, and (d) build a rapport with the expert. This interview (as with all sessions with experts) is recorded on either audiotape or videotape.

Transcribe the initial interview and analyze the resulting protocol. Create a concept ladder of the resulting knowledge to provide a broad representation of the knowledge in the domain. Use the ladder to produce a set of questions that cover the essential issues across the domain and

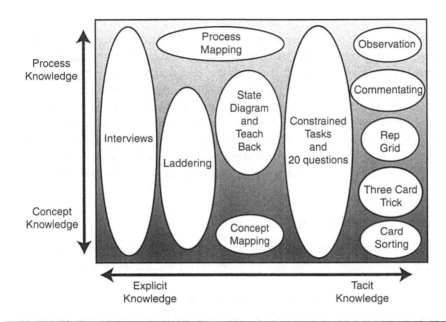

Figure 2.4   Knowledge Acquisition Techniques (Epistemics Web site.[4] Used with permission.)

that serve the goals of the knowledge acquisition project. Conduct a semistructured interview with the expert using the preprepared questions to provide structure and focus.

Transcribe the semistructured interview and analyze the resulting protocol for the knowledge types present. Typically, these would be concepts, attributes, values, relationships, tasks, and rules. Represent these knowledge elements using the most appropriate knowledge models, e.g., ladders, grids, network diagrams, hypertext. In addition, document anecdotes, illustrations, and explanations in a structured manner using hypertext and template headings.

Use the resulting knowledge models and structured text with contrived techniques such as laddering, think-aloud problem solving, 20 questions, and repertory grid to allow the expert to modify and expand on the knowledge already captured. Repeat the analysis, model building, and acquisition sessions until the experts and knowledge engineer are happy that the goals of the project have been realized.

Validate the knowledge acquired with other experts and make modifications where necessary.

This is a very brief description of what happens. It does not assume any previous knowledge has been gathered or that any generic knowledge can be applied. In reality, the aim would be to reuse as much previously acquired knowledge as possible. Techniques have been developed to assist in this, such as the use of ontologies and problem-solving models. These provide generic knowledge to suggest ideas to the expert such as general classes of objects in the domain and general ways in which tasks are performed. This reuse of knowledge is the essence of making the knowledge acquisition process as efficient and effective as possible. This is an evolving process. Hence, as more knowledge is gathered and abstracted to produce generic knowledge, the whole process becomes more efficient. In practice, knowledge engineers often mix this theory-driven (top-down) approach with a data-driven (bottom-up) approach.

Recent Developments

A number of recent developments are continuing to improve the efficiency of the knowledge acquisition process. Four of these developments are examined below.

First, methodologies have been introduced that provide frameworks and generic knowledge to help guide knowledge acquisition activities and to ensure that the development of each expert system is performed in an efficient manner. A leading methodology is CommonKADS. At the heart of CommonKADS is the notion that knowledge engineering projects should be model driven. At the level of project management, CommonKADS advises the use of six high-level models:

1. Organization model
2. Task model
3. Agent model
4. Expertise model
5. Communications model
6. Design model

To aid development of these models, a number of generic models of problem-solving activities are included. Each of these generic models describes the roles that knowledge plays in the tasks, hence providing guidance on what types of knowledge to focus on. As a project proceeds, CommonKADS follows a spiral approach to system development, such that phases of reviewing, risk assessment, planning, and monitoring are visited and revisited. This provides for rapid prototyping of the system, such that risk is managed and there is more flexibility in dealing with uncertainty and change.

A second important development is the creation and use of ontologies. Although there is a lack of unanimity in the exact definition of the term *ontology*, it is generally regarded as a formalized representation of the knowledge in a domain taken from a particular perspective or conceptualization. The main use of ontology is to share and communicate knowledge, both between people and between computer systems. A number of generic ontologies have been constructed, each having application across a number of domains, which enables the reuse of knowledge. In this way, a project need not start with a blank sheet of paper, but with a number of skeletal frameworks that can act as predefined structures for the knowledge being acquired. As with the problem-solving models of CommonKADS, ontologies also provide guidance to the knowledge engineer regarding the types of knowledge to be investigated.

A third development has been an increasing use of software tools to aid the acquisition process. Software packages, such as PCPACK4 by Epistemics, contain a number of tools to help the knowledge engineer analyze, structure, and store the knowledge required. The use of various modeling tools and a central database of knowledge can provide various representational views of the domain. Software tools can also force good knowledge engineering discipline on the user, so that even novice practitioners can perform knowledge acquisition projects. Software storage and indexing systems can also facilitate the reuse and transfer of knowledge from project to project. More recently, software systems that make use of generic ontologies are under development to provide for automatic analysis and structuring of knowledge.

A fourth recent development is the use of knowledge engineering principles and techniques in contexts other than the development of expert systems. A notable use of the technology in another field is as an aid to KM and construction of KMSs.

This approach has been a major influence in the past few years as companies recognize the vital need to manage their knowledge assets. A number of principles and techniques from knowledge engineering have been successfully transferred to aid in KM initiatives, such as the construction of Web sites for company intranet systems. This is an important precedent for the aim of this thesis to apply practices from knowledge engineering to the realm of personal knowledge.

What Is Knowledge?

To develop a framework to capture knowledge we must first know what knowledge is. Although we have given our definition of knowledge, which was established earlier in this chapter — "knowledge enables the user of information to make a decision or learn something from the information, which has been presented" — it really depends on the person's perspective. To some, knowledge is a commodity; others consider it a learning tool, and still others see it as a set of best practices.

Notes

1. Clare, M. Solving the Knowledge-Value Equation (Part One), *Knowledge Management Review* 5 (2), May/June 2002.
2. Ibid.
3. Ibid.
4. Epistemics. Information on knowledge acquisition. Available online: http://www.epistemics.co.uk/Notes/63-0-0.htm (Accessed November 2002).

Chapter 3

Declarative Knowledge

Declarative knowledge is the knowing of basic facts and the recall of stored information. It is the what, which means knowing what something is and what it is meant to do. When writing declarative knowledge we often use the words *explain, describe, summarize,* and *list.* Declarative knowledge is obtained in the following way:

- New knowledge is presented by some medium and consumed by the individual.
- The material presented is translated by the individual into propositions (ideas). Individuals then make relative connections within their memories.
- The individual then generates elaborations as new connections stimulate the making of inferences.

Declarative knowledge is broken into three subtypes:

1. Labels and names — Individuals mentally make a connecting link between two elements. This link could be prepositional or image based.
2. Facts and lists — A fact describes a relationship between or among concepts. A list is a group of elements, which may or may not be important.
3. Organized discourse — Discourse involves the comprehension of a thread of meaning that runs through an extensive body of information.

Declarative knowledge is often broken down into three cognitive activities:

1. Linking new information to existing knowledge — To learn and recall new information individuals have to tie new knowledge to knowledge they already possess. By linking new information to existing knowledge, individuals make the information more meaningful. To store this knowledge into long-term memory, an individual must make it meaningful. Incoming information will become meaningful when there is some prior knowledge that links to it. A result of linking is construction of meaning, which is at the heart of declarative knowledge.
2. Organizing — Putting new information into groups also helps in the learning of declarative knowledge. This placement of information also involves placing it into different areas of the memory. As information is received we actively organize it by grouping things together, separating one group from another, and subordinating and making relationships among groups. Phone numbers are an example: the phone number 17025551212 is grouped and separated in our mind as 1 (702) 555-1212. Organization often adds meaning by placing new unfamiliar material into some existing order.
3. Elaborating — Making connections among the information being received as well as connecting new information to existing knowledge. Elaborating is a basic process by which links are made within information being received as well as for connecting new information to existing knowledge and structures.

Declarative Knowledge Learning

The conditions needed to support declarative knowledge learning depend on the instructional strategy tool being used. Organization strategies, classification frames, concept mapping, advance organizers, metaphoric techniques, rehearsal strategies, mnemonics, and imagery are all strategy tools that can be used during a declarative knowledge lesson.

Declarative knowledge is represented explicitly and symbolically and should be independent of the methods to perform inferences on it. The forms of declarative knowledge representations are predicate logic, production rules, semantic nets, and frames. They all have one thing in common: They do not contain control information about how and in which order to use the knowledge.

A declarative knowledge representation has the following advantages:

- High modularity and modifiability.
- Easy reusability.
- High-level reasoning, which is the possibility to acquire knowledge automatically (learning) and use metaknowledge.
- Introspective explanation.

A declarative knowledge representation has the following drawbacks:

- Limited descriptive vocabulary (shallow knowledge)
- Low efficiency and performance

Declarative Knowledge Representation

An excellent way to represent declarative knowledge is to use concept maps (see Chapter 8). Concept maps are tools for organizing and representing knowledge.

> They include concepts, usually enclosed in circles or boxes of some type, and relationships between concepts or propositions, indicated by a connecting line between two concepts. Words on the line specify the relationship between the two concepts. We define concept as a perceived regularity in events or objects, or records of events or objects, designated by a label. The label for most concepts is a word, although sometimes we use symbols such as + or %. Propositions are statements about some object or event in the universe, either naturally occurring or constructed. Propositions contain two or more concepts connected with other words to form a meaningful statement. Sometimes these are called semantic units, or units of meaning.[1]

Any description of the behavior of an individual or a system in a declarative programming language takes the form of a set of implications. If one set of statements is true (the antecedents), then another set of statements is true (the consequents). The *antecedents* describe in general terms the state in which the consequents are true. The *consequents* could describe new characteristics of the state, including the results of specific actions undertaken by individuals. In either event, the antecedent-consequent coupling describes one step or one set of parallel steps to be taken in a particular state.

It is usual for both antecedent and consequent statements to contain variables. The antecedent's variables are unified with particular values either by matching statements already on a database or by inferring values from such unified statements. A standard example is that the antecedent-consequent couple `isa ?x person` `loves ?x mary` means every person loves Mary. So the statement on a database `loves john mary` is true by implication if the statement `isa john person` is on the database. There can be a set of such statements that depend on one another including, in this example, an antecedent with the consequent `isa ?x person` that unifies the variable `?x with john`.

Because the sequence in which these implications are found to be true for particular instances (i.e., the order in which these implications are instantiated) is not imposed *a priori* in the writing of the declarative model, they can be said to emerge by computation with the model. So when we run a declarative simulation model, the sequence of implications that are drawn, including implications that entail actions by individuals, emerges during the course of the run.

Whereas the processes are programmed to determine the resulting states in a procedural model, the states determine the processes in a declarative model.

An Example

Let us consider what knowledge an alphabetical sorter would need:

- Implicit knowledge that A comes before B, etc.
- This is easy — real integer comparison of (ASCII) codes for <???>.
- All programs contain procedural knowledge of this sort.
- The procedural information here is that knowledge of *how to alphabetize* is represented explicitly in the alphabetization procedure.

A declarative system might need to have explicit facts as A comes before B, B comes before C, etc.

Gathering Declarative Knowledge

There are many ways to gather declarative knowledge:

- Advanced organizers, metaphoric devices, and review can be used to activate prior knowledge.
- Associational techniques (mnemonics, images, and analogies), organizational techniques (graphic and advance organizers), and elaborative techniques can be used for the processing of information.
- Underlining, listing, and reflecting as well as the use of questions help focus attention.

- Mnemonics, elaboration strategies, imagery, analogy, organization, chunking, linking, graphic organizers, and rehearsals are all learning strategies that can be employed.
- Practice should involve paraphrased or verbatim recall. This recall should take place over a period of time. The more exposure people have to new material, the more likely they are to remember it.
- Feedback should evaluate whether the information given is complete and correct. If an error has been made, the feedback should point out the error and offer suggestions on how to fix the mistake.

Declarative knowledge is knowledge of what is true and can be communicated directly to other individuals. For example, an Englishman may have both procedural and declarative knowledge about the game of cricket. He can explain the rules of the game and describe or show a novice how to stand at the wicket or where to stand if he is to play off-stump, or what to do if he is the wicketkeeper, or the necessity of keeping the bowling arm straight at the elbow. All of this knowledge is declarative.

To hit the ball successfully and place it where the batsman wants the ball to land, or to spin-bowl so that the ball hits the ground and bounces so that it hits the wicket without coming into the range of the bat, require abilities that can only be attained by practice. However well a person might know the rules and be able to describe the practices of cricket, that person will not be able actually to play cricket without acquiring substantial procedural knowledge. Interestingly, Edith Penrose also made this distinction in her seminal (1959) analysis of the direction of the growth of the firm, although she called the two types of knowledge objective and subjective.[2] However, her distinction between the two was couched in the same terms as Anderson's discussion of the distinction between procedural and declarative knowledge. Discussions of core competencies and capabilities in the business strategy literature are based on the belief that organizations have procedural knowledge, which cannot simply be imitated by other organizations.

A similar, though by no means identical, distinction is made by computer scientists between declarative and procedural programming and programming languages. Procedural programming languages include C, Pascal, Fortran, and Basic. All of these languages require the programmer to write out the sequence of steps required to fulfill the objectives of the program in the order in which they are required to be completed. Declarative programming languages include Prolog (which also has procedural features) and SDML (strictly declarative modelling language). Programming in these languages entails the writing of statements and relationships among statements that are "true" (in the sense of being tautologies). A statement can be represented by clauses on databases, and the relationships can be represented as rules. Typically, there are rules in such languages that state that one set of statements is true if some other set of statements is true. A virtue of forward chaining is that statements demonstrated by rules to be true are stored on a database for future retrieval.

These two uses of the declarative-procedural distinction are seen to be mutually reinforcing in relation to computational models and the interpretation of the behavioral elements of these models by social scientists. That is, the distinctions between procedural and declarative programming and between procedural and declarative knowledge, respectively, are closely related in computational modeling.

Methods for Eliciting Declarative Knowledge

Table 3.1 through Table 3.11 list several methods used to elicit declarative knowledge.

Table 3.1   Card Sorting (Method for Eliciting Declarative Knowledge)

Description	Knowledge engineer obtains sets of concepts that broadly cover the domain (derived from glossary, text, or gleaned from introductory tutorial talk) and then transfers each concept to a card. The SME then sorts the cards into common groups or functions according to similarity. The SME creates the sorting criteria. The groups themselves are grouped until eventually a hierarchy is formed.
Type of representation	Hierarchical cluster diagram — This method yields a tree of related concepts, with the bottom level holding basic components of the domain and progressing through different levels of abstraction to higher-order concepts relating to them.
Subprocess in decision making and application	Knowledge structures — concepts or categories, goals, principles, values, and relationships. This method applies when a large set of concepts exists, and concepts range across the whole domain and require a suitable structuring to become manageable.
Knowledge type or nature	Declarative or indirect method
Strengths	Gives structure to large concepts sets, and is easy to do.[a] Appropriate for systems with natural hierarchical organization.[b] Apart from detailed knowledge, which experts bring to bear on specialized areas, experts are likely also to have a more global structuring of the domain. Concept or card sorting helps identify this metaknowledge.[c]
Limitations	Requires prep work to create concepts. Requires knowledge engineer trained in interpretation. Requires computer. Hierarchy may be too restrictive. Permits only one view per sort. Some aspects may be distorted and lost.[a]

[a] Converse and Kahler, 1992.

[b] Tullis, 1985.

[c] Gammock and Young, 1985.

Source: McDonald, Dearholt, Paap, and Schvanevedt, 1986.

Table 3.2 Data Flow Modeling (Method for Eliciting Declarative Knowledge)

Description	Expert interviewed. Knowledge engineer draws data flow diagram using data gathered from interview. Expert verifies diagram.
Type of representation	Data flow diagram defines the processes that are required to be part of the elicited knowledge base; the data or knowledge that exists within the knowledge base.
Subprocess in decision making and application	Knowledge structures — goals, schema, concepts, categories, strategies, relationships.
Knowledge type or nature	Declarative (input and outputs). Procedural (processing flow of inputs and outputs) or direct.
Strengths	Method defines boundary between knowledge that needs to be explicit and knowledge that does not.
Limitations	Expert's task being modeled may not have a sequential flow. Requires two knowledge engineers: one to interview, one to draw the diagram.[a] Requires training in data flow diagram methodology.[b]

[a] Swaffield and Knight, 1990.

[b] Converse and Kahler, 1992.

Source: Gane and Sarson, 1977.

Table 3.3   Document Analysis (Method for Eliciting Declarative Knowledge)

Description	Knowledge engineer translates information from a document into a conceptual graph. Propositions are translated into nodes and arcs of the conceptual graph.
Type of representation	Conceptual graph.
Subprocess in decision making and application	Knowledge structures — goals, schema, concepts or categories, rules.
Knowledge type or nature	Declarative (conceptual graph is taxonomic, spatial region hierarchy, or causal network). Procedural (goal hierarchy) or direct.
Strengths	Method can detect missing information, inconsistent information, and ambiguous statements.
Limitations	None

Source: Gordon, Schmierer, and Gill, 1993.

Table 3.4   Entity-Relationship Modeling (Method for Eliciting Declarative Knowledge)

Description	Expert uses software to identify concepts, problem-solving techniques, and tasks used to achieve domain objectives. Data used to create a conceptual graph.
Type of representation	Conceptual graph.
Subprocess in decision making and application	Knowledge structures — principles or values, goals, schema, concepts or categories, relationships.
Knowledge type or nature	Declarative (concept graph is taxonomic, spatial region hierarchy, or causal network). Procedural (concept graph is goal hierarchy) or direct.
Strengths	Can be used to build a domain model before using specific knowledge acquisition tools.
Limitations	Requires cognosis software and computer hardware.

Source: Woodward, 1990.

Table 3.5 Entity Life Modeling (Method for Eliciting Declarative Knowledge)

Description	Expert is interviewed. Knowledge engineer draws entity life-cycle diagram using data gathered from interview. Expert verifies diagram.
Type of representation	Entity life-cycle diagram — Represents the allowable status changes of an entity and the events that cause those changes.
Subprocess in decision making and application	Knowledge structures — goals, schema, concepts or categories, rules, relationships.
Knowledge type or nature	Declarative (allowable entity status changes). Procedural (events that cause those changes) or direct.
Strengths	None
Limitations	Difficult to represent inheritance through control relationships. Requires two knowledge engineers: one to interview and one to create diagrams.[a] Requires knowledge engineers to be trained in entity life-cycle modeling.[b]

[a] Swaffield and Knight, 1990.

[b] Converse and Kahler, 1992.

Source: Swaffield and Knight, 1990.

Table 3.6 Interviewing (Method for Eliciting Declarative Knowledge)

Description	Most familiar method of elicitation. In a fairly simple manner, it generates quickly a lot of knowledge that indicates the terminology and main components of the domain.
Type of representation	Varies depending on knowledge engineer.
Subprocess in decision making and application	Knowledge structures — principles or values, goals, schema, concepts or categories, rules, strategies and relationships.
Knowledge type or nature	Declarative or direct.
Strengths	None
Limitations	Knowledge may not be directly communicable in interview situations. Instead, it must be inferred using other techniques.[a]

[a] Cammock and Yound, 1985.

Sources: Cammock and Yound, 1985; Graessar and Gordon, 1991; Evans, 1988; Visser and Morals, 1991; Gordon, Schmierer, and Gill, 1993.

Table 3.7   Laddered Grids (Method for Eliciting Declarative Knowledge)

Description	Elicitors question the expert. Domain concepts and relations are graphed.
Type of representation	Rules, graphs of nodes, and labeled arcs.
Subprocess in decision making and application	Knowledge structures — concepts or categories, goals, relationships.
Knowledge type or nature	Declarative or direct.
Strengths	Highly similar to interview format
Limitations	Requires knowledge engineers trained in rule analysis.[a]

See Chapter 8.

[a] Converse and Kahler, 1992.

Source: Shadbolt and Burton, 1989.

Table 3.8   Object Oriented Modeling (Software) (Method for Eliciting Declarative Knowledge)

Description	Expert fills in computer forms detailing objects and events. Data collection includes scripts, types, aspects, relations, and attributes. Network of objects is created.
Type of representation	Network of objects (types, aspects, attributes).
Subprocess in decision making and application	Knowledge structures — schema, concept or categories, relationships.
Knowledge type or nature	Declarative or direct.
Strengths	None
Limitations	Experts must be comfortable in terms of objects. Requires specific computer software and hardware.[a]

[a] Converse and Kahler, 1992.

Source: Riekert, 1991.

Table 3.9 Ratings Analyzed by Multidimensional Scaling (MDS) (Method for Eliciting Declarative Knowledge)

Description	Expert rates similarity between concept pairs. MDS algorithm assigns set of spatial coordinates for each concept. It considers the relationship of each concept to all other concepts and places the concepts along dimensions of space in a way that reflects these relationships. MDS summarizes data into a spatial configuration. Expert identifies dimensions of MDS graph.
Type of representation	Spatial structure — MDS focuses on global information about the conceptual structure that cannot be gleaned from the original ratings nor from other scaling techniques.[a]
Subprocess in decision making and application	Knowledge structures — concepts or categories, relationships.
Knowledge type or nature	Declarative or indirect.
Strengths	MDS captures interconcept global relationships. MDS creates a metric (distance between concepts in multidimensional space) that has useful applications.[b]
Limitations	MDS can distort local distance relationships (within a concept pair). MDS requires expert interpretation. Requires MDS algorithm.[a] Requires advance identification of concepts.[c]

[a] Schvaneveldt et al., 1985.

[b] Gammock and Young, 1985.

[c] Converse and Kahler, 1992.

Source: Schvaneveldt et al., 1985.

Table 3.10 Repertory Grid (General) (Method for Eliciting Declarative Knowledge)

Description	Method of deriving object descriptions. Expert makes comparisons among groups of selections (typically triadic). These comparisons are used to identify attributes. A repertory grid is then constructed with attributes as rows and selections as columns. Using a rating scale, the expert rates the match between each selection and attribute pair on the grid.[a]
Type of representation	Repertory grids — Can be analyzed with cluster analysis, Pathfinder, or MDS
Subprocess in decision making and application	Knowledge structures — concepts or categories, relationships. Repertory grid method is appropriate when numerous closely related concepts require expertise to discriminate among them.[b]
Knowledge type or nature	Declarative or indirect.
Strengths	Validated by using grid analysis results to predict performance on cognitive tasks within the domain. Statistical techniques identify hidden patterns, grid permits expert to compare understanding to the analysis results to evaluate agreement level. Experts may make adjustments for special cases. Appropriate when numerous closely related concepts require expertise to discriminate among them.[b]
Limitations	Memory drain on expert.[c] Little procedural knowledge provided.[d]

[a] Chignell and Peterson, 1988.

[b] Gammock and Young, 1985.

[c] Converse and Kahler, 1992.

[d] Evans, 1988.

Sources: Mitta, 1989; Evans, 1988; Mitchell, 1987; Gardner, 1990; Gammock and Young, 1985; McCloskey, Geiwitz, and Kornell, 1991.

Table 3.11 Semantic Nets (Method for Eliciting Declarative Knowledge)

Description	Expert interacts with software to build a semantic net. Data collected includes relationships among objects.
Type of representation	Semantic nets.
Subprocess in decision making and application	Knowledge structures — concepts or categories, relationships.
Knowledge type or nature	Declarative or direct.
Strengths	Domain expert not required to know any programming language, artificial intelligence schema, rule semantics, or other computer science abstractions. Software increased productivity of potential expert system users 30 times that of previous methods.
Limitations	Requires semantic net software and compatible hardware.[a]

[a] Converse and Kahler, 1992.

Source: Atkins 1990.

Note

1. Novak, J.D. The Theory of Underlying Concept Maps and How to Construct Them. Available online: http://cmap.coinst.uwf.edu/info/printer.html.
2. Pitelis, C. *The Growth of the Firm: The Legacy of Edith Penrose* (Oxford: Oxford University Press, 2001).

Chapter 4

Procedural Knowledge

Procedural knowledge or *know-how* is the knowledge of how to perform some task. It focuses on the "way" needed to obtain a result. Typical examples are procedural programming languages, which allow the specification of the actions or operations needed to obtain something. Remember that procedural knowledge is typically incorporated in an algorithm or a program.

Procedural knowledge comes in many forms, for example, in legal systems, procedural knowledge or know how is considered *intellectual property*. This property can be transmitted, transferred, or sold. One limitation of procedural knowledge is that it is job dependent; thus, it tends to be less general in nature. For example, a computer expert might have knowledge about a computer algorithm in multiple languages, or in pseudocode, whereas a Visual Basic® development system programmer might only know how to run a specific implementation of that algorithm, written in Visual Basic. Thus, the hands-on expertise and experience of the Visual Basic programmer might be of commercial value only to Microsoft® job shops, for example.

The following are other aspects of procedural knowledge:

- It can involve more senses, such as hands-on experience, practice at solving problems, understanding of the limitations of a specific solution, etc.
- Know-how can frequently eclipse theory.
- Has high efficiency.
- Has low modifiability.
- Has low cognitive adequacy (which is considered better for knowledge engineers).

Knowing how the strategy works or is implemented is called procedural knowledge. What are the steps, the process, and the procedure? What do I do first, then next, and then following? Knowing that a strategy exists does only so much good if you do not know how to implement it.

The following are aspects of procedural representation:

- Control information that is necessary to use the knowledge is embedded in the knowledge itself (e.g., how to find relevant facts, make inferences, etc.).
- Requires an interpreter to follow instructions specified in knowledge.

Procedural issues are commonly relegated to ways to change representations rather than to be representations of the actions themselves. Logic is stuck with *logical inference*, which is a set of syntactic rules that map onto commonly accepted natural inference results. Perhaps *modus ponens* is the most obvious and useful of these, but there are many others. Inference rules are permissive, which means that they can be applied whenever the knowledge engineer chooses. They are inadequate for capturing the intricacies of human thought, but they have formed the basis of many problem-solving systems that do operate to produce a sequence of actions that mimic human problem solving in some aspects. Actually, it is a testament to the true universality of the rules of inference that this is possible at all. We should marvel at a system that solves a puzzle just by proving a theorem, which is a way to characterize the applications of inference rules to achieve a desired result.

The generalization of inference into the rule set of an expert system also follows this pattern. Now a rule does not change the logical form of a representation, but a rule is allowed to change the state of objects and their relationships. The sequencing of the application of rules in the rule set can again be mapped onto sequences of actions, but again the temporal aspect arises out of the behavior of the rule engine and is not represented explicitly. The attempt to represent and control the behavior of the rule engine (so-called control knowledge) did not really solve the temporal problem, because what was being represented was the rule engine itself (a program), not real-world actions. Frame systems also fall into this category. Typically a frame system will do well in representing declarative relationships, some of an epistemological nature, such as the IS-A link, but then introduce actions, and therefore time, through add-on functions, or demons, which are programs much like the rules in a rule system. In fact, the hybrid knowledge representation system was very popular for a time, combining a declarative frame system and an attached rule system using the demon notion to provide procedural capability knowledge engineering environment (KEE), a frame-based expert system.

We perceive an imbalance between declarative and procedural issues, not only in the amount of effort applied, but also in the nature of the solutions. We believe this stems from the nature of human cognition and its emphasis on visual, therefore spatial, and thus declarative issues.

Process Maps

A hierarchical method for displaying processes illustrates how a product or transaction is processed. It is a visual representation of the workflow within a process or an image of the whole operation. Process mapping comprises a stream of activities that transforms a well-defined input or set of inputs into a predefined set of outputs (see Figure 4.1).

The High Level Process Map — "30,000 feet overviews," "Medium image" — is differentiated from the Detailed Process Map — "homing in," "zooming in," "Micro Map." The High Level Process Map is utilized in determining the scope of a Six Sigma project and establishing boundaries, while a detailed process map will be used by the analyst to analyze (identify potential causes) and improve (optimize) the process.

A good process map should:

■ Allow people unfamiliar with the process to understand the inter-action of causes during the workflow.
■ Contain additional information per critical step about input and output variables, time, cost, DPU value.

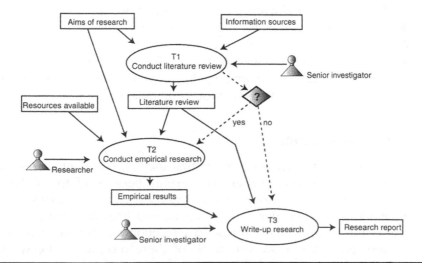

Figure 4.1   Process Map for Procedural Knowledge. (Epistemics Web site.[1] Used with permission.)

Process Defined

A *process* is a transformation; it transforms its inputs into its outputs. It is a picture showing how the transformation is carried out. It shows the inputs and outputs (best described using nouns), the activities in between (best described using verbs), and for each of the activities, the inputs and outputs used and produced.

A process is not just about what people do; it is also about what people produce. Historically, there has been a lot of emphasis attached to the study of the way people perform their jobs (i.e., the activities they carry out) or the verbs in the process map.

Two organizations competing for the same customers are differentiated on how well they manage to perform their processes. How well, for example, they transform market research into product design and development, or prospective customer interest into professional sales follow-up, and raw materials into product build. An organization with effective processes will meet or exceed customer expectation, whereas organizations with ineffective processes will fail to meet customer expectation and will therefore fail to retain those customers.

Requirements for Representing Procedural Knowledge

To represent procedural knowledge, the knowledge engineer should:

- Use process map notation.
- Base the process map on an ontology of action.
- Use visual formalism for control flow (next action).
- Be able to handle parallelism.
- Incorporate existing actor formalism for functions.
- Use all standard programming language features — conditionals, looping, program state (memory), modularity.

Visual Representation

One way to look at process maps are that they are just another notation for logic, in most cases a better one, mainly because of the ability to represent contexts in a more precise fashion. There are many visual representations for procedures. Flow charts and Petri nets are two such examples, the first for single threaded execution and the latter suitable for parallel processes. However, none of these methods addresses the ontological issues that are vitally important.

Programs

Computer programs are representations of a sequence of events (machine code instructions), where each event can be assumed to execute atomically. Clearly, programs have the necessary dynamic characteristics to support procedural knowledge as long as we can use the ideas in programming languages to support the requirements for representing procedural knowledge listed above. Most programming languages are text based, and the understanding of a program written in one of these languages relies on two factors mentioned before. Standard reading order says that events happen sequentially because one statement or command follows another down the page, and this order can only be subverted by special control-flow mechanisms, which allow jumping from one part of the page to another. However, using such a text-based language precludes the advantages offered by a visual representation, and in any case, there is no direct representation of control flow in these languages; control is represented declaratively, not procedurally.

If a process is specified in advance of its being undertaken, it is in effect an algorithm with ordered steps carried out in some specified, though often conditional, sequence. An economist, for example, would model the demand for particular goods as the result of applying an algorithm for the maximization of a consumer's utility subject to the constraints of known prices and incomes. An operational researcher would specify the steps required to maximize outputs or minimize costs within the constraints imposed by a specified technology, prices, and available resources. Economists have long denied that individuals actually apply constrained-optimization algorithms to the determination of the goods they consume or the labor they offer. The conventional wisdom among economists in particular is that individuals act as if they apply such algorithms in reaching their consumption and labor-supply decisions. In effect, the constrained-optimization algorithms are procedural descriptions (in the programming sense) of procedural knowledge (in the cognitive science sense) of individual agents in the economy. It is important to note in this context that procedural modeling applies the description of a specified process to determine the state that will emerge. The process itself cannot emerge from the model precisely because it is a well-defined algorithm already embedded in the model.

Architectures with procedural representations encode how to do some task. In other words, procedural knowledge is skill knowledge. A simple example of human procedural knowledge is the ability to ride a bike. The specifics of bicycle riding may be difficult to articulate but one can perform the task. One advantage of procedural representations is possibly faster usage in a performance system. *Productions* are a common means of representing procedural knowledge.

Procedural knowledge representation contrasts with *declarative* representation, which stores knowledge in a more flexible but harder to immediately use format.

Use of procedural knowledge in an agent raises the questions of whether the agent can "know what it knows" and the issue of *penetrability* of the knowledge. Use of this knowledge may not preclude the agent from this form of metaknowledge, and it certainly does not imply cognitive impenetrability. That the agent can demonstrate that it "knows what it knows" is illustrated in a *Soar system*, which includes the ability to explain its actions. Cognitive impenetrability is not implied because for any operator learned, new, improved operators can be learned along with preference rules that lead to the emergence of cognitive penetrability. The precise bits corresponding to the original operator are neither understood nor changed, but the behavior exhibited by the operator has been penetrated.

Capturing Procedural Knowledge

Procedural knowledge acquisition via task analysis is a reasonable candidate for graphical representation modes. Decomposing a complex set of steps that make up a specific mission or task requires cognitive visualization and the ability to formulate and reformulate the decomposition of those steps or actions. The specific heuristic procedures that most SMEs employ share certain levels of organization and recall. The path in which a procedure evolves starts with specific agendas and goals. The last or final action of reaching or satisfying those actual goals would end the procedure. On the other hand, any actions that would restart a process (e.g., a loop) would occur before the goal-oriented or last action.

Decisions may be made during a task that direct the expert along alternative paths that may or may not be taken in other performances of the same task. In cases where the processes offer one or more options to complete a task, the process diverges into as many paths as necessary to meet the optional requirements. Each path would then contain specific values for technique evaluation or other modes of feedback. These types of complexities lend themselves to representation in a visual form.

Process Definition

A *process* is the representation of a business process in a form that supports automated manipulation, such as modeling, or enactment by a workflow management system. The process definition consists of a network of activities and their relationships, criteria to indicate the start and termination of the process, and information about the individual activities, such as participants, associated information technology (IT) applications and data, etc.

Usage

The process definition:

- Results from work during the process definition mode and may include both manual and workflow (automated) activities.
- May contain references to subprocesses, separately defined, which make up part of the overall process definition.
- May make reference to a separate organization or resource model to enable participants to be indirectly defined, for example, by reference to attributes such as role or organizational position.

Activity

An *activity* is the description of a piece of work that forms one logical step within a process. Activity can be atomic, compound, or a route one. An activity is typically the smallest (i.e., atomic) unit of work that is scheduled by a workflow manager during process enactment. A compound activity is usually expressed as a subprocess.

For every activity, its performer is assigned. There can be more than one activity performer. An activity performer is represented as a workflow participant. An activity can be executed as an application and use data according to the data types that are defined.

Usage

A process definition consists of many process activities, which are logically related in terms of their contribution to the overall realization of the business process.

Transition

A *transition* is a point during the execution of a process instance where one activity completes and the thread of control passes to another, which starts. A transition defines the order between two activities.

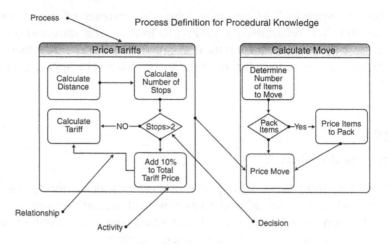

Figure 4.2 Process Definition for Procedural Knowledge

The activity in one process cannot start before the previous process has been finished. The ordering construct enforces sequential execution of activities.

A transition may be unconditional, which means that after completion of the "from" activity, the transition is executed and then the "to" activity starts. If a transition includes a transition condition, it means that the transition is executed and then the "to" activity starts only if its transition condition is satisfied. A transition condition includes functions that operate on relevant, control, as well as workflow data (see Figure 4.2).

Declarative and Procedural Knowledge

Knowledge is often expressed in two forms (see Figure 4.3):

- Declarative knowledge (knowing "what") — This takes the form of relatively simple and clear statements, which can be added and modified without difficulty. It is knowledge of facts and relationships. For example, a car has four tires; Peter is older than Robert.
- Procedural knowledge (knowing "how") — This explains what to do to reach a certain conclusion. For example, to determine if Peter or Robert is older, first find their ages. This knowledge concept will be detailed in Chapter 5.

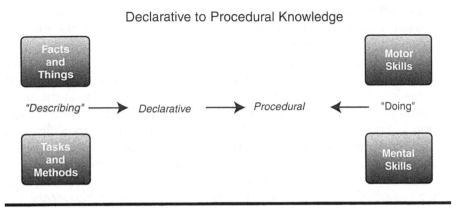

Figure 4.3   Declarative to Procedural Knowledge. (The Knowledge in Knowledge Management Web site.[2] Used with permission.)

We differentiate between procedural and declarative knowledge. Procedural knowledge is typically incorporated in an algorithm or a program, whereas declarative knowledge is represented explicitly and symbolically and should be independent of the methods to perform inferences on it.

Expert systems initially separated declarative knowledge from procedural knowledge. Declarative information was stored in a knowledge base, and the procedural instructions were stored in the inference engine. Object-oriented programming has resulted in changes to this system because its modular structure allows objects to be created that contain both the declarative knowledge and the procedural code directly associated with that data. This has allowed the previous separate knowledge types to be incorporated into a single object.

Declarative Knowledge and Procedural Knowledge Difference

There is a fundamental difference between declarative and procedural knowledge. Declarative knowledge refers to factual knowledge and information that a person knows. Procedural knowledge is knowing how to perform certain activities. According to John Anderson of Carnegie-Mellon University, all knowledge starts out as declarative information and procedural knowledge is acquired through inferences from already-existing knowledge. This is not to say that all procedural knowledge is higher-order knowledge. It is often done without any attention to what we are doing or why we are doing it, for example, driving a car.

Any skill being learned starts out as declarative knowledge. For example, when learning to play tennis, you first learned all about the rules of the game, where to come into contact with the ball on the racket, how to make the ball go where you wanted to by the follow-through, and how to position your body for a backhand stroke. This is a set of factual information. Putting those facts into practice will help you gain the skills to transform a series of declarative knowledge into procedural knowledge. Simply being told would not enable you to learn the necessary skills. You can gain the skills only after actively putting them into practice and being monitored by a coach who was constantly providing feedback.

In education, there is a mix of declarative and procedural knowledge being presented. It is important to remember that declarative knowledge has to be present to form procedural knowledge, but it should not be the only type of knowledge taught. Learning the declarative knowledge helps set the stage for the procedural knowledge. Teaching students to use the facts and information they have gained in context helps ensure long-term retention. Table 4.1 lists some of the benefits of emphasizing declarative knowledge and procedural knowledge differences.

Figure 4.4 illustrates the connection of declarative and procedural knowledge. Procedural knowledge depends on having built the prior, or declarative, knowledge.

Table 4.1 Declarative Knowledge and Procedural Knowledge Differences

Declarative Knowledge	Procedural Knowledge
Reliant on authoritative instruction.	Reliant on coaching and modeling from teacher.
Lends itself to elaborate grading system and ability groupings.	Flexible and open ended, spontaneous, progressiveness, dialogic context.
Fosters dependency, tell-me-what-to-do-and-think attitude.	Self-directed, personal efficacy.
Easily forgotten.	Long-term retention.
Stifles creativity and discourages independent problem solving and strategy building.	Yields creative, reflective thought and promotes critical thinking and independent decision making.
Teacher's role as dispenser and arbiter of knowledge.	Teacher's role as enabler, facilitator, stage manager, guide, resource.

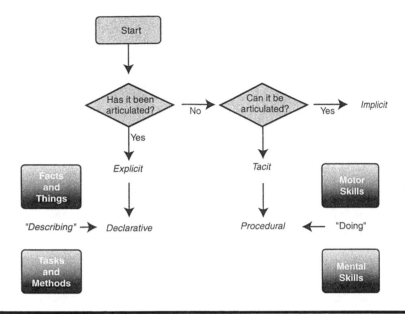

Figure 4.4 Explicit to Declarative to Tacit to Procedural Knowledge (The Knowledge in Knowledge Management Web site.[2] Used with permission.)

Notes

1. Epistemics. Available online: http://www.epistemics.co.uk/Notes/63-0-0.htm (Accessed November 2002).
2. The Knowledge in Knowledge Management. Available online: http://home.att.net/~nickols/knowledge_in_KM.htm

Chapter 5

Tacit Knowledge

The concept of *tacit knowing* comes from scientist and philosopher Michael Polanyi. Michael Polanyi was

> a world-class physical chemist who turned to philosophy at the height of his scientific career because he was dismayed at the abuses and restrictions that materialist philosophy, especially in its Marxist guise, was inflicting on scientific research. The influential approach to the philosophy of science he articulated in response to this crisis was thoroughly non-reductive in character. He illustrated how philosophical, religious, psychological, sociological, and scientific concerns interact to affect each other's development, arguing that each perspective is essential and that none can be reduced to any other. Polanyi extended this multi-leveled analysis into his discussion of complexity in nature, arguing, for example, that the sort of complexity exhibited in biology could never be reduced to the laws of physics and chemistry. The information content of a biological whole exceeds that of the sum of its parts.[1]

By definition, tacit knowledge is not easily shared. One of Polanyi's famous aphorisms is "We know much more than we can tell." From the basis of Polanyi's research we know that tacit knowledge resides in the minds of individuals. This knowledge is the most difficult to capture. This knowledge takes the form of insights, intuitions, and inspiration. As such, this knowledge is less tangible and is deeply embedded into an individual as well as the organization's operating practices.

Tacit knowledge remains as the key component to KM and KMSs. This component will promote the reuse of knowledge across the enterprise. Currently, getting access to tacit knowledge has relied solely on employees filling out endless questionnaires, conducting interviews with knowledge engineers, conducting brainstorming sessions, and facilitating JAD and JAR sessions. Capturing tacit knowledge has led to the following:

- Creation of knowledge repositories — Knowledge repositories are collections of factual, procedural knowledge that include manuals, best practices, discussion threads, corporate directories, and SME directories.
- Communities of practice — An environment that people can organize their learning around the social communities in which they belong. The knowledge of the community is integrated in the life of communities that share values, beliefs, languages, and ways of doing things.
- Enterprise knowledge portals — The enterprise knowledge portal is a single infrastructure solution that supports the distributed KM objectives of the organization.

Varieties of Tacit Knowledge

The distinction between tacit knowledge and explicit knowledge has sometimes been expressed in terms of

> knowing-how and knowing-that, respectively, or in terms of a corresponding distinction between embodied knowledge and theoretical knowledge. On this account knowing-how or embodied knowledge is characteristic of the expert, who acts, makes judgments, and so forth without explicitly reflecting on the principles or rules involved. The expert works without having a theory of his or her work; he or she just performs skillfully without deliberation or focused attention.
>
> Knowing-that, by contrast, involves consciously accessible knowledge that can be articulated and is characteristic of the person learning a skill through explicit instruction, recitation of rules, attention to his or her movements, etc.[2]

According to Polanyi, when we acquire a skill, we acquire a corresponding understanding that defies articulation. This becomes a part of our collection of tacit knowledge.

However, the distinction between knowing how and knowing that appears to collapse on further examination.

> Knowing-how involves more than just a certain technical or physical 'know-how;' it also involves knowing how to obtain desired end-states, knowing what to do in order to obtain them, and knowing when to do it. Implied in all this is that knowing how to perform an action means knowing that certain things are the case regarding that action. If this is the case, then knowing-how would seem to be closely bound up with, if not dependent on, some variety of knowing-that.[2]

In rejecting the distinction between knowing how and knowing that, we are not denying the existence of tacit knowledge, but rather we are questioning its exclusive identification with procedural operations that may in the end have little to do with knowledge as such. What is rejected is not the idea that skillful (or other) activities may rely on content states that are inaccessible to consciousness (or that conscious attention is not necessary for the exercise of a given skill), but rather the notion that a given behavior or performance stands as the proper criterion for possession of the tacit knowledge in question. Certainly, there is no reason to suppose that the knowing that, which would seem to come into play even in expert performance, cannot be tacit.

> That an exhaustive equation of tacit knowledge with pre-the-oretical, skilled expertise cannot be maintained becomes particularly clear when we consider that one widely accepted paradigm of tacit knowledge is to be found in language competence. In contrast to the variety of tacit knowledge described above, knowledge of language is not understood to constitute a skill, and thus to consist in a capacity to do something and consequently to have possession predicated on the appropriate behavioral criteria, but rather is a properly cognitive capacity, and therefore defined in terms of mental states and structures that are not always or reliably manifested in behaviors or performances.[2]

Tacit knowledge deals with presuppositions or stances, which many of our actions and behaviors commit us to. Such stances are not current beliefs, although they may be expressed as current beliefs under the appropriate circumstances. Rather, they constitute a kind of cognitive background or disposition to believe that certain things are the case. An example of this kind of tacit knowledge is that of knowing an object to be blue. We all may formulate that this object is blue by observation. Because such knowledge is expressible as propositional content, it would seem to be a case of tacit knowing that. These tacit stances or presuppositions are perhaps best described as tacit beliefs or hypotheses that can be falsified under the appropriate conditions.

While the kinds of tacit knowledge underlying skills or expert performances, on the one hand, and cognitive competences like knowledge of language, on the other, appear to be domain specific, this third type of tacit knowledge would appear to be more generally applicable. It seems that the cognitive content associated with tacit beliefs comes into play across a diverse set of activities and domains.

Tacit Knowledge and Explicit Belief

As with ascriptions of rule following, the ascription of tacit knowledge states to people is a theoretical move meant to explain behavior or cognitive operations (see Chapter 9). What makes ascriptions of tacit knowledge distinctive is the asymmetry between the richness of the ascribed content state and the relative poverty of the subjective experience corresponding to that state. Simply put, the person to whom we ascribe tacit knowledge has little or no conscious experience of what it is we claim is causing his or her activity. Although the relation between the cognitive unconscious and conscious states is complex, we might offer the following observations.

First, at least some forms of tacit knowledge would appear to differ little from ordinary knowledge, outside of their being tacit.

> This would seem to be true of much of the tacit knowledge assigned to the third category above, and possibly true as well of knowledge of language.

> Regarding the latter, that knowledge of grammar involves propositional knowledge and belief as does ordinary knowledge. In addition, it has been observed that a speaker's tacit knowledge of grammar is inferentially available to interact with his or her other systems of knowledge and belief as speakers' decisions to use their tacit knowledge are influenced by their "goals, beliefs, expectations, and so forth.[2]

Regarding the former (i.e., the third variety of tacit knowledge described above), it seems essential that such general content as appears to be involved should be available for integration into a person's beliefs and other attitude states. Far from existing behind a kind of firewall separating it from ordinary beliefs and other attitude states, at least some forms of tacit knowledge would seem to have to be a part of a person's overall network of attitude states and to exert influence on as well as to be influenced by those states.

Also, it may be the case that many ordinary beliefs themselves are largely dispositional or tacit. Our having consciously thought about or avowed a belief may be a purely contingent fact about us rather than a necessary feature of beliefs. When a belief of ours is brought to our attention, we do, under ordinary circumstances, tend to recognize it as such. The dispositional aspect thus consists in this: when confronted with a statement or other formulation of what appears to be a person's tacit knowledge that the object is blue, that person ordinarily will be disposed to feel/hold/agree that the object is indeed blue.

There is thus reason to suppose that at least some but not all forms of tacit knowledge can behave like ordinary dispositions to believe, and accordingly can be brought to awareness given the proper circumstances. We can conclude, however, that these kinds of tacit knowledge are tacit to the extent that they are initially inaccessible to the person to whom they are attributed, but that given the proper conditions, this inaccessibility can be converted to the kind of accessibility enjoyed by our ordinary knowledge.

Tacit Knowledge Capture

Tacit knowledge capture is a process by which the expert's thoughts and experiences are captured. Tacit knowledge capture involves the transfer of problem-solving expertise from some knowledge source to a repository or a program. A knowledge developer collaborates with an expert to convert expertise into a form in which it can be used to distribute the knowledge across the enterprise (e.g., KMS, expert system).

It is the tacit knowledge that is never quantified into a manual or other accessible form, but resides in the minds of the people who have worked with and developed that information. The problem is that when someone leaves the company or takes a different assignment within the company, the intellectual capital in that person's mind leaves also. To capture this tacit knowledge, knowledge acquisition techniques must be utilized.

Capturing the tacit knowledge of individuals in a way that can be leveraged by an organization is perhaps one of the most challenging aspects of KM. Organizations that successfully tap into this invaluable source of knowledge will receive great benefits in the performance of individuals within the organization and ultimately the organization itself.

Because tacit knowledge is difficult to track and capture, many organizations are not realizing its value. Tacit knowledge capture has been largely ignored in traditional KM systems, which focus on creating knowledge bases for use in customer self-service. Such systems are predicated on the highly structured and lengthy workflow of content authoring, approval, and publishing.

Tacit knowledge can only be captured when it is found. Therefore, the key to successfully leveraging tacit knowledge within an organization is to accurately find the right people to solve that particular situation. Expertise management becomes a central tenet of tacit knowledge.

Organizations that can identify and link experts who can share their tacit knowledge will benefit by providing higher quality solutions faster and at a lower overall cost. It applies in markets that are challenged with business-critical situations, including customer support, IT help desk, strategic account management, team selling, professional services, and research and development (R&D).

To begin to capture tacit knowledge you can channel informal discussions into a collaborative workspace (i.e., collaboration tools). Doing this replaces ad hoc interactions like sidebar conversations and blasting e-mail threads with a single, well-organized place where people can work together as teams that may extend to customers and partners. In this environment, people can share information about a current issue, problem, or topic. Workspaces have become much more integrated into communication channels typically used throughout the day, such as e-mail and instant messaging, so ease of adoption concerns have been dramatically reduced.

By doing this, tacit knowledge is automatically captured and immediately usable. Therefore, the next time there is a similar critical business situation, knowledge workers can tap into these workspaces to retrieve relevant information to increase the quality of resolution while reducing resolution time.

The following are some aspects about capturing tacit knowledge and about the experts that we seek out for this knowledge within the organization:

- Knowledge developers should focus on how experts approach a problem by looking beyond the facts or the heuristics.
- When modeling the tacit knowledge, reevaluate how well knowledge developers understand the problem domain and how accurately they are modeling it.
- Understand the qualifications of a good domain expert:
  - Peers regard expert's decisions as good decisions.
  - Every time there is a problem, the expert is consulted.
  - Expert sticks to the facts and works with a focus.

 – Expert has a knack for explaining things.
 – Expert exhibits an exceptional quality in explanations.
 – Expert knows when to follow hunches and sees the big picture.
 – Expert possesses good communication skills and thinks creatively.
 – Expert maintains credibility.
 – Expert operates within a schema-driven orientation.
 – Expert uses chunked knowledge.
 – Expert generates motivation and enthusiasm.
 – Expert shares expertise willingly.

Pros and Cons of Using a Single Expert

Advantages of using a single expert include:

- Ideal when building a simple KM system where a problem is in a restricted domain.
- Better facilitates the logistics aspect of coordinating arrangements for knowledge capture.
- Shares more confidentiality with project-related information than do multiple experts.

Drawbacks to using a single expert include:

- The expert's knowledge is not easy to capture.
- Single experts provide a single line of reasoning, which makes it difficult to evoke in-depth discussion of the domain.
- Single experts are more likely to change scheduled meetings than experts who are part of a team.
- Expert knowledge is sometimes dispersed.

Pros and Cons of Using Multiple Experts

Advantages of using multiple experts include:

- Complex problem domains benefit from the expertise of more than one expert.
- Working with multiple experts stimulates interaction.
- Listening to a variety of views allows the knowledge developer to consider alternative ways of representing knowledge.
- Formal meetings are frequently a better environment for generating thoughtful contributions.

Drawbacks to using multiple experts include:

■ Scheduling difficulties.
■ Disagreements frequently occur among experts.
■ Confidentiality issues.
■ Requires more than one knowledge developer.
■ Process loss in determining a solution.

Developing Relationships with Experts

To develop good relationships with experts, the knowledge engineer should:

■ Create the right impression.
■ Not underestimate the expert's experience.
■ Prepare well for the session.
■ Decide where to hold the session.

Styles of Expert Expression

Experts may express their knowledge in different ways. The expert may be a:

■ Procedure type — Methodical approach to the solution.
■ Storyteller — Focuses on the content of the domain at the expense of the solution.
■ Godfather — Feels compelled to take over the session.
■ Salesperson — Spends most of the time explaining why his or her solution is the best.

Approaching Multiple Experts

There are a few ways to approach experts:

■ Individual approach — Holding a session with one expert at a time.
■ Primary and secondary experts — Start with the senior expert first and work on down to others in the hierarchy. Alternatively, start from the bottom and go up for verification and authentication of knowledge gathered.
■ Small groups approach — Experts gathered in one place to provide a pool of information. Each expert is tested against the expertise of others in the group.

Analogies and Uncertainties in Information

Knowledge engineers should be aware of the analogies and uncertainties involved in obtaining information:

- Experts use analogies to explain events.
- An expert's knowledge is the ability to take uncertain information and use a plausible line of reasoning to clarify the fuzzy details.
- Understanding experience — Knowledge in cognitive psychology is helpful background.
- Language problem — Reliable knowledge capture requires understanding and interpreting an expert's verbal description of information, heuristics, and so on.

Things to Consider during the Interview Process

There are some important things that the knowledge engineer should know about the interview process:

- It is commonly used in the early stages of tacit knowledge capture.
- The voluntary nature of the interview is important.
- A major benefit of the interview process is behavioral analysis.
- Interviewing as a tool requires training and preparation.
- It is a great tool for eliciting information about complex subjects.
- It is a convenient tool for evaluating the validity of information acquired.

Types of Interviews

There are three kinds of interviews:

1. Structured — Questions and responses are definitive. Used when specific information is sought.
2. Semistructured — Predefined questions are asked but experts are allowed some freedom in expressing the answers.
3. Unstructured — Neither the questions nor their responses specified in advance. Used when exploring an issue.

Variations of Structured Questions

Here are some of the variations of structured questions:

- Multiple-choice questions offer specific choices, faster tabulation, and less bias by the way answers are ordered.
- Dichotomous (yes or no) questions are a special type of multiple-choice question.
- Ranking scale questions ask experts to arrange items in a list in order of their important or preference.

Guidelines to Consider for Successful Interviewing

For a successful interview, the knowledge engineer should:

- Set the stage and establish rapport
- Phrase the questions properly — question construction is important
- Listen closely and avoid arguments
- Evaluate session outcomes

What Things to Avoid during the Interview Session

The knowledge engineer should avoid the following during the interview:

- Taping a session without advance permission from the expert (this is illegal!)
- Converting the interview into an interrogation
- Interrupting the expert
- Asking questions that put the domain expert on the defensive
- Losing control of the session
- Pretending to understand an explanation when the knowledge engineer actually does not
- Promising something that cannot be delivered
- Bringing up items not on the agenda

Tacit Knowledge as a Source of Competitive Advantage

Tacit knowledge underlies many competitive capabilities. The experience, stored as tacit knowledge, often reaches consciousness in the form of insights, intuitions, and flashes of inspiration. The marvelous capacity of your mind to make sense of your previous collection of experiences and to connect patterns from the past to the present and future is essential to the innovation process. "The creativity necessary for innovation derives not only from obvious and visible expertise, but from invisible reservoirs of experience."[1]

Tacit knowledge, or implicit knowledge, as opposed to explicit knowledge, is far less tangible and is deeply embedded into an organization's operating practices. It is often called *organizational culture*.

> Tacit knowledge includes relationships, norms, values, and standard operating procedures. Because tacit knowledge is much harder to detail, copy, and distribute, it can be a sustainable source of *competitive advantage* ... What increasingly differentiates success and failure is how well you locate, leverage, and blend available explicit knowledge with internally generated tacit knowledge.[2]

Inaccessible from explicit expositions, tacit knowledge is protected from competitors unless key individuals are hired away.

Innovation Process: Diversion and Conversion of Ideas

"The process of innovation is a rhythm of search and selection, exploration and synthesis, cycles of divergent thinking followed by convergence."[2]

Divergence, or creative synthesis, is the interlocking of previously unrelated skills or matrices of thought. The creation of such intellectual ferment is important to innovation — the more options offered, the more likely that an out-of-the-box perspective will be available for selection. Just hearing a different perspective challenges the mindset of others sufficiently that they will search beyond what initially appears to be an obvious solution. This is a reason that intellectually heterogeneous *cross-functional teams* are more innovative than homogenous functional ones.

As soon as a sufficient choice of innovative ideas has been generated, a solution — convergence on acceptable action — needs to be defined and agreed on. Confining the discussion here to managing the tacit dimensions of knowledge, three types of tacit knowledge — overlapping specific, collective, and guiding — need to be managed.

Managing Tacit Knowledge

Managing tacit knowledge is a significant challenge in the business world, and it requires more than mere awareness of barriers. During the new idea generation (divergent thinking) phase, people create a wealth of possible solutions to a problem. "Chaos succeeds in creating newness because it takes place in a system that is non-linear."[1] In a well-managed development process, where a group of diverse individuals addresses a common challenge, varying perspectives foster creative abrasion, intellectual conflict between diverse viewpoints producing energy that is channeled into new ideas.

Mechanisms by which collective tacit knowledge is created and tapped include brainstorming, concept extraction, and automatic categorization.

Brainstorming

Brainstorming involves gathering a set of experts with diverse skills, preferably including client representatives. The main rules to be followed during the idea generation phase are defer judgments, build on the ideas of others, one conversation at one time, stay focused on the topic, and think outside the box — encourage wild ideas. All ideas should be recorded and discussed during the selection (convergent thinking) phase.

In large organizations that are conceived as a collective of communities, separate community perspectives can be amplified by interchanges to increase divergent thinking. Out of this friction of competing ideas can come the sort of improvisational sparks necessary for igniting organizational innovation. Managers and innovation team leaders can use tacit knowledge to aid convergent thinking by creating guiding visions and concepts for teams involved in innovation.

Key to capturing tacit knowledge are the other two breakthroughs — the automatic extraction of concepts rather than keywords and the automatic categorization of information according to the key concepts it contains.

The combination of tacit knowledge and explicit knowledge is key to KM. The latter can be derived from sources such as company manuals, memoranda, corporate intranets, notes, spreadsheets, e-mails, faxes, and news feeds. To date, getting access to tacit knowledge has relied solely on employees filling out endless questionnaires. Autonomy Corporation's approach, however, is more powerful and totally automatic. Autonomy makes it possible to identify an employee's area of expertise from a personal profile automatically derived from the issues an individual researches, as well as the ideas in the documents and e-mail messages they send and receive. This helps facilitate virtual workgroups, encourages communication, and reduces duplication of effort.

Concept Extraction

By applying its Dynamic Reasoning Engine (DRE) to KM, Autonomy is designed to be able to understand concepts and the real meaning of words in their correct context, providing its KM products with an unrivaled level of automation and precision. Most technologies analyze keywords only and fail to recognize the context or meaning of searches.

Autonomy's approach is based on analyzing the body of text and identifying key concepts within it, through an understanding of the frequency and relationships of terms that closely correlate with meaning. Once key concepts are identified, they are encoded as "concept agents," which can then be employed to look for matches to the concepts they contain in any source of text or to find people with agents that contain similar concepts.

For example, an employee may want to find out about electronic commerce and selling products over the Internet. Initiating a query would deliver information on the subject from a variety of sources, which might include an e-mail, an employee with relevant experience, a company memo, an analyst report, or a variety of company documents on the subject.

Automatic Categorization

The third principle relates to the automatic sorting and categorization of information using these concept agents. Once a company deploys Autonomy's technology, all the knowledge held on computer systems can be automatically categorized by the core engine without the labor intensive and expensive process currently used, where every single piece of information needs to be read and then tagged manually. For example, to manually index 10,000 documents could take more than eight weeks; however, Autonomy can achieve this automatically within minutes resulting in a huge reduction in administrative costs while ensuring a greater degree of accuracy and flexibility.

Notes

1. Atherton, J.S. 2003. Learning and Teaching: Tacit Knowledge and Implicit Learning. Available online: http://www.dmu.ac.uk/~jamesa/learning/tacit.htm (Accessed: July 5, 2004).
2. Barbiero, D. 2004. Tacit Knowledge, Philosophy of Mind. Available online: http://www.artsci.wustl.edu/~philos/MindDict/tacitknowledge.html#belief (Accessed July 5, 2004).

Chapter 6

Explicit Knowledge

A widely recognized distinction in KM is Polanyi's distinction between tacit knowledge (knowledge contained in the minds of humans, sometimes called personal knowledge) and explicit knowledge (which has been referred to as codified knowledge). Polanyi has also indicated that much tacit knowledge can be made explicit even though much of it will remain unexpressed (see Figure 6.1). Therefore, for knowledge to become explicit it must first have been tacit. In this chapter, we explore explicit knowledge in more detail.

Explicit knowledge is knowledge that can be transmitted in formal, systematic language. It is discrete or "digital." It is captured in records of the past such as libraries, archives, and databases and is assessed on a sequential basis. It can be expressed in words and numbers and shared in the form of data, scientific formulations, specifications, manuals, etc. This kind of knowledge can be readily transmitted between individuals formally and systematically.

Explicit knowledge is knowledge that has been articulated and, more often than not, captured in the form of text, tables, diagrams, product specifications, and so on.

> In a well-known and frequently cited 1991 Harvard Business Review article titled 'The Knowledge Creating Company,' Ikujiro Nonaka refers to explicit knowledge as 'formal and systematic' and offers product specifications, scientific formulas and computer programs as examples. An example of explicit knowledge with which we are all familiar is the formula for finding the

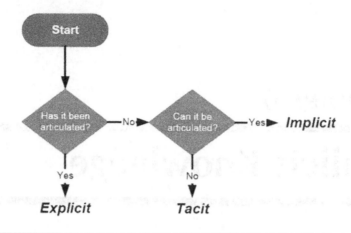

Figure 6.1   Explicit-Tacit-Implicit. (*Distance Consulting*, 2003.[1] Used with permission.)

area of a rectangle (i.e., length times width). Other examples of explicit knowledge include documented best practices, the formalized standards by which an insurance claim is adjudicated and the official expectations for performance set forth in written work objectives.[1]

In a KMS, explicit knowledge takes the form of data servers and traditional knowledge bases. Explicit knowledge fits well into call centers that handle a large volume of similar requests that have relatively simple answers. However, it falls short in business critical situations that generate complicated discussions requiring a variety of expertise, with interactions that often extend across multiple organizations. To capture explicit knowledge to be used in a KMS, we must first recognize where explicit knowledge exists.

Explicit knowledge exists in many sources. The following represents areas where explicit knowledge exists.

Literature

Additional sources of information may come in the form of printed documents such as reports, regulations, guidelines, books, etc. At a minimum, if these documents exist, the knowledge engineer should review them to gain an overview understanding of the problem area. These documents can also be helpful in defining and clarifying the terminology of the problem domain. Moreover, they can often provide details on the business rules that will eventually be used in the final system. Such documents are additionally valuable in that they are an excellent source to provide insight into the major issues that will need to be addressed.

However, printed materials should never be considered as sufficient sources of information for the development of a rules-based application. These materials are only valuable as supplementary sources of information and should never replace an experienced business analyst.

Company Policy Manuals and Regulations

Company policy manuals and printed regulations are by far the best source for supplementary information about the problem area for a rules-based application. Such documents are generally formatted and organized in a manner that is analogous to the format and organization of business rules specifications. All existing policy and regulation documentation should be made available to the knowledge engineer as early as is possible in the elicitation phase of development.

Reports, Memos, and Guidelines

Although reports, memoranda, and other printed guidelines do have value to the knowledge elicitation process, these types of documents are generally not formatted and organized in a manner that is useful to the elicitation process. Documents such as these will require a substantial amount of explanation and clarification from the business analysts or other content providers on the development team.

Published Books and Journal Articles

Published sources are generally the least useful forms of documentation to the elicitation process. Essentially, the only realizable value of these types of documents is as a source for high-level information about a problem area. Two valuable types of high-level information that can be obtained from published materials are clarifications of terminology and overview descriptions of the problem area.

Existing Application Code

The least useful alternative source for information about a problem area is application source code. Many rules-based development efforts are actually upgrades to existing applications that already solve parts of the problems to be addressed with business rules automation. Customers often believe that providing source code for the existing components is an effective means of communicating the business rules to be incorporated into the upgraded system. This is not the case. Most application source code is formatted in a way that is effectively useless to the knowledge elicitation process.

Database-Stored Procedures

Database-stored procedures are definitely the lesser evil. Well-designed stored procedures are generally rule oriented. Such stored procedures are designed to answer specific questions that are asked by the application. The knowledge engineer may have some success in extracting business rules from stored procedures. However, this is far from an ideal approach. Most importantly, stored procedures should never be provided as the sole source of information about a problem area.

Program Source Code

COBOL (Common Business-Oriented Language) or other programming language source code is generally of no use to the business rules elicitation process. Programming languages are algorithmic and procedural in nature; even object-oriented languages like C++ and Java tend to follow an algorithmic approach to problem solving. Procedural analysis and algorithmic thinking is not conducive to business rules automation. These sources should never be relied on as a source for information about a problem area.

Once knowledge is explicit, it should be organized in a structured document that will enable multipurpose use. The best KM tools fit the needs of multimedia contact centers by being channel agnostic and enabling knowledge creation once and then leveraging it across multiple channels, including phone, e-mail, chat, Web self-service, interactive voice response (IVR), and any new channels that come online.

Organizations that have already experienced the pain of updating content in one repository for e-mail, another repository for phone, and yet another one for FAQs on a Web site should look at ways to centralize their support KM practices.

Acquiring Explicit Knowledge

The result of acquiring explicit knowledge can be attained with different techniques that share the generality and the robustness features that we expect from the implementation of a computer programming language. For example, the tasks comprising scientific theories have been studied in this approach. The scientific theories have the additional appealing feature of been obtained by a system that mimics the logic of the scientific discovery as described by the philosophy of science.

Explicit knowledge, which in this case is symbolic in nature, is present in scientific theories and can be represented by means of logical expressions or — equivalently — by computer programs. For example, in the representation of list processing (LISP) programs, or LISP S-expressions, can represent the explicit primarily symbolic knowledge contained in scientific theories.

LISP programs are written in the form of LISP S-expressions, which are ordered sets of operators and arguments within a well-formed parenthesization. The argument of a LISP expression can be another LISP expression, and so forth. It is this modularity that makes it easy to feed S-expressions to genetic operators obtaining new conjectures in return.

The compiler then translates any list in an executable program, which can be tested against the observed data, to get a fitness mark. The central machinery is the same as that described in the previous section. The individuals are the S-expressions whose shape and dimensions change during the process. The genetic operators are analogous of mutation and crossover (some caution is needed to ensure that only legal expressions are output). The fitness function is defined by the degree of consistency of the (compiled) S-expression with respect to the data. The evolutionary process is performed in the identical manner, with the initial population generated randomly (starting from a predefined set of atomic functions), and the iterative refinement procedure induced by the selection of the fittest individuals at each generation.

The final output is a computer program (i.e., a symbolically expressed theory about the original data). The method has been successfully applied to the task of scientific laws induction from empirical data.

The same approach has been successfully applied also to time series analysis problems, which are another representation of scientific discovery tasks. More recently, work has been done in the direction of evolving Prolog formulas in a population of agents that explore a large database. Such agents are also provided with specific heuristics, which help them to produce new hypothesis (i.e., standard learning algorithms). However, they have features (like being subjected to a selective pressure and performing crossover reproduction) that could make them related to typical evolutionary systems.

Capturing Explicit Knowledge for Knowledge Management Systems

Expert personnel are extremely valuable organizational assets because they harbor unique and specialized knowledge that enables them to perform tasks more efficiently and effectively than other personnel. Energy companies use various means to capture expert knowledge and disseminate it to other workers, including embedding the knowledge in decision aids and expert systems; transferring the knowledge through mentoring, job rotation, and cross training; and having experts update existing or prepare new procedures and practices to reflect their knowledge.

The article "Capturing Undocumented Knowledge of Industry Personnel" outlines a practical process for explicit, but particularly tacit knowledge capture that was developed based on extensive background research and field-testing activities conducted during 2001. The report also characterizes existing and emerging techniques for knowledge elicitation, storage, retrieval, and presentation.

> The field tests provided experience in eliciting valuable knowledge from experts with a variety of responsibilities at a range of facilities, ensuring the guidance report's applicability throughout the energy sector," says Hanes. "Practical information on capture, storage, retrieval, and presentation approaches should also prove useful for energy companies and other organizations engaged in knowledge management activities.

The report culminates the three-year project on capturing undocumented worker-job knowledge under EPRI's (Electric Power Research Institute's) Strategic Human Performance Program. The project was launched to address a growing concern within the energy industry, as well as other industries and the public sector.

> After extended periods of employment within complex work environments, some personnel become seemingly irreplaceable: They know things others don't, and they can do things others can't," says Madeleine Gross, manager of EPRI's Strategic Human Performance Program. "With this project, we set out to address a critical question: When experts leave an organization — at the end of their shift, for vacation, or forever — how do we prevent their expertise from also walking out the door?

> In initial strategic work, four major tasks were performed: needs analysis, industry survey, literature and background review, and development of a prototype knowledge capture process. Results from these tasks are reported in the 1999 and 2000 status reports for the project. The needs analysis, which included site visits to several energy facilities, was conducted to determine the perceived importance of capturing valuable undocumented

knowledge within the energy industry. Discussions indicated that at least some of the information valuable to the work performed at generating stations and transmission and distribution (T&D) facilities reside in the "heads" of experienced workers, rather than in documentation or training programs.

The industry survey involved managers and workers from 21 energy companies. Nearly all (92%) respondents indicated that loss of unique valuable expertise within the next 5 years would pose a problem, while only 30% of respondents indicated that a formalized planning effort is in place to address the expected loss of expert knowledge.

The literature and background review covered the fields of knowledge management, cognitive psychology, applied psychology, artificial intelligence, and expert systems. The review evaluated current practice and the state of the art in capturing, storing, and making available undocumented knowledge. It indicated that some knowledge elicitation, storage, retrieval, and presentation techniques being explored for or being applied successfully in industrial, defense, corporate, and other settings have not yet penetrated the energy sector. For example, the concept mapping method has been used to elicit and display concepts that reflect the cognitive processes of experts.[2]

A concept map provides a visual representation of the expert's knowledge relevant to specific concepts (see Concept Maps in Chapter 9).

Business Value of Acquired Knowledge

When explicit knowledge is acquired and used in a KMS, certain business value is created. Some of the business values created are as follows:

- They facilitate the collection, recording, organization, filtering analysis, retrieval, and dissemination of explicit knowledge. This explicit knowledge consists of all documents, accounting records, and data stored in computer databases. This information must be widely and easily available for an organization to run smoothly. A KMS is valuable to a business to the extent that it is able to do this.
- They facilitate the collection, recording, organization, filtering, analysis, retrieval, and dissemination of implicit or tacit knowledge. This knowledge consists of informal and unrecorded procedures,

practices, and skills. This how-to knowledge is essential because it defines the competencies of employees. A KMS is of value to a business to the extent that it can codify these "best practices," store them, and disseminate them throughout the organization as needed. It makes the company less susceptible to disruptive employee turnover. It makes tacit knowledge explicit.

■ They can also perform an explicitly strategic function. In a fast-changing business environment, many feel only one strategic advantage is truly sustainable: to build an organization that is so alert and so agile that it can cope with any change, no matter how discontinuous. This agility is only possible with an adaptive system like a KMS, which creates learning loops that automatically adjust the organization's knowledge base every time it is used.

Notes

1. Nickols, F. The Knowledge in Knowledge Management. *Distance Consulting*, 2003. Available online: http://home.att.net/~nickols/articles.htm.
2. Capturing Undocumented Knowledge of Industry Personnel. *EPRI Journal Online*, 2002. Available online: www.epri.com/journal/details.asp?doctype=features&id=389.

Chapter 7

Process Knowledge and Concept Knowledge

Process Knowledge

KM and process automation are closely linked, but are often seen as unrelated disciplines, largely because there are two vastly different perspectives for business processes. Most companies organize, automate, and manage work from a functional context. A much smaller percentage of companies have organized their workers into collaborative teams responsible for the completion of an entire process from end to end. Companies that are organized to support cross-functional business processes learn that it is essential to share product-related and process-related knowledge across functional boundaries.

Workflow software can have a significant role in facilitating knowledge. Workflow software can be used as a repository for business rules, making it possible for organizations to change business logic without rewriting applications, while enabling the organization to collect, disseminate, and enhance their process knowledge (see Figure 7.1). Organizations automating complex processes will increasingly rely on workflows embedded in KMSs (see Figure 2.3) to give them the flexibility needed to disseminate knowledge.

Organizations should not overlook the value and challenges of capturing process knowledge. Managing and automating work processes is extremely difficult; incorporating a workflow solution will greatly alleviate this difficulty. More simply put, most organizations are not organized by

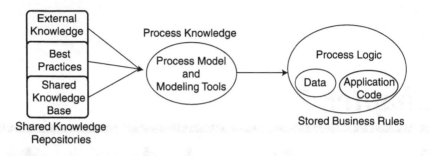

Figure 7.1 Process Knowledge Workflow

processes: managers are not rewarded for overseeing processes, employees are not trained to understand processes, and IT seldom focuses on automating processes. For this to change, organizations must focus on procedures and policies that will encourage, stimulate, and instruct their workforce on how to capture process knowledge and the benefits on doing so.

Despite many challenges, visionary organizations with process awareness will begin to develop knowledge repositories for managing, automating, and continuously improving processes. These repositories will contain internal and external best practices, process templates, and process patterns for workgroups and individuals that will be reused as processes evolve. This transformation across the entire enterprise will take a commitment in collaboration with management as part of their strategic plan and with employees and resources geared toward meeting that plan.

A *process* is knowledge about how something works. It answers the question, "What happens?" Processes are often taught at an information-about level. The process is sometimes demonstrated, but the learner frequently has an incomplete or inaccurate mental model of the process.

The components of a process include its name and description, a consequence that is defined as a change in a property value with the corresponding change in the portrayal of the entity (what happens?), and a set of conditions that is defined as values on properties (when?). A knowledge structure for a process's causal network is illustrated in Figure 7.1. This structure is called a PEAnet for process, entity, and activity network. This structure is a generic knowledge structure that can be used to represent almost any process. Processes are defined in terms of properties. A condition for a process is some value on a property. A consequence for a process is a change in the value of a property. When the value of a property of an entity changes the portrayal, either its appearance or its behavior also changes in a corresponding way.

Process Knowledge Applications

Process knowledge capture and deployment applications are often Web-based applications (see Figure 7.1). When developing a decision support application that includes process knowledge, there are a number of advantages obtained by making process knowledge available on the Web. These advantages include:

- Ensuring best practices are followed. If the best practices are published and easily accessible, everyone will be able to use them.
- Increasing process compliance — Having the process knowledge published helps to ensure consistency.
- Users who are not domain experts can reuse knowledge. This means that any user can get access to the expert knowledge any time and any place. No longer will an unavailable expert cause delays.
- Users can capture and store design results for future business risk and value analytics. This means that the process model can be saved for future reference.
- Users can capture and leverage intellectual capital globally. This means that companies with global operations can both access the process knowledge created anywhere but also, if necessary, update the process knowledge model from anywhere.
- Technical experts are freed up to do more value-added tasks.

Decision support applications that capture and deploy knowledge also tend to suffer from a number of disadvantages and issues. These disadvantages include:

- Problem of knowledge transfer from the domain expert to the knowledge engineer — It is time consuming for a knowledge engineer to learn and understand everything that a process expert knows. Things will be overlooked. Depending on their significance, these can have a tremendous impact on the overall usefulness of the system.
- The additional time and cost of IT personnel to develop the application — Having IT resources create an end-user application is generally expensive and time consuming.
- Business processes often change. Modifying a custom-built application whenever the rules change is a time-consuming task. With time, the knowledge tends to get out of synchronization with the data, resulting in the usefulness of the application being diminished.
- Software maintenance issues — Having IT maintain custom-built applications is both costly and inefficient.

Concept Knowledge

To begin with, we can state that concepts seem to be the stuff that reasoning and other cognitive processes have as their basis. However, it is possible to distinguish several functions of human concepts. Some of them are:

- Stability functions
- Cognitive economical functions
- Linguistic functions
- Metaphysical functions
- Epistemological functions
- Inferential functions

Concepts give our world stability in the sense that we can compare the present situation with similar past experiences. For instance, when confronted with a wasp, we can compare this situation with a situation some years ago when another wasp stung us and consequently take the appropriate measures. Actually, there are two types of stability functions — intrapersonal and interpersonal. Intrapersonal stability is the basis for comparisons of cognitive states within an agent, whereas interpersonal stability is the basis for comparisons of cognitive states between agents.

By partitioning the world into categories, in contrast to always treating each individual entity separately, we decrease the amount of information we must perceive, learn, remember, communicate, and reason about. In this sense, we can say that categories (and thus concepts) promote cognitive economy. For instance, by having one representation of the category wasp instead of having a representation for every wasp we have ever experienced, we do not have to remember that the wasp we saw yesterday has a stinger or that it has a nervous system.

Here, and in the following, "wasp" refers to the black- and yellow-striped wasp (yellow jacket). The linguistic function is mainly providing semantics for linguistic entities (words), so that they can be translated and synonymies relations be revealed. For instance, the fact that the English word "wasp" and the Swedish word "geting" have the same meaning enables us to translate "wasp" into "geting" and vice versa. Furthermore, it seems that it is the linguistic function together with the interpersonal stability function that make it possible for us to communicate (by using a language).

In philosophy, metaphysics deals with issues concerning how the world is, and epistemology deals with issues concerning how we know how the world is. Thus, we might say that the metaphysical functions of a concept are those that determine what makes an entity an instance of a particular category. For example, we say that something actually is a wasp if it has a particular genetic code or something like that. The epistemological functions then, are those that determine how we decide whether the entity is an instance of a particular category. For instance, we recognize a wasp by color, body shape, and so on.

Finally, concepts allow us to infer nonperceptual information from the perceptual information we get from an entity and to make predictions concerning it. Thus, we can say that concepts enable us to go beyond the information given. For instance, by perceptually recognizing a wasp we can infer that it is able to hurt us. We know that all wasps have a stinger and that a stinger can be used for hurting other animals.

Functions of Concepts in Artificial Autonomous Agents

The functions of concepts are not pertinent in AI literature. The main reason for this is probably that AI researchers often do not study problems from an autonomous agent perspective. Instead, they assume that the concepts acquired are to be used for some classification task under human supervision. Typically, the task can be described as finding a concept description such that the system correctly can classify the given training instances (described by a number of observable features). Thus, in my terms, the function of the acquired concept is mainly of an epistemological nature. The other functions are to a great extent taken cared of by the human supervisor. In my opinion, this leads to a narrow view of the problem where several difficulties are ignored. To get a broader view, I will base the discussion of functions of concepts on my own reflections on the previous section.

The functions of intrapersonal stability and cognitive economy are, of course, important, but they are trivial in the sense that they emerge more or less automatically for the agent just by having concepts independent of the choice of representation. By analogy with the stability functions, we can say that an agent can have both intrapersonal and interpersonal linguistic functions. The intrapersonal function is a rather weak one, which is implied only by the fact that the concepts have names internal to the agent.

Representation of Concepts

Traditionally in AI, categories are treated as equivalence classes that can be characterized in terms of necessary and sufficient conditions. This is a rather strong version of what cognitive psychology calls the classical view.

The Classical View

According to the classical view, all instances of a category share common features that are singly necessary and jointly sufficient for determining category membership. Thus, it would be possible to represent a concept by these features. Categorization would then be a matter of straightforward application of this "definition." Some of the representation languages that have been used for such definitions are logic-based notation (attribute-value pairs), decision trees, and semantic networks.

However, as is often noted in recent cognitive science literature, there are some problems with the classical view. The most serious problem is probably that it is often not possible to find necessary and sufficient features for natural categories, in contrast to artificial categories. This problem is sometimes called the ontological problem. Moreover, there are unclear cases of category membership. For instance, it is hard to decide for some objects whether they are a bowl or a cup.

Furthermore, assuming that a classical definition exists for a category, it is interesting to notice that instead of using the classical definition we often use nonnecessary features to categorize objects of the category. Thus, it seems that humans, at least, do not use classical definitions to implement the epistemological function.

Finally, it is generally believed that some exemplars of a category are more typical than others. Prototype usually refers to the best representatives or most typical instances of a category as opposed to the treatment of categories as equivalence classes. For instance, it has been shown that (at least for the experiment subjects) robins are prototypical birds whereas penguins are not.

Thus, it seems clear that the classical view cannot explain all aspects of natural concepts. In response to this, the probabilistic and the exemplar view that have been presented by artificial categories are typically categories that are constructed for a particular experiment, whereas natural categories are those that have evolved in a natural way through everyday use. Artificial categories are often constructed to be specified by a short and simple definition in terms of necessary and sufficient conditions. Cognitive scientists view these categories as more realistic and consistent with empirical findings. Some scientists working in the artificial intelligence (AI) field have also adopted these views.

Nonclassical Views

According to the probabilistic view, concepts are represented by a summary representation in terms of features that may be only probable or characteristic of category members. Membership in a category is graded rather than all-or-none. Better members have more characteristic properties than the poorer ones. An object will be categorized as an instance of some category if, for example, it possesses some critical number of properties, or sum of weighted properties, included in the summary representation of that category. Followers of the probabilistic view in AI are, for instance, de la Maza who calls his type of representation-augmented prototypes. Fisher's probabilistic concept tree represents a taxonomy of probabilistic concepts.

Those in favor of the exemplar view argue that some may represent categories of their individual exemplars, and that concepts thus are represented by representations of these exemplars. A new instance is then categorized as a member of a category if it is sufficiently similar to one or more of the category's known exemplars. There are several models consistent with the exemplar view. One such model is the proximity model that simply stores all instances. An instance is categorized as a member of the category that contains its most similar stored exemplar. Another model is the best examples model. It only stores selected, typical instances. This model assumes that a prototype exists for each category and that it is represented as a subset of the exemplars of the category. Another possible alternative is that the prototype is a nonexistent average instance that is derived from the known instances.

In AI, Kibler and Aha have experimented with both the proximity model and selected examples models where a subset of the instances is stored. Systems that use this kind of representation often use some version of the nearest-neighbor algorithm to classify unknown instances. That is, a novel instance is classified according to its most similar known instance. Musgrove and Phelps have chosen to have a singular representation of the average member (not necessarily an actual instance) of the category, which they call the prototype. Nagel presents a best examples model that, in addition to the prototypes, stores transformations that change less typical instances to a prototype. Learning systems that use specific instances rather than abstractions to represent concepts have been labeled instance-based systems.

Michalski takes a different approach to nontraditional concept representation and his colleagues. Their representation has two components, the base concept representation (BCR) and the inferential concept interpretation (ICI). The BCR is a classical representation that is supposed to capture typical and relevant aspects of the category, whereas the ICI should handle exceptional or borderline cases. When categorizing an unknown object, the object is first matched against the BCR. Then, depending on the outcome, the ICI either extends or specializes the BCR to see if the object really belongs to the category.

These nontraditional representations are sometimes commonly called prototype-based representations. In addition to what is normally called prototype-based representations, there has in the last few years been a growing optimism about the capability of neural networks for dealing with concepts. For instance, back-propagation networks have been suggested for the learning and representation of concepts.

Discussion

So, how should autonomous agents represent concepts? Should we use logic-based representations, decision trees, instance-based or probabilistic representations, or maybe neural networks? Let us analyze these questions in terms of the functions that the concepts should be able to serve, starting with the epistemological function.

The epistemological function of concepts is what makes an agent able to classify objects based on the perceptual input that it receives from the environment. It was mentioned earlier that it is not possible to find a definition based on necessary and sufficient conditions for all natural categories (the ontological problem). Even if such a definition exists, as is true for many categories, it is often based on features that under normal circumstances are not detectable by an agent's perceptual system. Examples of such features are atomic structure, genetic code, and functionality (of the instances of the category). Thus, classical definitions are not adequate for perceptual classification and consequently not appropriate for supporting the epistemological function. Contrary to this conclusion, it is common in ML to try to make a classical definition of a category based directly on the perceptual data. The metaphysical function of concepts, on the other hand, is what determines if an object actually is an instance of a particular category. Such crucial conditions for category membership might not exist for all categories (an obvious consequence of the ontological problem). Also, these conditions must hold for every instance of the category and must be explicitly stated. This implies that prototype-based representations are not adequate for supporting the metaphysical function.

Finally, to implement the inferential function we must have some encyclopedic knowledge about the category and its members. Kirsh has called this collection of knowledge "a package of associated glop." It includes mainly declarative knowledge, in contrast to the more procedural classification knowledge. Concerning the representation of this knowledge, it is obviously not adequate to use classical definitions or prototype-based representations. They should, of course, be used for classification purposes only (representing classification knowledge).

The Idea of a Composite Structure

The discussion above makes clear that it is not possible for a single and simple structure to capture all the relevant aspects of a concept. We need a richer composite representation that, in some way, is structured according to the functions of the concept to be represented. For instance, in daylight wasps can be recognized by their look, whereas they must be recognized by their sound when it is dark. Let us illustrate the idea of composite representation using the category "wasp." The kind of information that the epistemological representation may include are that wasps are black- and yellow-striped, cylinder-shaped, approximately two centimeters long and half a centimeter in diameter, hum, have two wings, and so on. The metaphysical representation on the other hand, may include information of the genetic code of wasps. The kinds of encyclopedic knowledge that the associated glop would include are, for instance, that they can hurt other animates with their stings and that they live in collectives. The internal designator could be something like `organism.animate.xxx`, whereas the external designator would be "wasp" (in an environment where communication is based on the English language, that is).

There are no sharp distinctions between what information is included in these representations in the sense that they may contain redundant information. For example, besides being an essential part of the epistemological representation, the fact that wasps have wings is a rather natural part of the encyclopedic knowledge represented in the associated glop. However, the fact is probably not represented in the same way in these representations. For instance, it may be implicitly represented in a prototype-based representation for the epistemological representation and explicitly represented in a logic-based notion for the associated glop.

This composite structure enables concepts to serve all the functions listed before. The epistemological and metaphysical representations support the epistemological and metaphysical functions, respectively. The associated glop supports the inferential function. The internal designator supports the intrapersonal stability, whereas the external designator supports both the interpersonal stability and the linguistic function.

An issue that is not yet discussed is how these concept structures should be organized and how they relate to each other. We know that categories can be hierarchically organized in taxonomies. For instance, "fruit" is a superclass category to "apple," whereas "Red Delicious" is a subordinate category. Taxonomies serve an important function by promoting cognitive economy. Because categories inherit features from their superclass categories, it is possible to reduce the amount of information that have to be stored at each level in the hierarchy. For instance, if we know that all fruits are sweet, we do not have to remember that apples are sweet (if we know that apples are fruits).

Thus, how to complete the choice of the internal designator is entirely up to the system, it should be as convenient and effective as possible for the system. However, it seems that it is mainly encyclopedic knowledge that can be inherited in this manner. It is not clear how this could be done with classification knowledge (epistemological and metaphysical). If it is possible, composite representation suggested above with taxonomical information, so that the concepts together form a tree structure.

Depending on the situation, the composite concept representation is accessed (or retrieved) in different ways. External stimuli in the form of direct perception of objects access the concept via the epistemological representation. Thus, the epistemological representation reminds of percepts as described by Sowa in the context of his theory of conceptual graphs. If, on the other hand, the external stimuli are on the linguistic level, as when communicating with other agents, the concept is accessed via the external designator. Finally, if the stimulus is internal, like in the case of reasoning, the concept is accessed via the internal designator.

How Should the Components Be Represented?

We now know what information should be included in the different parts of the composite structure, but not how it should be represented. Classical definitions are not adequate for supporting the epistemological function. Moreover, the bulk of research on this matter in cognitive science suggests that humans probably use some kind of prototype-based representations for this purpose. Thus, it seems that a prototype-based representation would be a good choice for the epistemological representation. Because there exist several such representations — probabilistic, instance-based, and different types of neural networks — it is a subject for future research to find the best choice of these or invent better ones.

The reasons for not using prototype-based representations to support the metaphysical function were that the crucial condition for category membership must hold for every instance and be explicitly stated. Thus, the implementation of the metaphysical function demands, almost by definition, a classical definition. The most common ways to express such a definition are either in a logic-based notation, such as predicate logic, or by a decision tree. To support the inferential function we need some encyclopedic knowledge about the category and its members. This knowledge might be seen as a collection of universal or probabilistic rules. Seen from this perspective, it seems natural to express it in some logic-based notation. However, alternative approaches exist, for instance, semantic networks and frames. (In fact, one might see the composite structure suggested above as a "metaframe" where the five parts correspond to slots to be filled in.)

The knowledge components for a concept (kind) are name, description, and definition (list of property values). A knowledge structure for a concept identifies the relationships among these knowledge components.

This concept knowledge structure attempts to show the following relationships. A concept (kind) is always some subclass of another class (the superclass). There must always be at least two kinds of coordinate classes. Each subordinate coordinate class shares a set of properties with the superclass. Properties that have different values for two more of the subordinate (coordinate) classes are called discriminating properties. Not all properties are discriminating properties, only those that have different values for different coordinate classes are. Class membership in a given coordinate class is determined by the set of values that the discriminating properties assume for members of this class.

The concept map is an instructional tool that has been devised on the basis of Ausubel's learning theory.[1] Concept maps serve to clarify links between new and old knowledge and force the learner to externalize those links. Concept maps are useful tools to help students learn about their knowledge structure and the process of knowledge construction (metaknowledge). In this way, concept maps also help the student learn how to learn (metalearning). Concept mapping requires the learner to operate at all six levels of Bloom's (1956) educational objectives according to Novak and Gowin.[2]

Concept maps can make clear to the student (and instructor for curriculum development purposes) how small the number of truly important concepts they have to learn. Voluminous prose can be distilled into essential and linked ideas. Concept maps externalize a person's knowledge structure, therefore, concept maps can serve to point out any conceptual misconceptions the person may have concerning the knowledge structure. This explicit evaluation of knowledge and subsequent recognition of misconceptions allows for finely targeted remediation. Furthermore, because concept maps are visual images they tend to be more easily remembered than text.[2]

Notes

1. Novak, J. Applying Learning Psychology and Philosophy to Biology Teaching. *The American Biology Teacher* 43(1), 1981, pp. 12–20.
2. Novak, J., and Gowin, D. *Learning How to Learn* (New York: Cambridge University Press, 1984).

Chapter 8

Case-Based Reasoning

A discussion about types of knowledge would not be complete without mentioning case-based reasoning (CBR). CBR is an intelligent-systems method that enables information managers to increase efficiency and reduce cost by substantially automating processes such as diagnosis, scheduling, and design. CBR works by matching new problems to "cases" from a historical database and then adapting successful solutions from the past to current situations. Many government agencies and corporate organizations have made use of CBR in applications such as customer support, quality assurance, automobile maintenance, help desk, process planning, and decision support. CBR components can be added to existing information systems.

CBR is a problem-solving paradigm that in many respects is fundamentally different from other major AI approaches. Instead of relying solely on general knowledge of a problem domain, or making associations along generalized relationships between problem descriptors and conclusions, CBR is able to utilize the specific knowledge of previously experienced, concrete problem situations (cases). Finding a similar past case and reusing it in the new problem situation solves a new problem. A second important difference is that CBR also is an approach to incremental, sustained learning, because a new experience is retained each time a problem has been solved, making it immediately available for future problems.

What is CBR? CBR solves a new problem by referring to a previous similar situation and reusing information and knowledge of that situation. To illustrate this lets look at the following examples:

- A computer operator, after discovering a system error causing the nightly database update to stop, examines the error and compares it against a database of previously experienced errors of this kind. After examining the error, it is determined that a similar error has occurred, the solution is displayed to the operator, and the operator corrects the error and processing continues.
- A doctor examining a patient will ask the patient a series of questions about what problem the patient is experiencing. After ascertaining the symptoms the patient is experiencing, the doctor would compare it to a host of ailments that exhibit similar symptoms to come up with a diagnosis and subsequent treatment.
- An auto mechanic before working on a customer's vehicle would ask the customer a series of questions to get a basis of where to start to diagnosis the problem and determine what has to be repaired. After obtaining the information the mechanic, based on previous experience (previous case), would know where to look to determine the exact problem and solution for the repair.

Case-Based Problem Solving

As the above examples indicate, reasoning by reusing past cases is a powerful and frequently applied way to solve problems for humans. This claim is also supported by results from cognitive psychological research. Part of the foundation for the case-based approach is its psychological plausibility. Several studies have given empirical evidence for the dominating role of specific, previously experienced situations (what we call cases) in human problem solving.

> Schank developed a theory of learning and reminding based on retaining of experience in a dynamic, evolving memory structure. Anderson has shown that people use past cases as models when learning to solve problems, particularly in early learning. Other results (e.g., by W.B. Rouse) indicate that the use of past cases is a predominant problem solving method among experts as well. A study of problem solving by analogy (e.g., [Gentner, Carbonell]) also shows the frequent use of past experience in solving new and different problems. Case-based reasoning and analogy are sometimes used as synonyms (e.g., by Carbonell).[1]

CBR can also be considered a form of intradomain analogy. In CBR terminology, a case is associated with a problem situation. A previously experienced situation, which has been captured and learned in a way that it can be reused in the solving of future problems, is referred to as a past case, previous case, stored case, or retained case. Correspondingly, a new case or unsolved case is the description of a new problem to be solved. CBR is basically a cyclic problem-solving process. CBR will constantly add new cases, in effect learning from new experiences and adding these cases to the knowledge base.

Learning in Case-Based Reasoning

An important feature of CBR is its coupling to learning. The driving force behind case-based methods has largely come from the machine-learning community, and CBR is also regarded a subfield of machine learning. Thus, the notion of CBR does not only denote a particular reasoning method, irrespective of how the cases are acquired, it also denotes a machine-learning paradigm that enables sustained learning by updating the case base after a problem has been solved. Learning in CBR occurs as a natural by-product of problem solving. When a problem is successfully solved, the experience is retained to solve similar problems in the future. When an attempt to solve a problem fails, the reason for the failure is identified and remembered to avoid the making same mistake in the future.

CBR favors learning from experience, because it is usually easier to learn by retaining a concrete problem-solving experience than to generalize from it. Still, effective learning in CBR requires a well worked out set of methods to extract relevant knowledge from the experience, integrate a case into an existing knowledge structure, and index the case for later matching with similar cases.

Combining Cases with Other Knowledge

By examining theoretical and experimental results from cognitive psychology, it seems clear that human problem solving and learning in general are processes that involve the representation and utilization of several types of knowledge and the combination of several reasoning methods. If cognitive plausibility is a guiding principle, an architecture for intelligence, where the reuse of cases is at the center, should also incorporate other and more general types of knowledge in one form or another. This is an issue of current concern in CBR research.

History of the Case-Based Reasoning Field

The roots of CBR in AI are found in the works of Roger Schank on dynamic memory and the central role that a reminding of earlier situations (episodes, cases) and situation patterns (scripts, memory organization packets [MOPs]) has in problem solving and learning. Other trails into the CBR field have come from the study of analogical reasoning, and from theories of concept formation, problem solving, and experiential learning within philosophy and psychology (e.g., Wittgenstein, Tulving, Smith). Wittgenstein observed "natural concepts": concepts that are part of the natural world, such as a bird, an orange, a chair, a car, etc., are polymorphic. This means "their instances may be categorized in a variety of ways, and it is not possible to come up with a useful classical definition, in terms of a set of necessary and sufficient features, for such concepts. An answer to this problem is to represent a concept extensionally, defined by its set of instances or cases."[1]

The first system that might be called a case-based reasoner was the CYRUS system, developed by Janet Kolodner, at Yale University. CYRUS was based on Schank's dynamic memory model and MOP theory of problem solving and learning. It was basically a question-answering system with knowledge of the various travels and meetings of former U.S. Secretary of State Cyrus Vance. The case memory model developed for this system has later served as basis for several other CBR systems (including MEDIATOR, PERSUADER, CHEF, JULIA, CASEY).

Bruce Porter and his group at the University of Texas–Austin, developed another basis for CBR and another set of models. They initially addressed the machine-learning problem of concept learning for classification tasks. This led to the development of the PROTOS system, which emphasized integrating general domain knowledge and specific case knowledge into a unified representation structure. The combination of cases with general domain knowledge was pushed further in GREBE, an application in the domain of law.

CBR work has been strongly coupled to expert systems development and knowledge acquisition research. Among the earliest results was the work on CBR for complex technical diagnosis within the MOLTKE system, done by Michael Richter together with Klaus Dieter Althoff and others at the University of Kaiserslautern. This led to the PATDEX system, with Stefan Wess as the main developer, and later to several other systems and methods. At IIIA (Institut d'Investigació en Intel·ligència Artificial) in Blanes, Enric Plaza and Ramon Lopez de Mantaras developed a case-based learning apprentice system for medical diagnosis, and Beatrice Lopez investigated the use of case-based methods for strategy-level reasoning.

Fundamentals of Case-Based Reasoning Methods

Central tasks that all CBR methods have to deal with are to identify the current problem situation, find a past case similar to the new one, use that case to suggest a solution to the current problem, evaluate the proposed solution, and update the system by learning from this experience. How this is done and what type of problems drive the methods will vary considerably, however.

The CBR paradigm covers a range of different methods for organizing, retrieving, utilizing, and indexing the knowledge retained in past cases. Cases may be kept as concrete experiences, or a set of similar cases may form a generalized case. Cases may be stored as separate knowledge units or split up into subunits and distributed within the knowledge structure. Cases may be indexed by a prefixed or open vocabulary and within a flat or hierarchical index structure. The solution from a previous case may be directly applied to the present problem or modified according to differences between the two cases. The matching of cases, adaptation of solutions, and learning from an experience may be guided and supported by a deep model of general domain knowledge, by more shallow and compiled knowledge, or be based on an apparent, syntactic similarity only. CBR methods may be purely self-contained and automatic, or they may interact heavily with the user for support and guidance of its choices. Some CBR methods assume a large amount of widely distributed cases in their case base, while others are based on a more limited set of typical ones. Past cases may be retrieved and evaluated sequentially or in parallel. Other terms related to CBR are discussed next.

Exemplar-Based Reasoning

> The term is derived from a classification of different views to concept definition into 'the classical view,' 'the probabilistic view,' and 'the exemplar view.' In the exemplar view, a concept is defined extensionally, as the set of its exemplars. CBR methods that address the learning of concept definitions (i.e., the problem addressed by most of the research in machine learning), are sometimes referred to as exemplar-based. Examples are early papers by Kibler and Aha [Kibler-87], and Bareiss and Porter.[1]

In this approach, solving a problem is a classification task (i.e., finding the right class for the unclassified exemplar). The class of the most similar past case becomes the solution to the classification problem. The set of classes constitutes the set of possible solutions. Therefore, modification of a solution found is outside the scope of this method.

Instance-Based Reasoning

This is a specialization of exemplar-based reasoning into a highly syntactic CBR approach. To compensate for lack of guidance from general background knowledge, a relatively large number of instances are needed to close in on a concept definition. The representation of the instances are usually simple (e.g., feature vectors), because a major focus is to study automated learning with no user in the loop. Instance-based reasoning labels recent work by Kibler and Aha and colleagues and serves to distinguish their methods from more knowledge-intensive exemplar-based approaches (e.g., PROTOS' methods). Basically, this is a nongeneralization approach to the concept learning problem addressed by classical, inductive machine-learning methods.

Memory-Based Reasoning

This approach emphasizes a collection of cases as a large memory and reasoning as a process of accessing and searching in this memory. Memory organization and access is a focus of the case-based methods. The utilization of parallel processing techniques is a characteristic of these methods and distinguishes this approach from the others. The access and storage methods may rely on purely syntactic criteria, as in the MBR-Talk system, or they may attempt to utilize general domain knowledge, as in PARADYME and the work done in Japan on massive parallel memories.

Case-Based Reasoning

Although CBR is used as a generic term in this chapter, the typical CBR methods have some characteristics that distinguish them from the other approaches listed here. First, a typical case is usually assumed to have a certain degree of richness of information contained in it and a certain complexity with respect to its internal organization. That is, a feature vector holding some values and a corresponding class is not what we would call a typical case description. What we refer to as typical case-based methods also have another characteristic property: They are able to modify or adapt a retrieved solution when applied in a different problem-solving context. Paradigmatic case-based methods also utilize general background knowledge — although its richness, degree of explicit representation, and role within the CBR processes vary. Core methods of typical CBR systems borrow a lot from cognitive psychology theories.

Analogy-Based Reasoning

This term is sometimes used, as a synonym for CBR, to describe the typical case-based approach just described. However, it is also often used to characterize methods that solve new problems based on past cases from a different domain. Typical case-based methods focus on indexing and matching strategies for single-domain cases. Research on analogy reasoning is therefore a subfield concerned with mechanisms for identification and utilization of cross-domain analogies. The major focus of study has been on the reuse of a past case, what is called the mapping problem: finding a way to transfer or map the solution of an identified analogue (source or base) to the present problem (target).

Case-Based Reasoning Problem Areas

As for AI in general, there are no universal CBR methods suitable for every domain of application. The challenge in CBR as elsewhere is to come up with methods that are suited for problem solving and learning in particular subject domains and for particular application environments. Core problems addressed by CBR research can be grouped into five areas.

1. Knowledge representation
2. Retrieval methods
3. Reuse methods
4. Revise methods
5. Retain methods

In the next five sections, we give an overview of the main problem issues related to these five areas and exemplify how they are solved by some existing methods. Our examples will be drawn from the six systems PROTOS, CHEF, CASEY, PATDEX, BOLERO, and CREEK. In the recently published book by Janet Kolodner, these problems are discussed and elaborated to substantial depth, and hints and guidelines on how to deal with them are given.

Representation of Cases

CBR is heavily dependent on the structure and content of its collection of cases, which is often referred to as its case memory. Because a problem is solved by recalling a previous experience suitable for solving the new problem, the case search and matching processes need to be both effective and reasonably time efficient. Further, because the experience from a problem just solved has to be retained in some way, these requirements also apply to the method of integrating a new case into the memory. The representation problem in CBR is primarily the problem of deciding what to store in a case, finding an appropriate structure for describing case contents, and deciding how the case memory should be organized and indexed for effective retrieval and reuse. An additional problem is how to integrate the case memory structure into a model of general domain knowledge to the extent that such knowledge is incorporated.

In the following section, two influential case memory models are briefly reviewed: the dynamic memory model of Schank and Kolodner and the category-exemplar model of Porter and Bareiss.

The Dynamic Memory Model

As previously mentioned, the first system that may be referred to as a case-based reasoner was Kolodner's CYRUS system, based on Schank's dynamic memory model. The case memory in this model is a hierarchical structure of what is called "episodic memory organization packets" (E-MOPs, also referred to as generalized episodes [GEs]). This model was developed from Schank's more general MOP theory. The basic idea is to organize specific cases that share similar properties under a more general structure (a GE). A GE contains three different types of objects — norms, cases, and indexes. Norms are features common to all cases indexed under a GE. Indexes are features that discriminate between a GE's cases. An index may point to a more specific GE or directly to a case. An index is composed of two terms — an index name and an index value.

When a new case description is given and the best matching is searched for, the input case structure is "pushed down" the network structure, starting at the root node. The search procedure is similar for case retrieval as for case storing. When one or more features of the case matches one or more features of a GE, the case is further discriminated based on its remaining features. Eventually, the case with the most features in common with the input case is found. During storage of a new case, when a feature of the new case matches a feature of an existing case, a GE is created. The two cases are then discriminated by indexing them under different indexes below this GE. If during the storage of a case, two cases (or two GEs) end up under the same index, a new GE is automatically created. Hence, the memory structure is dynamic in the sense that similar parts of two case descriptions are dynamically generalized into a GE, and the cases are indexed under this GE by their difference features.

Finding the GE with most norms in common with the problem description retrieves a case. Indexes under that GE are then traversed to find the case that contains most of the additional problem features. Storing a new case is performed in the same way, with the additional process of dynamically creating GEs, as described above. Because the index structure is a discrimination network, a case (or pointer to a case) is stored under each index that discriminates it from other cases. This may easily lead to an explosive growth of indexes with an increased number of cases.

Therefore, most systems using this indexing scheme put some limits to the choice of indexes for the cases. In CYRUS, for example, only a small vocabulary of indexes is permitted.

CASEY stores a large amount of information in its cases. In addition to all observed features, it retains the causal explanation for the diagnosis found, as well as the list of states in the heart failure model for which there was evidence in the patient. These states, referred to as generalized causal states, are also the primary indexes to the cases.

The primary role of a GE is as an indexing structure for matching and retrieval of cases. The dynamic properties of this memory organization, however, may also be viewed as an attempt to build a memory structure, which integrates knowledge from specific episodes with knowledge generalized from the same episodes. Therefore, it is claimed that this knowledge organization structure is suitable for learning generalized knowledge as well as case-specific knowledge and that it is a plausible — although simplified — model of human reasoning and learning.

Case Retrieval

The retrieve task starts with a (partial) problem description and ends when a best-matching previous case has been found. Its subtasks are referred to as identify features, initially match, search, and select, and are executed in that order. The identification task basically comes up with a set of relevant problem descriptors. The goal of the matching task is to return a set of cases that are sufficiently similar to the new case, given a similarity threshold of some kind. The selection task works on this set of cases and chooses the best match (or at least a first case to try out).

> While some case-based approaches retrieve a previous case largely based on superficial, syntactical similarities among problem descriptors (e.g., the CYRUS system, ARC, and PATDEX-1 systems), some approaches attempt to retrieve cases based on features that have deeper, semantically similarities (e.g., the PROTOS, CASEY, GREBE, CREEK, and MMA systems). Ongoing work in the FABEL project, aimed to develop a decision support system for architects, explores various methods for combined reasoning and mutual support of different knowledge types.[1]

To match cases based on semantic similarities and relative importance of features, an extensive body of general domain knowledge is needed to produce an explanation of why two cases match and how strong the match is. Syntactic similarity assessment (sometimes referred to as a "knowledge-poor" approach) has its advantage in domains where general domain knowledge is difficult or impossible to acquire. On the other hand, semantically oriented approaches (referred to as "knowledge-intensive") are able to use the contextual meaning of a problem description in its matching, for domains where general domain knowledge is available.

A question that should be asked when deciding on a retrieval strategy is the purpose of the retrieval task. If the purpose is to retrieve a case that is to be adapted for reuse, this can be accounted for in the retrieval method. Approaches to "retrieval for adaptation" have been suggested for retrieval of cases for design problem solving and for analogy reasoning.

Identify Feature

To identify a problem may involve simply noticing its input descriptors, but often — and particularly for knowledge-intensive methods — a more elaborate approach is taken, in which an attempt is made to understand the problem within its context. Unknown descriptors may be disregarded or requested to be explained by the user. In PROTOS, for example, if an input feature is unknown to the system, the user is asked to supply an explanation that links the feature into the existing semantic network (category structure). To understand a problem involves filtering out noisy problem descriptors, inferring other relevant problem features, checking whether the feature values make sense within the context, generating expectations of other features, etc. Other descriptors than those given as input may be inferred by using a general knowledge model or by retrieving a similar problem description from the case base and using features of that case as expected features. Checking of expectations may be done within the knowledge model (cases and general knowledge) or by asking the user.

Initially Match

The task of finding a good match is typically split into two subtasks: an initial matching process that retrieves a set of plausible candidates and a more elaborate process of selecting the best one among these. Finding a set of matching cases is done by using the problem descriptors (input features) as indexes to the case memory in a direct or indirect way. There are, in principle, three ways of retrieving a case or a set of cases:

1. Following direct index pointers from problem features
2. Searching an index structure
3. Searching in a model of general domain knowledge

A domain-dependent, but global similarity metric is used to assess similarity based on surface match. Dynamic memory-based systems take the second approach, but general domain knowledge may be used in combination with searches in the discrimination network. PROTOS and CREEK combine the first and third ways, because direct pointers are used to hypothesize a candidate set that in turn is justified as plausible matches by use of general knowledge.

Cases may be retrieved solely from input features or also from features inferred from the input. Cases that match all input features are, of course, good candidates for matching, but — depending on the strategy — cases that match a given fraction of the problem features (input or inferred) may also be retrieved. PATDEX uses a global similarity metric with several parameters that are set as part of the domain analysis. Some tests for relevance of a retrieved case are often executed, particularly if cases are retrieved on the basis of a subset of features. For example, a simple relevance test may be to check if a retrieved solution conforms to the expected solution type of the new problem. A way to assess the degree of similarity is needed, and several similarity metrics have been proposed, based on surface similarities of problem and case features.

Similarity assessment may also be more knowledge intensive, for example, by trying to understand the problem more deeply and by using the goals, constraints, etc., from this elaboration process to guide the matching. Another option is to weigh the problem descriptors according to their importance for characterizing the problem during the learning phase. In PROTOS, for example, each feature in a stored case has assigned to it a degree of importance for the solution of the case. A similar mechanism is adopted by CREEK, which stores both the predictive strength (discriminatory value) of a feature with respect to the set of cases, as well as a features criticality (i.e., what influence the lack of a feature has on the case solution).

Select

From the set of similar cases, a best match is chosen. This may have been done during the initial match process, but more often a set of cases is returned from that task. The best-matching case is usually determined by evaluating the degree of initial match more closely. This is done by an attempt to generate explanations to justify nonidentical features, based on the knowledge in the semantic network. If a match turns out not to be strong enough, an attempt to find a better match by following different links to closely related cases is made. This subtask is usually a more elaborate one than the retrieval task, although the distinction between retrieval and elaborate matching is not distinct in all systems. The selection process typically generates consequences and expectations from each retrieved case and attempts to evaluate consequences and justify expectations. This may be done by using the system's own model of general domain knowledge or by asking the user for confirmation and additional information. The cases are eventually ranked according to some metric or ranking criteria. Knowledge-intensive selection methods typically generate explanations that support this ranking process, and the case that has the strongest explanation for being similar to the new problem is chosen. Other properties of a case that are considered in some CBR systems include relative importance and discriminatory strengths of features, prototypically of a case within its assigned class, and difference links to related cases.

Case Reuse

The reuse of the retrieved case solution in the context of the new case focuses on the following two aspects:

1. The differences between the past and the current case
2. What part of a retrieved case can be transferred to the new case

Copy

In simple classification tasks, the differences are abstracted away (they are considered nonrelevant but similarities are relevant) and the solution class of the retrieved case is transferred to the new case as its solution class. This is a trivial type of reuse. However, other systems have to take into account differences in item 1 (see list under Case Reuse), and thus the reused part (item 2) cannot be directly transferred to the new case but requires an adaptation process that takes into account those differences.

Adapt

There are two main ways to reuse past cases:

1. Reuse the past case solution (transformational reuse).
2. Reuse the past method that constructed the solution (derivational reuse).

In transformational reuse, the past case solution is not directly a solution for the new case but there exists some knowledge in the form of transformational operators (T), such that applied to the old solution they transform it into a solution for the new case. A way to organize these T operators is to index them around the differences detected among the retrieved and current cases. An example of this is CASEY, where a new causal explanation is built from the old causal explanations by rules with condition-part indexing differences and with a transformational operator T at the action part of the rule. Transformational reuse does not look at how a problem is solved but focuses on the equivalence of solutions. This requires a strong domain-dependent model in the form of transformational operators plus a control regime to organize the operator's application.

Derivational reuse looks at how the problem was solved in the retrieved case. The retrieved case holds information about the method used for solving the retrieved problem, including a justification of the operators used, subgoals considered, alternatives generated, failed search paths, etc. Derivational reuse then reinstantiates the retrieved method to the new case and replays the old plan into the new context (usually general problem-solving systems can be seen here as planning systems). During the replay, successful alternatives, operators, and paths will be explored first and filed paths will be avoided; new subgoals are pursued based on the old ones, and old subplans can be recursively retrieved for them. An example of derivational reuse is the Analogy/Prodigy system that reuses past plans guided by commonalities of goals and initial situations and resumes a means-ends planning regime if the retrieved plan fails or is not found.

Case Revision

When a case solution generated by the reuse phase is not correct, an opportunity for learning from failure arises. This phase is called case revision and consists of two tasks: (1) evaluate the case solution generated by reuse; if successful, learning from the success, otherwise (2) repair the case solution using domain-specific knowledge.

Evaluate Solution

The evaluation task takes the result from applying the solution in the real environment (asking a teacher or performing the task in the real world). This is usually a step outside the CBR system, because it — at least for a system in normal operation — involves the application of a suggested solution to the real problem. The results from applying the solution may take some time to appear, depending on the type of application. In a medical decision support system, the success or failure of a treatment may take from a few hours up to several months. The case may still be learned and be available in the case base in the intermediate period, but it has to be marked as a nonevaluated case. A solution may also be applied to a simulation program that is able to generate a correct solution. This is used in CHEF, where a solution (i.e., a cooking recipe) is applied to an internal model assumed to be strong enough to give the necessary feedback for solution repair.

Repair Fault

Case repair involves detecting the errors of the current solution and retrieving or generating explanations for them. The best example is the CHEF system, where causal knowledge is used to generate an explanation of why certain goals of the solution plan were not achieved. CHEF learns the general situations that will cause the failures using an explanation-based learning technique. This is included into a failure memory that is used in the reuse phase to predict possible shortcomings of plans. This form of learning moves detection of errors in a post hoc fashion to the elaboration plan phase where errors can be predicted, handled, and avoided. A second task of the revision phase is the solution repair task. This task uses the failure explanations to modify the solution in such a way that failures do not occur. For instance, the failed plan in the CHEF system is modified by a repair module that adds steps to the plan that will ensure that the causes of the errors will not occur. The repair module possesses general causal knowledge and domain knowledge about how to disable or compensate causes of errors in the domain. The revised plan can then be retained directly (if the revision phase ensures its correctness) or it can be evaluated and repaired again.

Case Retainment — Learning

This is the process of incorporating what is useful to retain from the new problem-solving episode into the existing knowledge. The learning from success or failure of the proposed solution is triggered by the outcome of the evaluation and possible repair. It involves selecting which information from the case to retain, in what form to retain it, how to index the case for later retrieval from similar problems, and how to integrate the new case in the memory structure.

Extract

In CBR, the case base is updated no matter how the problem was solved. If it was solved by use of a previous case, a new case may be built or the old case may be generalized to subsume the present case as well. If the problem was solved by other methods, including asking the user, an entirely new case will have to be constructed. In any case, a decision needs to be made about what to use as the source of learning. Relevant problem descriptors and problem solutions are obvious candidates. However, an explanation or another form of justification of why a solution is a solution to the problem may also be marked for inclusion in a new case. In CASEY and CREEK, for example, explanations are included in retained cases and reused in later modifications of the solution. CASEY uses the previous explanation structure to search for other states in the diagnostic model, which explains the input data of the new case, and to look for causes of these states as answers to the new problem. This focuses and speeds up the explanation process, compared to a search in the entire domain model. The last type of structure that may be extracted for learning is the problem-solving method (i.e., the strategic reasoning path), making the system suitable for derivational reuse.

Failures (i.e., information from the revise task) may also be extracted and retained as separate failure cases or within total-problem cases. When a failure is encountered, the system can then get a reminding to a previous similar failure, and use the failure case to improve its understanding of — and correct — the present failure.

Indexing

The indexing problem is a central and much-focused problem in CBR. It amounts to deciding what type of indexes to use for future retrieval and how to structure the search space of indexes. Direct indexes, as previously mentioned, skip the latter step, but there is still the problem of identifying what type of indexes to use. This is actually a knowledge acquisition problem and should be analyzed as part of the domain knowledge analysis and modeling step. A trivial solution to the problem is of course to use all input features as indexes. This is the approach of syntax-based methods within instance-based and memory-based reasoning. In the memory-based method of CBR-Talk, for example, relevant features are determined by matching, in parallel, all cases in the case base, and filtering out features that belong to cases with few features in common with the problem case.

In CASEY, a two-step indexing method is used. Primary index features are — as referred to in the section on representation — general causal states in the heart failure model that are part of the explanation of the case. When a new problem enters, the features are propagated in the heart failure model, and the states that explain the features are used as indexes to the case memory. The observed features themselves are used as secondary features only.

Integrate

This is the final step of updating the knowledge base with new case knowledge. If no new case and index set has been constructed, it is the main step of retain. By modifying the indexing of existing cases, CBR systems learn to become better similarity assessors. The tuning of existing indexes is an important part of CBR learning. Index strengths or importance for a particular case or solution are adjusted due to the success or failure of using the case to solve the input problem. For features that have been judged relevant for retrieving a successful case, the association with the case is strengthened, but it is weakened for features that lead to retrieval of unsuccessful cases. In this way, the index structure has a role of tuning and adapting the case memory to its use. PATDEX has a special way to learn feature relevance: A relevance matrix links possible features to the diagnosis for which they are relevant and assigns a weight to each such link. The weights are updated, based on feedback of success or failure, by a connectionist method.

In knowledge-intensive approaches to CBR, learning may also take place within the general conceptual knowledge model, for example, by other machine-learning methods (see next section) or through interaction with the user. Thus, with a proper interface to the user (whether a competent end user or an expert) a system may incrementally extend and refine its general knowledge model, as well as its memory of past cases, in the normal course of problem solving. This is an inherent method in the PROTOS system, for example. All general knowledge in PROTOS is assumed to be acquired in such a bottom-up interaction with a competent user.

Reentering the initial problem and see whether the system behaves as wanted may finally test the case just learned.

Integrated Approaches

Most CBR systems make use of general domain knowledge in addition to knowledge represented by cases. Representation and use of that domain knowledge involves integration of the case-based method with other methods and representations of problem solving, for instance, rule-based systems or deep models like causal reasoning. The overall architecture of the CBR system has to determine the interactions and control regime between the CBR method and the other components. For instance, the CASEY system integrates a model-based causal reasoning program to diagnose heart diseases. When the case-based method fails to provide a correct solution, CASEY executes the model-based method to solve the problem and stores the solution as a new case for future use. Because the model-based method is complex and slow, the case-based method in CASEY is essentially a way to achieve speed-up learning. The integration of model-based reasoning is also important for the case-based method itself: The causal model of the disease of a case is what is retrieved and reused in CASEY.

An example of integrating rules and cases is the:

> BOLERO system. BOLERO is a meta-level architecture where the base-level is composed of rules embodying knowledge to diagnose the plausible pneumonias of a patient, while the meta-level is a case-based planner that, at every moment, is able to dictate which diagnoses are worthwhile to consider. Thus in BOLERO the rule-based level contains domain knowledge (how to deduce plausible diagnosis from patient facts) while the meta-level contains strategic knowledge (it plans, from all possible goals, which are likely to be successfully achieved).[1]

Therefore, the case-based planner is used to control the space searched by the rule-based level, achieving a form of speed-up learning. The control regime between the two components is interesting: The control passes to the metalevel whenever some new information is known at the base level, ensuring that the system is dynamically able to generate a more appropriate strategic plan. This control regime in the metalevel architecture ensures that the case-based planner is capable of reactive behavior (i.e., of modifying plans reacting to situation changes). Also, the clear separation of rule-based and case-based methods in two different levels of computation is important; it clarifies their distinction and their interaction.

The integration of CBR with other reasoning paradigms is closely related to the general issue of architectures for unified problem solving and learning. This approach is a current trend in machine learning with architectures such as Soar, Theo, or Prodigy. CBR as such is a form of combining problem solving (through retrieval and reuse) and learning (through retainment). However, as we have seen, other forms of representation and reasoning are usually integrated into a CBR system and thus the general issue is an important dimension into CBR research. In the CREEK architecture, the cases, heuristic rules, and deep models are integrated into a unified knowledge structure. The main role of the general knowledge is to provide explanatory support to the case-based processes; rules or deep models may also be used to solve problems on their own if the case-based method fails. Usually the domain knowledge used in a CBR system is acquired through knowledge acquisition in the normal way for knowledge-based systems. Another option would be to also learn that knowledge from the cases. In this situation, it can be learned in a case-based way or by induction. This line of work is currently being developed in Europe by systems like the Massive Memory Architecture (MMA) and INRECA. These systems are closely related to the multistrategy learning systems; the issues of integrating different problem-solving and learning methods are essential to them.

MMA is an integrated architecture for learning and problem solving based on reuse of case experiences retained in the systems memory. A goal of MMA is understanding and implementing the relationship between learning and problem solving into a reflective or introspective framework: The system is able to inspect its own past behavior to learn how to change its structure so as to improve is future performance.

> Case-based reasoning methods are implemented by retrieval methods (to retrieve past cases), a language of preferences (to select the best case) and a form of derivational analogy (to reuse the retrieved method into the current problem). A problem in the MMA does not use one CBR method, since several CBR methods can be programmed for different subgoals by means of specific retrieval methods and domain-dependent preferences.[1]

Note

1. Aamodt, A., and Plaza, E. *AICom — Artificial Intelligence Communications* 7, Sec. 1, 1994, pp. 39–59.

Chapter 9

Knowledge Modeling

Knowledge modeling has emerged as one of the major achievements from the field of AI. Knowledge engineers can graphically represent knowledge in a variety of ways based on the type of knowledge being depicted. By conceptualizing aspects of the domain, it enables the knowledge engineer to see readily how tasks are performed and problems are solved. A well-diagramed domain makes the task of communicating to SMEs and non-experts less of an issue.

However, the type of knowledge one encounters further complicates the task of knowledge modeling. Due to the fact there are many classifications of knowledge, the appropriate modeling method used to capture specific knowledge will change from one form of knowledge to another. The type of knowledge that must be captured will fall into one or more classifications. The following represents several classifications of knowledge that can be captured:

- Declarative knowledge — Knowledge of facts (see Chapter 3)
- Procedural knowledge — Knowledge of how to do things (see Chapter 4)
- Tacit knowledge — Knowledge contained within humans that cannot be articulated easily (see Chapter 5)
- Explicit knowledge — Knowledge contained in documents, computer programs, databases, etc., which can be articulated easily (see Chapter 6)

- Process knowledge — Knowledge contained in processes (see Chapter 7)
- Concept knowledge — Knowledge contained in concepts (see Chapter 7)

The knowledge gathered by the knowledge engineer will be a combination of one or more of the knowledge classifications listed above. In the process of developing the knowledge model, the knowledge engineer will identify several "low-level" knowledge objects. These low-level knowledge objects include concepts, instances, processes, attributes and values, rules, and relationships.

The following further defines the types of low-level knowledge objects.

Concepts

Concepts are the things that constitute a domain (e.g., physical objects, ideas, people, and organizations). Each concept is described by its relationships to other concepts in the domain (e.g., in a hierarchy) and by its attributes and values. From a grammatical perspective, concepts are usually equivalent to nouns.

Instances

An *instance* is an instantiated class. For example, "my car" is an instance of the concept "car." Instances only have the attributes of their class (including inherited attributes). They may override any or all of the default values. For example, the "my car" attribute "maximum speed" may be 90 mph, overriding the default of 100 mph for all cars.

Processes (Tasks, Activities)

Processes are sets of actions performed to satisfy a goal or set of objectives. Some examples are:

- Ship a package
- Admit a patient
- Withdraw money from an ATM

Processes are described using other knowledge objects, such as inputs, outputs, resources, roles, and decision points.

Attributes and Values

Attributes and values describe the properties of other knowledge objects. *Attributes* are the generic properties, qualities, or features belonging to a class of concepts (e.g., weight, cost, age, and ability). *Values* are the specific qualities of a concept such as its actual weight or age. Values are associated with a particular attribute and can be numerical (e.g., 120 kg, 6 years old) or categorical (e.g., heavy, young). From a grammatical perspective, values are equivalent to adjectives.

Rules

Rules are statements of the form "IF ... THEN...." Some examples are:

- IF the temperature in the room is hot, THEN open the window or switch the fan on.
- IF the rate of compression of the engine is low, THEN increase the oil flow.

Relationships (Relations)

Relationships represent the way knowledge objects (such as concepts and tasks) are related to one another. Important examples include "IS A" to show classification, "PART OF" to show composition, and those used in various knowledge models such as process map or state transition network. Relationships are often represented as arrows on diagrams. From a grammatical perspective, relationships are usually equivalent to passive verbs.

To obtain a broader perspective on knowledge objects, the following discusses the concept of knowledge objects and how to construct them.

Knowledge Objects

A *knowledge object* is a precise way to describe the subject matter content or knowledge that is gathered. A knowledge object is a framework for identifying necessary knowledge components. A knowledge object is a way to organize a knowledge base of content resources (e.g., text, audio, video, graphics, etc.) to reflect the knowledge being gathered. Knowledge objects should consist of components that are not specific to a particular subject matter domain. It is desirable to have the same knowledge object components (knowledge object syntax) for representing a variety of domains (e.g., mathematics, science, humanities, technical skills, etc.). It is desirable to have a predetermined knowledge syntax rather than have user-defined knowledge components. Predetermined knowledge object syntax enables prespecified and preprogrammed instructional algorithms (strategies). User-defined knowledge components seriously limit the ability to generalize a knowledge base.[1]

A knowledge object can be used for presentation, exploration, practice, and simulation. The same knowledge object can also support parts-of, kinds-of, how-to, and what-happens types of knowledge. A knowledge object consists of a set of fields (containers) for the components of knowledge required to implement a variety of knowledge classifications.

> These components include: the name, information about, and the portrayal for some entity; the name, information about, and the portrayal for parts of the entity; the name, information about, values, and corresponding portrayals for properties of the entity; the name, and information about activities associated with the entity; and the name and information about processes associated with the entity. In the following paragraphs we will attempt to clarify these components.[1]

To clarify the components of knowledge objects, we have broken a knowledge object into five major components. These include the following:

1. Entity, some device, person, creature, place, symbol, object, thing
2. Parts of the entity
3. Properties of the entity (properties are qualities or quantities associated with the entity)
4. Activities associated with the entity (activities are actions that can be performed by the learner on, with, to, the entity)
5. Processes associated with the entity (processes are events triggered by an activity or another process that change the value of properties of the entity)

The five major components of a knowledge object are examined in more detail below.

Information Components of a Knowledge Object

All knowledge objects have a name and a portrayal and may have other associated information. Consider in the case of a transportation system, "Tariff" as a knowledge object. The name of the object will be Tariff. Information about the Tariff might include a definition: "rules associated with transporting goods across state lines." There are many possible portrayals of a Tariff: "A tariff charge of .01 cent per cubic will be charged for all goods transported between Colorado and Nevada."

Parts Component of a Knowledge Object

All entities can be subdivided into smaller entities or parts. Parts have a name, associated information, and portrayal as do entities. Parts can be subdivided into parts of parts, etc., for as many levels as may be necessary to adequately represent the entity.

For example:

- Part — Name = subject.
- Information about — "tells whom or what the sentence is about."
- Portrayal — The words, "these words," are the subject of the sentence, "These words are a sentence."
- Part of a part — Name = simple subject.
- Information about — "the main word in the complete subject."
- Portrayal — The word, "words," is the simple subject of the sentence, "These words are a sentence."
- Part — Name = predicate.
- Information about — "The part that says something about the subject."
- Portrayal — The words, "are a sentence," are the predicate of the sentence, "These words are a sentence."
- Part of a part — Name = simple predicate.
- Information about — "The main word or word group in the complete predicate."
- Portrayal — The word, "are," is the simple predicate of the sentence, "These words are a sentence."

Properties Component of a Knowledge Object

Properties cannot stand alone but must always be associated with an entity, activity, or process. A property has a name. A property has a set of legal values that the property can assume. A property has some portrayal or indicator associated with each possible property value.

For example, a sentence can express one complete thought or more than one complete thought:

- Property — Number of complete thoughts.
- Values — One, more-than-one.

- Portrayal for value of one — "A sentence expresses a complete thought."
- Portrayal for value of more-than-one — "A sentence expresses a complete thought, starts with a capital letter, and ends with a period, question mark, or exclamation point."
- Property — Purpose.
- Values — Make-a-statement, ask-a-question, make-a-request, express-emotion.
- Portrayal for make-a-statement — "Sentences enable you to express your thoughts."
- Portrayal for as-a-question — "Are you able to express your thoughts in complete sentences?"
- Portrayal for make-a-request — "Please, write a complete sentence."
- Portrayal for express-emotion — "It drives me crazy when you don't use complete sentences!"
- Property of a part — Number of simple subjects.
- Values — One, more-than-one.
- Portrayal for one — "A period is used to end a declarative sentence."
- Portrayal for more-than-one — "A period, a question mark, or an exclamation point are used to end a sentence."

Kinds Component of a Knowledge Object

Many entities can be subdivided into different kinds or classes of things. Each of these classes shares the properties of the parent entity, but the members of one class have different values on one or more of these properties than the members of another class. Class membership is defined by values on these discriminating properties.

For example, automobiles can be divided into four classes — cars, trucks, vans, SUVs.

- Kind — Car
- Property — BMW
- Value — Sedan

- Kind — Truck
- Property — Ford
- Value — Pickup

- Kind — SUV
- Property — Lincoln Navigator
- Value — Premium SUV

- Kind — Van
- Property — Chevrolet
- Value — Cab/chassis

Examples for each of these different kinds are found by finding the portrayals, which share the value of the properties that define the class. In the automobile example, each kind is defined by a value on a single property. Often a kind (class) is defined by values on two or more properties.

Knowledge Base

A knowledge object is a way to organize a knowledge base of content resources (i.e., text, audio, video, and graphics) so that a given instructional algorithm (predesigned instructional strategy) can be used to teach a variety of different contents. A knowledge base is a set of multimedia resources that instantiate the knowledge object. *Instantiate* means that in the knowledge base there is a record for each instance of the knowledge object, and that the fields in this record provide values for each of the parts and properties of the knowledge object.

Creating Objects

There are actually many approaches to object creation; the following is the most direct approach thus far:[2]

> *Step 1* — Write a description of the situation being experienced. Determine the preconditions associated with the experience. A *precondition* is a condition that must exist before the situation can be experienced. Determine the postconditions associated with the experience. A *postcondition* is a condition that must exist after the situation has been experienced.
> *Step 2* — Write a set of short concise scenarios describing what goes on during the situation being experienced.
> *Step 3* — Determine who or what is initiating the situation and who or what is supporting it.
> *Step 4* — Are there additional statements that could be added to make the object more robust; that is more findable and more usable? Think about what the pattern affects and other things that have an affect on the pattern. Patterns do not exist in isolation and the connections are important. The addition of facts at this point also forms relevance linkages to other objects with the same facts.

Step 5 — Establish a title for the object being created. A title statement should be unique to the pattern described by the object. *Step 6* — Put all the pieces together for the completed object.[2]

Object Review

Once knowledge engineers have developed an object, they should go back and read the object as though they were the intended audience. If the user in need of assistance described the situation, would the answer provided be a sound basis for action. Remember that objects are developed to provide a basis for action for individuals who need to act. If the object does not accomplish this, what is the likelihood that the user will indicate that they found the object to be of value?

Knowlegde engineers should ask themselves some questions: If I were the person describing the situation that led to this object, would it actually provide me with a means of dealing with the situation? Have I defined a pattern for which the fix I provided is the only sensible response? If the fix provided is one of several possible fixes, then go back and add things to the pattern (additional fix, symptom, change, or cause statement) to make it unambiguous. If the fix provides generalities in some areas, then code additional objects, which provide additional specifics and indicate in the fix that the user can search for these additional details if they desire? Every solution need not be written so anyone can understand it.[1]

Common Problems

The following seem to be some common problems associated with the development of objects.

Statements vs. Sentences

Although goal and fix statements should be complete sentences, fact, symptom, change, and cause statements should be complete thoughts. They do not need to be complete sentences. The intent is for these statements to be as short and concise as possible and still contain a complete thought. As fact, symptom, change, and cause statements may be presented to the user for relevance clarification out of context, they must individually make sense out of context — thus the requirement for being a complete thought. The reason for wanting them to be as short and concise as possible is to improve the possibility that the statement may be used in more than one knowledge object. The shorter and more concise the statement is the more probable its reuse becomes.[1]

Fact Statements

Facts are used to define the context in which the rest of the object is considered valid. An object that is appropriate for a new business startup may be quite inappropriate for an advanced, stable enterprise. Facts could also be used to define the knowledge domain the solution is related to, such as business development, team dynamics, etc. Aspects of the situation that were true for the environment before the situation described and after the fix is applied are probably more appropriate as cause statements or as part of the fix.

Change Statements

Change statements represent things that have changed in the recent past and are probably reasons the causes now come into play. Change statements do not represent things that need to change in the future.

Goal–Fix Relationship

For a specific goal, there should be only one fix. If there are multiple possible approaches then there must be something that determines when one fix should be used rather than the other. This would imply a difference in some part of the pattern, so two separate objects should be coded, one for each approach. Do not worry about the redundancy. Knowledge engineers know they are sacrificing efficiency for effectiveness.

Symptom–Fix Relationship

For a specific set of symptoms, there should only be one fix. If there are multiple possible approaches, then there must be something that determines when one fix should be used rather than the other. This would imply a difference in some part of the pattern, and two separate objects should be coded, one for each approach.

Cause–Fix Relationship

For a specific cause, or set of causes, there should only be one fix. If there are multiple possible approaches, then there must be something that determines when one fix should be used rather than the other; this would mean a difference in some part of the pattern, and that two separate objects should be coded for the one goal.

Once the knowledge objects have been identified, the knowledge engineer begins the task of creating knowledge models to represent the knowledge of the domain.

Knowledge Models

One of the major achievements in AI is the advent of knowledge modeling. Knowledge modeling represents the diagram-based technique to knowledge acquisition. There are myriad ways in which to model knowledge. Therefore, a thorough understanding of how knowledge can be represented is needed to accurately capture the knowledge of a domain. Here we will explore four major representations of knowledge. These representations include ladders, network diagrams, tables and grids, and decision trees.

Ladders

Ladders are hierarchical (treelike) diagrams. Some important types of ladders are the concept ladder, composition ladder, decision ladder, and attribute ladder. Laddering provides a way to validate efficiently the knowledge of the domain.

Concept Ladder

A *concept ladder* shows classes of concepts and their subtypes. All relationships in the ladder are the IS-A relationship (e.g., car is a vehicle). A concept ladder is more commonly known as a taxonomy and is vital to representing knowledge in almost all domains. See Figure 9.1 for an example of a concept ladder.

Composition Ladder

A *composition ladder* shows the way a knowledge object is composed of its constituent parts. All relationships in the ladder are the HAS-PART or PART-OF relationship (e.g., wheel is part of car). A composition ladder is a useful way of understanding complex entities such as machines, organizations, and documents. See Figure 9.2 for an example of a composition ladder.

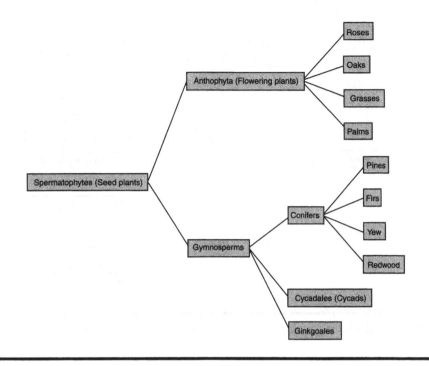

Figure 9.1 Concept Ladder. (Epistemics Web site.[3] Used with permission.)

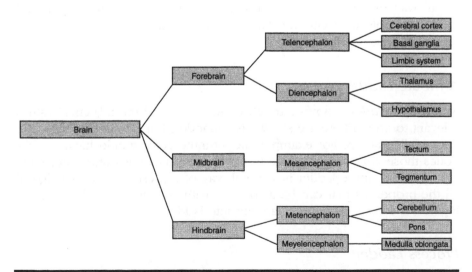

Figure 9.2 Composition Ladder. (Epistemics Web site.[3] Used with permission.)

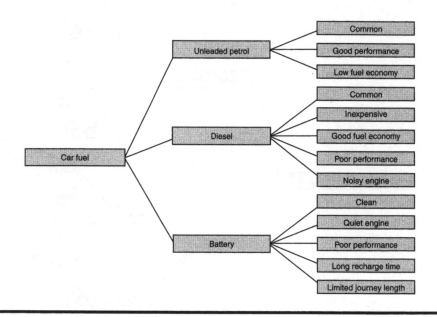

Figure 9.3   Decision Ladder. (Epistemics Web site.[3] Used with permission.)

Decision Ladder

A *decision ladder* shows the alternative courses of action for a particular decision. It also shows the pros and cons for each course of action, and possibly the assumptions for each pro and con. A decision ladder is a useful way of representing detailed process knowledge. See Figure 9.3 for an example of a decision ladder. This example determines the best type of fuel to use for a car.

Attribute Ladder

An *attribute ladder* shows attributes and values. All the adjectival values relevant to an attribute are shown as subnodes, but numerical values are not usually shown. For example, the attribute color would have as subnodes those colors appropriate in the domain as values (e.g., red, blue, green). An attribute ladder is a useful way of representing knowledge of all the properties that can be associated with concepts in a domain. See Figure 9.4 for an example of an attribute ladder.

Process Ladder

This ladder shows processes (tasks, activities) and the subprocesses (subtasks, subactivities) of which they are composed. All relationships are the

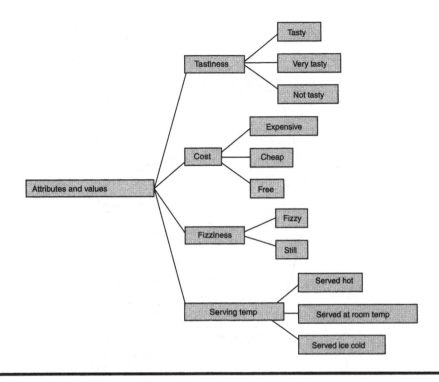

Figure 9.4   Attribute Ladder. (Epistemics Web site.[3] Used with permission.)

part of relationship (e.g., boil the kettle is part of make the tea). A process ladder is a useful way of representing process knowledge. See Figure 9.5 for an example of a process ladder.

Network Diagrams

Network diagrams show nodes connected by arrows. Depending on the type of network diagram, the nodes might represent any type of concept, attribute, value, or task, and the arrows between the nodes any type of relationship. The use of network diagrams is a useful technique when acquiring knowledge to develop object-oriented software. Examples of network diagrams include concept maps, process maps, and state transition networks.

Concept Map

A concept map is a type of diagram that shows knowledge objects as nodes and the relationships between them as links (usually labeled arrows). The knowledge objects (concepts) are usually enclosed in circles

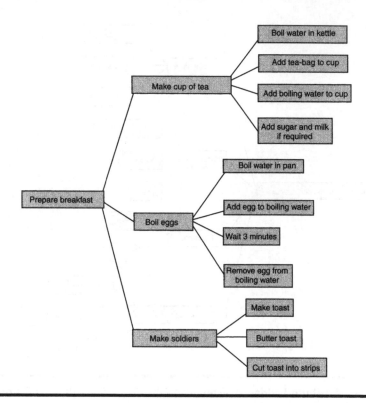

Figure 9.5   Process Ladder. (Epistemics Web site.[3] Used with permission.)

or boxes of some type, and relationships between concepts or propositions are indicated by a connecting line between two concepts. Words on the line specify the relationship between the two concepts.

> We define concept as a perceived regularity in events or objects, or records of events or objects, designated by a label. The label for most concepts is a word, although sometimes we use symbols such as + or %. Propositions are statements about some object or event in the universe, either naturally occurring or constructed. Propositions contain two or more concepts connected with other words to form a meaningful statement.[4]

Any types of concepts and relationships can be used. The concept map is similar to a semantic network used in cognitive psychology. An example of a concept map describing the structure of concept maps is shown below.

Concepts are represented in a hierarchical fashion with the most inclusive, most general concepts at the top of the map and the more specific, less general concepts arranged hierarchically below. The hierarchical structure for a particular domain of knowledge also depends on

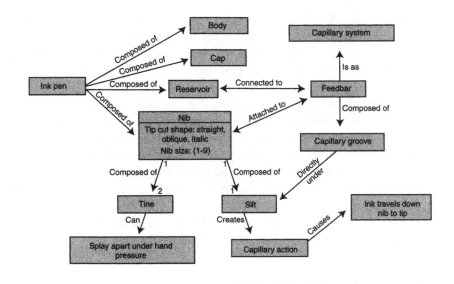

Figure 9.6   Concept Map. (Epistemics Web site.[3] Used with permission.)

the context in which that knowledge is being applied or considered. Therefore, it is best to construct concept maps with reference to some particular question we seek to answer or some situation or event that we are trying to understand through the organization of knowledge in the form of a concept map.

Another important characteristic of concept maps is the inclusion of "cross-links." These are relationships (propositions) between concepts in different domains of the concept map. Cross-links help us to see how some domains of knowledge represented on the map are related to each other. In the creation of new knowledge, cross-links often represent creative leaps on the part of the knowledge producer. There are two features of concept maps that are important in the facilitation of creative thinking: the hierarchical structure that is represented in a good map and the ability to search for and characterize cross-links. The final features that may be added to concept maps are specific examples of events or objects that help to clarify the meaning of a given concept; see Figure 9.6 as an example.

Epistemological Foundations

We defined concepts as perceived regularities in events or objects, or records of events or objects, designated by labels. What is coming to be generally recognized now is that the meaningful learning processes described above are the same processes used by scientists and mathematicians to construct new knowledge. In fact, knowledge construction is nothing other than a relatively high level of meaningful learning.[3,5]

As defined above, concepts and propositions are the building blocks for knowledge in any domain. We can use the analogy that concepts are like the atoms of matter and propositions are like the molecules of matter. There are now about 460,000 words in the English language, and these can be combined to form an infinite number of propositions; albeit most combinations of words might be nonsense, there is still the possibility of creating an infinite number of valid propositions. We shall never run out of opportunities to create new knowledge! As people create and observe new or existing objects or events, the creative people will continue to create new knowledge.

There is value in studying more extensively with the process of knowledge construction and the nature of knowledge.

Constructing Good Concept Maps

In learning to construct a concept map, it is important to begin with a domain of knowledge that is familiar to the person constructing the map. Because concept map structures depend on the context in which they will be used, it is best to identify a segment of a text, a laboratory activity, or a particular problem or question that one is trying to understand. This creates a context that will help to determine the hierarchical structure of the concept map. It is also helpful to select a limited domain of knowledge for the first concept maps.

Once a domain has been selected, the next step is to identify the key concepts that apply to this domain. These could be listed, and then from this list a rank order should be established from the most general, most inclusive concept for this particular problem or situation to the most specific, least general concept. Although this rank order may be only approximate, it helps to begin the process of map construction.

The next step is to construct a preliminary concept map. This can be done by writing all of the concepts on Post-it® notes or preferably by using this computer software program. Post-its allow a group to work on a whiteboard or butcher paper and to move concepts around easily. This is necessary as one begins to struggle with the process of building a good hierarchical organization. Computer software programs are even better in that they allow moving of concepts together with linking statements as well as the moving of groups of concepts and links to restructure the map. They also permit a computer printout, producing a nice product that can be easily shared (e.g., via e-mail) with collaborators or other interested parties.

It is important to recognize that a concept map is never finished. After a preliminary map is constructed, it is always necessary to revise this map. Good maps usually undergo three or more revisions. This is one reason why computer software is helpful. After a preliminary map is constructed, cross-links should be sought. These are links between different domains of knowledge on the map that help to illustrate how these domains are related to one another. Finally, the map should be revised, concepts positioned in ways that lend to clarity, and a "final" map prepared. When computer software is used, one can go back and change the size and font style to "dress up" the concept map.

It is important to help students recognize that all concepts are in some way related to one another. Therefore, it is necessary to be selective in identifying cross-links and to be as precise as possible in identifying linking words that connect concepts. In addition, one should avoid "sentences in the boxes," because this usually indicates that a whole subsection of the map could be constructed from the statement in the box. "String maps" illustrate either poor understanding of the material or an inadequate restructuring of the map.

Students often comment that it is hard to add linking words to their concept map. This is because they only poorly understand the relationship between the concepts and it is the linking words that specify this relationship. Once students begin to focus on good linking words, and also identification of good cross-links, they can see that every concept could be related to every other concept. This also produces some frustration, and they must choose to identify the most prominent and most useful cross-links. This process involves what Bloom (1956) identified as high levels of cognitive performance, namely evaluation and synthesis of knowledge. Concept mapping is an easy way to achieve high levels of cognitive performance, when the process is done well. This is one reason concept mapping can be a powerful evaluation tool.

Concept Maps for Evaluation

We are now beginning to see in many science textbooks the inclusion of concept mapping as one way to summarize understandings acquired by students after they study a unit or chapter. Change in school practices is always slow, but it is likely that the use of concept maps in school instruction will increase substantially in the next decade or two. When concept maps are used in instruction, they can also be used for evaluation. There is nothing written in stone that says multiple-choice tests must be used from grade school through university, and perhaps in time even national achievement exams will utilize concept mapping as a powerful evaluation tool. This is a chicken-and-egg problem because concept maps cannot be required on national achievement tests if most students have not been given opportunities to learn to use this knowledge representation tool. On the other hand, if state, regional, and national exams would begin to include concept maps as a segment of the exam, there would be a great incentive for teachers to teach students how to use this tool. Hopefully, by the year 2061, this will come to pass.

Process Map

Another important type of network diagram is a process map. This type of diagram shows the inputs, outputs, resources, roles, and decisions associated with each process or task in a domain. The process map is an excellent way of representing information of how and when processes, tasks, and activities are performed.

Process Defined

A *process* is a transformation; it transforms its inputs into its outputs. It is a picture showing how the transformation is carried out. It shows the inputs and outputs (best described using nouns), the activities in between (best described using verbs), and for each of the activities, the inputs and outputs used and produced.

A process is not just about "what people do," but also "what people produce." Historically, there has been a lot of emphasis attached to the study of the way people perform their jobs (i.e., the activities they carry out) or the verbs in the process map.

Process Map

A good process map should allow people unfamiliar with the process to understand the interaction of causes during the workflow. Also, a good process map should contain additional information relating to the project (i.e., information per critical step about input and output variables, time, cost, etc.), be understood at various levels of the organization, be able to model complex activities without ambiguity, be effective in analyzing a process, and be able to identify process-related issues.

To create a process map the following are key terms that the knowledge engineer should know:

- Alternative path — One or more options are presented that create the primary path.
- Decision criteria — If two or more options exist while incorporating alternative paths into a map, the question being asked should be specific.

- Inspection point — A pass or fail decision to test an output in process.
- Input — Information or other factors that are essential to the process.
- Output — The end result — the product or service that a customer receives.
- Parallel process — Another process that can be executed at the same time as the primary process.
- Primary process — The tasks must be carried out to achieve a desired output from given inputs.

In creating a process map, a good rule of thumb is to follow these six steps:

1. Select a process.
2. Define the process (goals, input, output).
3. Map the primary process:
   a. Define the tasks that will be required to reach the desired output.
   b. Incorporate appropriate symbols into the map.
   c. Make sure to show parallel processes.
4. Map alternative processes:
   a. Map points along the primary process where decisions are made.
   b. Recognize one or more alternative paths.
   c. Merge those paths back into the primary path.
5. Map inspection points:
   a. Use these points to error-proof the map.
   b. Useful to better satisfy customers or cut down on costs and time.
   c. Points could lead into rework loops or do-over loops.
6. Use the map to improve the process:
   a. Eliminate non-value-added steps.
   b. Set standards for the process.
   c. Ask what will pass and what will fail.

An example of a process map is shown in Figure 9.7. Process mapping symbols include:

- The rectangle represents each task of step within the map.
- The parallelogram represents inputs.
- The oval represents the process boundary.
- The diamond represents a decision.

State Transition Network

Another important type of network diagram is the state transition network. This type of diagram comprises two elements:

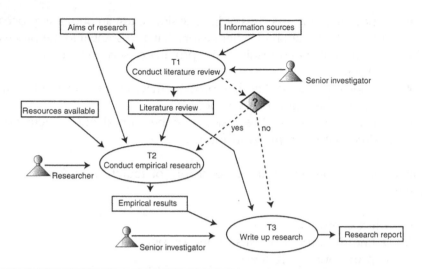

Figure 9.7   Process Map. (Epistemics Web site.[3] Used with permission.)

1. Nodes representing the states that a concept can be in.
2. Arrows between the nodes showing all the events and processes or tasks that can cause transitions from one state to another.

In many systems, transition networks are used to describe a set of states and the transitions that are possible between them. Common examples are such things as ATM control flows, editorial review processes, and definitions of protocol states. Typically, each of these transition networks has its own specific data format and its own specific editing tool. Given the rapid transition to pervasive networking and to application integration and interchange, a standard format for transition networks is desirable. This document defines such an interchange format, defined in Extensible Markup Language (XML) — the interchange language for the Internet.

A transition network is a set of states and the transitions between them. As noted above, they are good at capturing the notion of process. For example:

■ Control processes such as those in a digitally controlled heating system.
■ Processes controlling manufacture or design.
■ Workflow processes such as those found in product data management software.

They are also useful in modeling the behavior of systems and can be used in object-oriented analysis to create formal models of object interaction and larger system behavior.

Transition networks are closely related to finite state machines (FSMs) and to data flow diagrams (DFDs), but they are augmented with the following capabilities:

■ Transition networks are not limited to "accepting or rejecting their input." Transition networks may execute actions or fire off events during transitions.

■ Transition networks can interact with other objects, thereby affecting change in the transition network (or in other networks).

■ Transitions in transition networks can be controlled by guard conditions that prohibit or allow the transition to be followed.

■ These guard conditions can depend on any predicate involving objects from within the environment of the transition network.

As such, transition networks can be used to describe far more complex interactions or processes than either FSMs or DFDs allow.

What Are States?

A state within a transition network can loosely be defined as a point between transitions. In transition network diagrams, a state is typically depicted as a circle containing the name of the state. Although states are a point between transitions, there are some advantages to dealing with them explicitly:

■ Talking about states forms part of normal conversion. For example, people say, "my engine is off," meaning that the engine is in the off state. The principles of natural design call for states to be modeled explicitly.

■ There can often be multiple transitions into and, more importantly, out of, a state. As such, states can represent a branch in a process.

■ In some transition network formalisms, entry and exit from states can also execute actions and generate events.

Typically, states are defined in terms of the attributes of an object or objects in the system. For example, one would say that water has a number of states:

■ Frozen — When the temperature of the water is less than 0°.
■ Cold — When the temperature is less than 32°.
■ Hot — When the temperature is greater than 80°.
■ Boiled — When the temperature is greater than 100°.

One might also have the state "normal" as defined below:

■ Normal — The state is not frozen, cold, hot, or boiled.

The important point about the last example is that it shows one of the requirements of states: that they be exclusive. An object, or system, cannot be in two states at once.

Active and Passive States

In many processes, there is the notion of continuum, which is not completely captured by the above definition of state. For example, we have the notion of "thawing," where the word implies an ongoing and active state that is continually altering the system. This will be discussed further in the section on transitions.

Start and End States

Even though the process may allow entry and exit from multiple states, when describing the execution of a process, there is always a beginning and an end. Transition networks, likewise, require starting and ending states. Start and end states can be defined as follows:

■ Start state — A state that, in the context of a given execution, has no transitions preceding entry into the state.
■ End state — A state that has no transitions out of the state (no forward transitions).

Transitions

A transition is an atomic, directed connection between one state and another. Typically, transitions are represented as a line connecting two states. Bidirectional transitions (transitions both from A to B and B to A) are typically modeled as two separate transitions.

Transitions can be defined implicitly by the exclusionary nature of states. When the conditions defining one state become false and the conditions for another true, there is an implicit transition from one state to another; however, this model has only limited applicability.

Transitions and Active States

An active state can be looked on as a state that is being continually updated or a *gradual transition* from one state to another. As such, active states can be looked on as a form of continually evaluated transition.

Although using transitions to model active states does not capture the full semantics (because they are atomic and not continually updated), for most purposes this model suffices to capture the distinction.

Note that it is often useful to think at an even finer level of granularity and break transitions down into three discrete steps that form an atomic action. Those steps are:

1. Leaving a state — The point at which the state has been left, but traversal of the transition between states has not yet begun.
2. Transitioning between states — The act of traversing the transition between states.
3. Entering a state — The point at which the new state is entered, but before the "resting point" has been reached.

These three steps can be decomposed into a transition network.

Conditions, Actions, and Events

The main thing separating transition networks from FSMs is their active nature. This is captured in the notion of conditions, actions, and events.

Conditions

To control the set of transitions that are possible within a transition network, it is necessary to introduce the notion of a condition. Essentially, a condition is a set of predicates that guard entry to or exit from a given state. In other words, conditions filter the set of possible transitions.

In some systems, the conditions are placed solely on the transitions themselves; in others conditions can be placed upon states as a precondition to entry. These are essentially the same thing and are not mutually exclusive: In a system allowing both, the union of the guard conditions on the transition and the preconditions on the state form the total set of conditions to be met (i.e., this is an implicit "and" combination of the predicates). Likewise, it is possible to have postconditions on a state, thereby controlling the ability to transition from a state.

Given the above, there are three types of conditions found in transition network systems:

- State preconditions — Conditions that guard entry into a state.
- State postconditions — Conditions that guard exit from a state.
- Transition preconditions — Conditions guarding the transition from one state to another.

Actions

In transition networks, actions or operations allow processing to be associated with a transition. Typically, such actions will involve simple interaction with objects in the environment of the transition (getting and setting properties typically), though any arbitrary processing can be performed within the context of the environment. One rule must be obeyed, however: Altering the environment such that the guard conditions would now fail should not result in the transition failing. Transitions must always be regarded as atomic.

Typically, actions are associated with the transition, but it is often desirable to be able to specify actions at each of the three steps involved in making a transition. As such, there are three sets of actions that can be invoked:

- State postlude — The set of actions associated with the exit from a state.
- Transition body — The set of actions associated with transition traversal.
- State prelude — The set of actions associated with the entry into a state.

Events

Actions are scoped to the environment in which they are executed, and so they can only affect local state. Events or messages represent the interaction of the transition network with objects outside the local scope. Typically, they are modeled as actions that have the ability to send an event; see Figure 9.8.

Tables and Grids

Tabular representations make use of tables or grids. Four important types are forms, frames, timelines, and matrices or grids.

Forms

A more recent form of knowledge model is the use of hypertext and Web pages. Here relationships between concepts, or other types of knowledge, are represented by hyperlinks. This affords the use of structured text by making use of templates (i.e., generic headings). Different templates can be created for different knowledge types. For example, the template for a task would include such headings as description, goal, inputs, outputs, resources, and typical problems (see Figure 9.9).

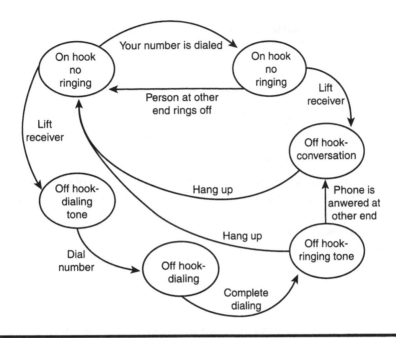

Figure 9.8 State Transition Network. (Epistemics Web site.³ Used with permission.)

Figure 9.9 Form — Hypertext Web Page. (A. J. Rhem & Associates, Inc.⁶ Used with permission.)

Frames

Frames are a way of representing knowledge in which each concept in a domain is described by a group of attributes and values using a matrix

Table 9.1 The Concept of "Car"

Cars	
Make	BMW
Model	740iL
Year	2004
Transmission	Automatic

representation. The left-hand column represents the attributes associated with the concept, and the right-hand column represents the appropriate values. When the concept is a class, typical (default) values are entered in the right-hand column. An example of a frame is shown in Table 9.1, which illustrates the concept "Car."

Timeline

A *timeline* is a type of tabular representation that shows time along the horizontal axis and such things as processes, tasks, or project phases along the vertical axis. It is useful for representing time-based process or role knowledge (see Figure 9.10).

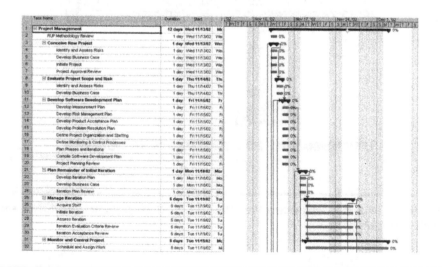

Figure 9.10   Timeline (Project Plan). (IBM.[7] Used with permission.)

Matrix

A *matrix* (or grid) is a type of tabular representation that comprises a two-dimensional grid with filled-in grid cells. One example is a problem-solution matrix that shows the problems that can arise in a particular part of a domain as the rows in the matrix and possible solutions as the columns. Ticks, crosses, or comments in the matrix cells indicate which solution applies to which problem. An example of a matrix used by knowledge engineers is a focus grid (see Figure 9.11).

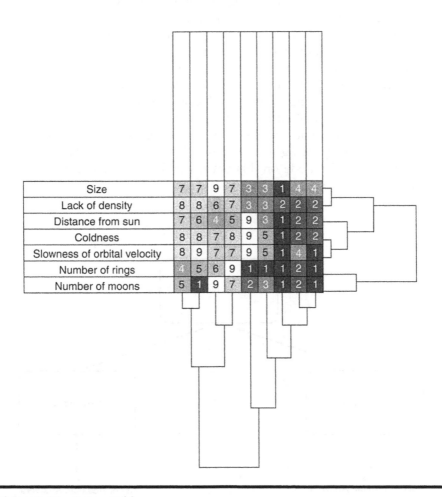

Size	7	7	9	7	3	3	1	4	4
Lack of density	8	8	6	7	3	3	2	2	2
Distance from sun	7	6	4	5	9	3	1	2	2
Coldness	8	8	7	8	9	5	1	2	2
Slowness of orbital velocity	8	9	7	7	9	5	1	4	1
Number of rings	4	5	6	9	1	1	1	2	1
Number of moons	5	1	9	7	2	3	1	2	1

Figure 9.11 Focus Grid

Decision Trees

Occam's Razor (Specialized to Decision Trees)

"The world is inherently simple. Therefore the smallest decision tree that is consistent with the samples is the one that is most likely to identify unknown objects correctly."[8]

A *decision tree* is an arrangement of tests that prescribes an appropriate test at every step in an analysis.

In general, decision trees represent a disjunction of conjunctions of constraints on the attribute values of instances. Each path from the tree root to a leaf corresponds to a conjunction of attribute tests and the tree itself to a disjunction of these conjunctions.

More specifically, decision trees classify instances by sorting them down the tree from the root node to some leaf node, which provides the classification of the instance. Each node in the tree specifies a test of some attribute of the instance, and each branch descending from that node corresponds to one of the possible values for this attribute.

An instance is classified by starting at the root node of the decision tree, testing the attribute specified by this node, then moving down the tree branch corresponding to the value of the attribute. This process is then repeated at the node on this branch and so on until a leaf node is reached (see Figure 9.12).

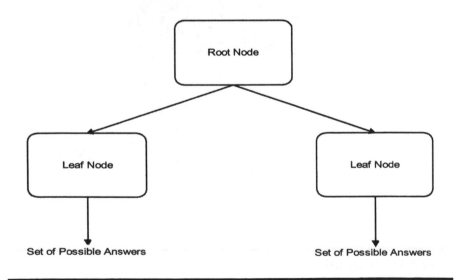

Figure 9.12   Decision Tree

Diagram

A decision tree creates a model as either a graphical tree or a set of text rules that can predict (classify) a given situation. A decision tree is a model that is both predictive and descriptive. It is called a decision tree because the resulting model is presented in the form of a tree structure. The visual presentation makes the decision tree model easy to understand and assimilate:

- Each nonleaf node is connected to a test that splits its set of possible answers into subsets corresponding to different test results.
- Each branch carries a particular test result's subset to another node.
- Each node is connected to a set of possible answers.

As a result, the decision tree has become a very popular data mining technique as indicated in Chapter 12.

For example decision trees graphically display the relationships found in data for example, IF Income = low and Years on job < 5 THEN Credit risk = Poor (see Figure 9.13). Decision-tree algorithms are similar to rule induction algorithms, which produce rule sets without a decision tree.

Problems Suited for Decision Trees

Decision trees are best suited for problems with the following characteristics:

- Decision trees are most commonly used for classification (predicting what group a case belongs to), but can also be used for regression (predicting a specific value).
- When instances are represented by attribute-value pairs.
  - Instances are described by a fixed set of attributes (e.g., temperature) and their values (e.g., hot).
  - The easiest situation for decision-tree learning occurs when each attribute takes on a small number of disjoint possible values (e.g., hot, mild, cold).
  - Extensions to the basic algorithm allow handling real-valued attributes as well (e.g., a floating point temperature).
- When the target function has discrete output values. A decision tree assigns a classification to each example.
  - Simplest case exists when there are only two possible classes (Boolean classification).
  - Decision-tree methods can also be easily extended to learning functions with more than two possible output values.
  - A more substantial extension allows learning target functions with real-valued outputs, although the application of decision trees in this setting is less common.

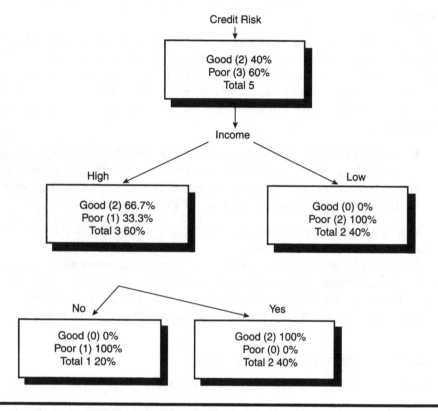

Figure 9.13 Credit Risk Decision Tree

- When disjunctive descriptions may be required.
  - Decision trees naturally represent disjunctive expressions.
- When the training data may contain errors.
  - Decision-tree learning methods are robust to errors — both errors in classifications of the training examples and errors in the attribute values that describe these examples.
- The training data may contain missing attribute values. Decision-tree methods can be used even when some training examples have unknown values.
- When you need to make a decision based on several factors (e.g., insurance underwriter determining the cost of damage, determining bankruptcy risk, determining stock portfolio risk).

Understanding the Output

The primary output of a decision-tree algorithm is the tree itself. The training process that creates the decision tree is called induction. Induction requires a small number of passes (generally far fewer than 100) through the training dataset. This makes the algorithm somewhat less efficient than "Naïve-Bayes algorithms," which require only one pass, but significantly more efficient than neural nets, which typically require a large number of passes, sometimes numbering in the thousands. "The number of passes required to build a decision tree is no more than the number of levels in the tree. There is no predetermined limit to the number of levels, although the complexity of the tree as measured by the depth and breadth of the tree generally increases as the number of independent variables increases."[3]

In a decision tree, the top node is called the root node. A decision tree grows from the root node, so you can think of the tree as growing upside down, splitting the data at each level to form new nodes. The resulting tree comprises many nodes, which are connected by branches. Nodes that are at the end of branches are called leaf nodes and play a special role when the tree is used for prediction.

Each node contains information about the number of instances at that node and about the distribution of dependent-variable values (credit risk). The instances at the root node are all of the instances in the training set (see Figure 9.13). This node contains five instances, of which 60 percent are good risks and 40 percent are poor risks. Below the root node (parent) is the first split that, in this case, splits the data into two new nodes (children) based on whether income is high or low.

The rightmost node (low income) resulting from this split contains two instances, both of which are associated with poor credit risk. Because all instances have the same value of the dependent variable (credit risk), this node is termed pure and will not be split further. The leftmost node in the first split contains three instances, 66.7 percent of which are good. The leftmost node is then further split based on the value of married (yes or no), resulting in two more nodes, which are each also pure. A tree that has only pure leaf nodes is called a pure tree. This condition does not lead to the best results because of limited training data. However, most trees are impure, that is, their leaf nodes contain cases with more than one outcome.

When to Stop

Once grown, a tree can be used for predicting a new case by starting at the root (top) of the tree and following a path down the branches until a leaf node is encountered. The path is determined by imposing the split rules on the values of the independent variables in the new instance. However, you may be wondering when to stop growing the tree?

There are tree-building rules that are used to determine when to stop growing the tree. These rules are usually based on several factors including maximum tree depth, minimum number of elements in a node considered for splitting, or the minimum number of elements that must be in a new node. In most implementations, the user can alter the parameters associated with these rules.

Pruning Trees

When using decision trees to perform data mining, a tree model, including one with stopping rules, may reveal nodes or subtrees that are undesirable because of overfitting or may contain rules that the domain expert feels are inappropriate. *Pruning* is a common technique used to make a tree more general. Pruning removes splits and the subtrees created by them. In some implementations, pruning is controlled by user-configurable parameters that cause splits to be pruned because, for example, the computed difference between the resulting nodes falls below a threshold and is insignificant. With such algorithms, users will want to experiment to see which pruning rule parameters result in a tree that predicts best on a test dataset.

We can see the effects of pruning even in our credit risk example. What if marital status has nothing to do with whether someone is a good risk? The split on marital status results from the applicants record (applicant has high income, but married is no and he has poor as the value for risk). Maybe the applicant turned out to be a poor credit risk because he is a gambler. However, because we have no data on whether or not loan applicants were gamblers, it is not possible to build a model taking this into account. The only data that the model has that differentiates the applicant from the other instances in the node is marital status, so that is what it uses.

If this second split is pruned, then the model will predict good for all people with high income regardless of marital status. The node used to make this prediction, although not pure, has good as the predominant value and, therefore, good will be the predicted value for instances that end on this node.

Testing a Tree

Before integrating your decision tree, you must test and validate the model using an independent dataset. Once accuracy has been measured on an independent dataset and is determined to be acceptable, the tree or its rules are ready to be used. However, be sure to retest the tree periodically to ensure that it maintains the desired accuracy.

Notes

1. Merrill, M.D. Knowledge Objects. Utah State University, *CBT Solutions,* March–April 1998, pp. 1–11.
2. Bellinger, G. The Way of Systems. OutSights, Inc., 2004.
3. Epistemics. Available online: http://www.epistemics.co.uk/Notes/90-0-0.htm
4. Novak, J. *A Theory of Education* (Ithaca, NY: Cornell University Press, 1977).
5. Novak, J. *The Theory Underlying Concept Maps and How to Construct Them* (Ithaca, NY: Cornell University Press, 1988).
6. A. J. Rhem & Associates, Inc. Available online: http://www.ajrhem.com/training.html
7. IBM, Rational Unified Process (RUP) Project Plan Template.
8. Mitchell, T. Decision Tree Learning, in *Machine Learning*, ed. T. Mitchell (New York: McGraw-Hill, 1997), pp. 52–78.

Chapter 10

UML — An Introduction

A Brief History

UML was pioneered by Jim Rumbaugh, Ivar Jacobson, and Grady Booch, who originally had their own competing methods (OMT — Object Modeling Technique, OOSE — Object Oriented Software Engineering, and Booch). Eventually, they joined forces and brought about an open standard. UML has become a standard modeling language for analysts, designers, and architects because it is programming-language independent. Also, the UML notation set is a language and not a methodology. As such, this language can easily fit into any company's way of conducting business without requiring change.

Because UML is not a methodology, it does not require any formal work products, or "artifacts" as they are sometimes called. Yet it does provide several types of diagrams that, when used within a given methodology, increase the ease of understanding an application under development. There is more to UML than these diagrams, but for the purpose of this book, the diagrams offer a good introduction to the language and the principles behind its use. By placing standard UML diagrams in your methodology's work products, you make it easier for UML-proficient people to join your project and quickly become productive. This is a particular benefit when introducing the knowledge modeling concepts presented in this book.

The most useful, standard UML diagrams that complement knowledge modeling are use case diagram, activity diagram, statechart diagram, class diagram, object diagram, sequence diagram, and collaboration diagram.

The heart of object-oriented problem solving is the construction of a model. The model abstracts the essential details of the underlying problem from its usually complicated real world. Several modeling tools are wrapped under the heading of the UML.

This introduction to UML will focus on the following diagrams:

- Use case diagram
- Activity flow diagram
- Statechart diagram
- Collaboration diagram
- Sequence diagram
- Class diagram
- Object diagram

Use Case Diagram

A use case illustrates a unit of functionality provided by the system. The main purpose of the use case diagram is to help development teams visualize the functional requirements of a system, including the relationship of "actors" (an actor could be a person, role, system, or anything that interacts with the system) to essential processes, as well as the relationships among different use cases. Use case diagrams generally show groups of use cases, either all use cases for the complete system, or a breakout of a particular group of use cases with related functionality (e.g., all security administration related use cases).

The use case diagram models system services determined through interviewing project stakeholders. The use case diagram consists of several widgets. These widgets consist of a stick figure, which represents an actor, an ellipse, which represents the use case itself and a line, which represents communication (see Figure 10.1).

An *actor* is who or what initiates the events involved in that task. Actors are simply roles that people or objects play.

The *communication* represents the relationship between actor and use case. A use case diagram shows the relationship among use cases within a system or other semantic entity and their actors (see Figure 10.2).

Semantics

Use case diagrams show actors and use cases together with their relationships. The use cases represent functionality of a system or a classifier, like a subsystem or a class, as manifested to external integrators with the system or the classifier.

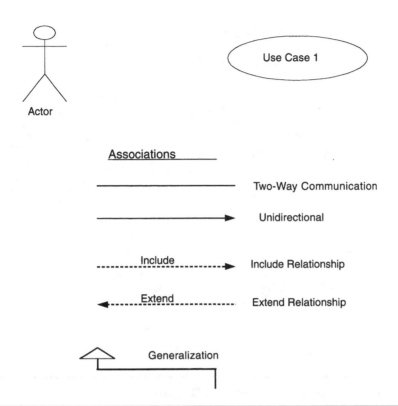

Figure 10.1   Use Case Diagram: Widgets

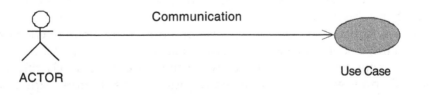

Figure 10.2   Communication Relationship

Notation

A use case diagram is a graph of actors, a set of use cases, possibly some interfaces, and the relationships between these elements. The relationships are associations between the actors and the use cases, generalizations between the actors, and the generalizations "extend" and "include" among the use cases. The use cases may be enclosed by a circle that represents the boundary of the containing system or its scope (see Figure 10.3).

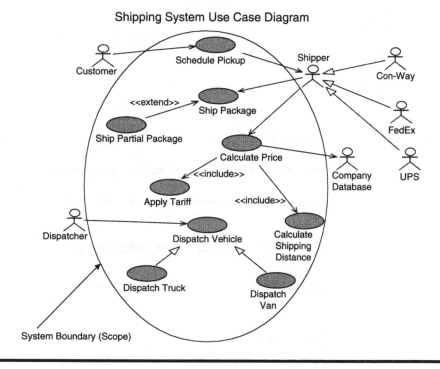

Figure 10.3 Shipping System Use Case Diagram

Mapping

A set of use case ellipses with connections to actor symbols maps to a set of use cases and actors corresponding to the use case and actor symbols, respectively. Each generalization arrow maps onto a generalization in the model, and each line between an actor symbol and a use case ellipsis maps to an association between the corresponding classifiers. A dashed arrow with the keyword «include» or «extend» maps to an include or extend relationship between use cases.

There are several standard relationships among use cases or between actors and use cases.

An association between an actor and a use case is shown as a solid line between the actor and the use case. It may have end adornments such as multiplicity. An extend relationship between use cases is shown by a dashed arrow with an open arrowhead from the use case providing the extension to the base use case. The arrow is labeled with the keyword «extend». The condition of the relationship is optionally presented close to the keyword.

An include relationship between use cases is shown by a dashed arrow with an open arrowhead from the base use case to the included use case. The arrow is labeled with the keyword «include». A generalization arrow — a solid line with a closed, hollow arrowhead pointing at the parent use case — shows the generalization between use cases. The relationship between a use case and its external interaction sequences is usually defined by an invisible hyperlink to sequence diagrams.

- Association — The participation of an actor in a use case; that is, instances of the actor and instances of the use case communicate with each other. This is the only relationship between actors and use cases.
- Extend — An extend relationship from use case "Ship Partial Package" to use case "Ship Package" indicates that an instance of use case "Ship Package" may be augmented (subject to specific conditions specified in the extension) by the behavior specified by "Ship Partial Package." The behavior is inserted at the location defined by the extension point in "Ship Package," which is referenced by the extend relationship (see Figure 10.3).
- Generalization — A generalization from use case "Dispatch Truck" to use case "Dispatch Vehicle" indicates that "Dispatch Truck" is a specialization of "Dispatch Vehicle."
- Include — An include relationship from use case "Calculate Price" to use case "Calculate Shipping Distance" indicates that an instance of the use case "Calculate Price" will also contain the behavior as specified by "Calculate Shipping Distance." The behavior is included at the location, which defined in "Calculate Price."

Actor Relationships

Semantics

There is one standard relationship among actors and one between actors and use cases.

- Association — The participation of an actor in a use case; that is, instances of the actor and instances of the use case communicate with each other. An association between an actor and a use case is shown as a solid line between the actor and the use case. This is the only relationship between actors and use cases (see associations in Figure 10.1).

■ Generalization — A generalization from an actor A to an actor B indicates that an instance of A can communicate with the same kinds of use case instances as an instance of B (see associations in Figure 10.1).

Each use case is textually described with a *use case specification*. The use case specification is where the behavior of the use case is described with text and in detail. *Use case diagrams* give a visual representation of a set of use cases. The use case will describe what a system does from the standpoint of an external observer. The emphasis is on what a system does rather than how.

Use case diagrams are closely connected to the scenarios described in the use case specification. A *scenario* is an example of what happens when someone interacts with the system. The following is an example scenario for searching for a policy within an insurance company: "An insurance agent receives a request to verify vehicle insurance by an underwriter. The agent then performs a search for the policyholder's insurance information." The following use case specification incorporates this as well as other scenarios when describing the behavior of this process (see Table 10.1).

Activity Flow Diagram

Activity diagrams are similar to a flow chart. They show the procedural flow of control between two or more class objects while processing an activity. Activity diagrams can be used to model higher-level business processes at the business unit levels or to model low-level internal class actions. Activity diagrams are best used to model higher-level processes, such as how the company is currently doing business or how it would like to do business. This is because activity diagrams are less technical in appearance and are easily communicated and understood by the business.

Activity diagrams when used with lower-level system processes are associated to a use case (use case specification). In fact, an activity diagram is used to visually represent the behavior, which is described in the use case specification. The activity diagram starts with a solid circle connected to the initial activity. The activity is modeled by drawing a rectangle with rounded edges, enclosing the activity's name. Activities can be connected to other activities through transition lines or to decision points that connect to different activities guarded by conditions of the decision point. Activities that terminate the modeled process are connected to a termination point.

Table 10.1 Use Case Specification

Use Case Specification: Search for a Policy

Description

This use case will describe what a user will need to accomplish to search for a policy through the system's Web interface.

Actors

Insurance agent — Someone who interacts with the insurer.

Underwriter — Someone who evaluates policies written by the agent.

Preconditions.

The user has access to the policy system.

Basic Flow of Events

1. User enters policy or vehicle search criteria.
2. Search criteria pass all edit checks (policy number is at least six characters long, insured name is at least three characters long, or the vehicle identification number (VIN) is at least six characters long).
3. Search results are found based on search criteria provided (match on six characters or more on the policy number, match first three characters or more on the insured name, match first six characters or more on the VIN).
4. The number of policies returned is greater than one and less than the maximum limit.
5. A list of policies is returned to the user and may be sorted by policy number, insured name, policy effective date, or policy expiration date.
6. Use case ends.

Alternate Flows

Alternate Flow 1

Refers to Step 2 in the Basic Flow: Search criteria do not pass edit checks.

The search criteria do not pass the edit checks (policy number is at least six characters long, insured name is at least three characters long, or the VIN is at least six characters long).

User is asked to correct the errors in the search criteria or to reenter the information.

Continue with Step 1 in Basic Flow.

Table 10.1 (continued)   Use Case Specification

Alternate Flow 2
Refers to Step 3 in the Basic Flow: Search results are not found.
No search results are found based on the search criteria provided (match on six characters or more on the policy number, match first three characters or more on the insured name, match first six characters or more on the VIN).
User is notified to refine search criteria.
Continue with Step 1 in Basic Flow.
Alternate Flow 3
Refers to Step 3 in the Basic Flow: Search results only return one policy.
The number of policies returned is equal to one.
The policy detail for the one policy is display (not a list of policies).
Alternate Flow 4
Refers to Step 3 in the Basic Flow: Returned results are greater than the maximum number of policies that should be returned.
The number of policies returned is greater than the maximum number of policies that should be displayed.
The user is notified to refine the search criteria.
Continue with Step 1 in Basic Flow.
Exception Flows
None

Semantics

An activity diagram shows a set of activities, the sequential or branching flow from activity to activity, and objects that act and are acted on. Activity diagrams are used to illustrate the dynamic view of the system. Activity diagrams are especially useful when modeling as-is and to-be functions of a system. Figure 10.4 shows widgets that are used to develop an activity flow diagram.

Activity Diagram Notation

An activity diagram graphically illustrated represents a collection of vertices, arcs, activity states, action states, transitions, objects with branches,

Activity Flow Diagram Widgets

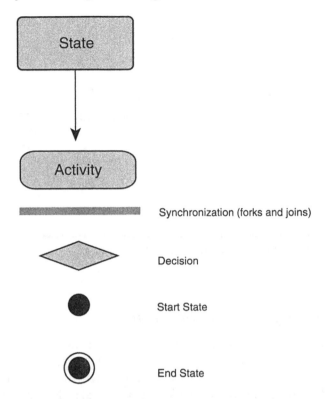

Figure 10.4   Activity Flow Diagram: Widgets

forks, and joins (see Figure 10.5). The entire activity diagram is attached (through the model) to a classifier, such as a use case, or to a package, or to the implementation of an operation. The purpose of this diagram is to focus on flows driven by internal processing (as opposed to external events). Activity diagrams are used in situations where all or most of the events represent the completion of internally generated actions (i.e., procedural flow of control).

Action States and Activity States

Action states are states that represent an execution of an action. Action states cannot be further decomposed. Alternatively, activity states can be further decomposed and represented by other activity diagrams.

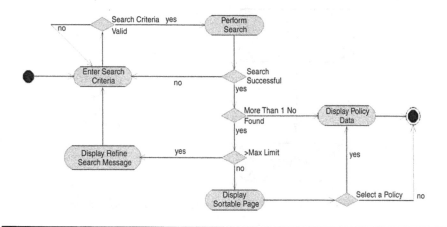

Figure 10.5   Activity Diagram: Search for a Policy

Activity Diagrams with Swimlanes

When modeling workflows of business processes it is helpful to partition the activity within the diagram into groups. Each group will represent the business organization responsible for those activities. In UML, each group is called a "swimlane" and is divided by a vertical solid line (see Figure 10.6).

In describing a workflow, swimlanes in an activity diagram are useful. Each object (business organization, system, department, etc.) that has a responsibility within the workflow will have its own swimlane. Therefore, each swimlane has a unique name, which is represented by some real-world entity. Each swimlane represents a part of the overall activity of the activity diagram and may be implemented by one or more classes. When an activity diagram is partitioned into swimlanes, every activity belongs to exactly one swimlane with transitions that may cross lanes. Swimlanes often correspond to organizational units in a business model.

Notation

An activity diagram may be divided visually into swimlanes, each separated from neighboring swimlanes by vertical solid lines on both sides. The relative ordering of the swimlanes has no semantic significance. Each action is assigned to one swimlane. Transitions may cross lanes. There is no significance to the routing of a transition path.

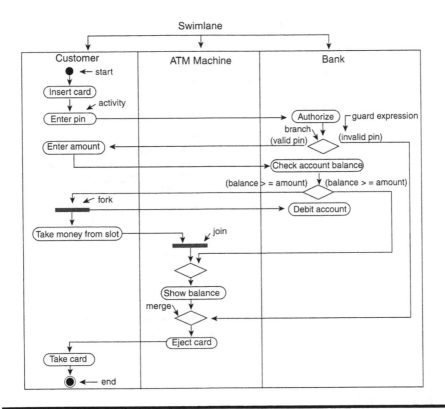

Figure 10.6 Activity Diagram with Swimlanes

Sequence Diagram

A sequence diagram, also called an interaction diagram, shows an interaction between a set of objects and their relationships. This also includes the messages that can be passed among them. Sequence diagrams emphasize the time ordering of messages. Sequence diagrams are used to model instances of classes, interface components, and nodes, along with the messages that are passed between them. This is done within the context of scenarios that illustrate behavior. A sequence diagram consists of objects, links, and messages (see Figure 10.7).

A sequence diagram is constructed by first placing the objects that participate in the interaction at the top of the diagram. You would typically place the object that initiates the interaction at the left and increasingly move subordinate objects to the right. When placing messages that these objects send and receive they will be placed along the y axis (time) to illustrate the movement of time. This will visualize the flow of control over time (see Figure 10.7).

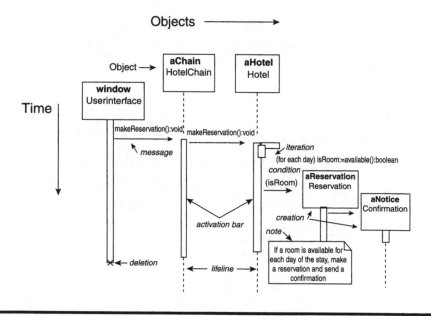

Figure 10.7 Simple Sequence Diagram with Concurrent Objects

Object Lifeline

Each object has an object lifeline. An object lifeline is a vertical dashed line that represents the existence of an object over a period of time. Most objects will be in existence for the duration of the interaction. Objects may be created during the interaction. Lifelines can start with a receipt of a message stereotyped as «create» and may be destroyed during the interaction stereotyped as «destroyed» with a visual cue of a large X marking the end of that object.

Semantics

In a sequence diagram, an object lifeline denotes an instance playing a specific role. Arrows between the lifelines denote communication between the instances playing those roles. Within a sequence diagram the existence and duration of the instance in a role is shown, but the relationships among the instances are not shown. The role is specified by a ClassifierRole; it describes the properties of an instance playing the role and describes the relationships an instance in that role has to other instances.

Notation

An instance is shown as a vertical dashed line called the lifeline. The lifeline represents the existence of the instance at a particular time. If the instance is created or destroyed during the period of time shown on the diagram, then its lifeline starts or stops at the appropriate point; otherwise, it goes from the top to the bottom of the diagram. An object symbol is drawn at the head of the lifeline. If the instance is created during the diagram, then the arrow, which maps onto the stimulus that creates the instance, is drawn with its arrowhead on the object symbol.

Flow of Control

Each sequence diagram will illustrate a flow of control. Focus of the control is depicted by a tall thin rectangle that shows the period of time during which an object is performing an action. This can be done either directly or through a subordinate procedure. The top of the rectangle is aligned with the start of the action, and the bottom is aligned with its completion. Nesting with the flow of control is illustrated by stacking another focus of control to the right of its parent.

The transition of flow of control between objects is illustrated with an arrow and label. The label of the arrow is mapped into the body attribute of the procedure or into a detailed action model. For the action model, the name of the operation to be invoked or signal to be sent is mapped onto the name of the operation or signal invoked by the actions in the procedure connected to the message. Different alternatives exist for showing the arguments of the stimulus. If references to the actual instances being passed as arguments are shown, these are mapped onto the arguments of the stimulus.

If the argument expressions are shown instead, and a detailed action model is used, then these are mapped into CodeActions in the procedure or additional actions that compute the values of the expressions. Finally, if the types of the arguments are shown together with the name of the operation or the signal, these are mapped onto the parameter types of the operation or the attribute types of the signal, respectively. A timing label placed on the level of an arrow endpoint maps into the name of the corresponding message or stimulus. A constraint placed on the diagram maps into a constraint on the entire interaction.

An arrow with the arrowhead pointing to an object symbol or role symbol within the frame of the diagram maps into a stimulus (message) dispatched by a CreateObjectAction. The interpretation is that an instance is created by dispatching the stimulus. If the target of the arrow is a classifier-role symbol, the instance will conform to the `ClassifierRole`. (Note that the diagram does not necessarily show from which classifier the instance originates, only that the newly created instance conforms to the `ClassifierRole`.) After the creation of the instance, it may immediately start interacting with other instances. This implies that the creation method (e.g., constructor, initializer) of the instance dispatches these stimuli.

If an object termination symbol (X) is the target of an arrow, the arrow maps into a stimulus that will cause the receiving instance to be removed. If the object termination symbol appears in the diagram without an incoming arrow, it maps into a procedure containing a `DestroyObjectAction`.

The order of the arrows in the diagram maps onto pairs of associations between the stimuli (messages). A predecessor relationship is established between stimuli (messages) corresponding to successive arrows in the vertical sequence. In case of concurrent arrows preceding an arrow, the corresponding stimulus (message) has a collection of predecessors. Moreover, each stimulus (message) has an activator association to the stimulus (message) corresponding to the incoming arrow of the activation.

In the case that the arrow maps onto a message, the sender and the receiver are specified by the sender and receiver `ClassifierRoles` of the message. The sender and receiver instances of a stimulus conform to these `ClassifierRoles`. Any condition or iteration expression attached to the arrow becomes, in a detailed action model, the test clause action in a `ConditionalAction` or `LoopAction` in the dispatching procedure. All arrows departing the nested activation map into stimuli (messages) with an activation association to the stimulus (message) corresponding to the arrow at the head of the activation. A return arrow departing the end of the activation maps into a stimulus (message) with the following:

- An activation association to the stimulus (message) corresponding to the arrow at the head of the activation.
- A predecessor association to the previous stimulus (message) within the same activation. A return must be the final stimulus (message) within a predecessor chain. It is not the predecessor of any stimulus (message).

To model a flow of control that includes objects and roles and the passing of messages over time, sequence diagrams are ideal. The following outlines the techniques used to create sequence diagrams:

- Set the context for the sequence diagram's interaction (i.e., system, subsystem, operation, class, or use case scenario).
- Identify which objects play a role in the interaction; align them on the sequence diagram from left to right based on importance.

- Set the lifeline for each object as appropriate and indicate their birth and death with the appropriately stereotyped messages.
- Starting with the messages that initiate the interactions, align each message from top to bottom, indicating the message properties.
- If needed, indicate any computations taking place along the specific lifeline.
- To indicate time and space constraints, each message should be adorned with this specific information.
- Also, to specify flow of control more formally, attach preconditions and postconditions to each message.

Typically, a single sequence diagram can show only one flow of control, and you will have a number of diagrams to indicate alternate paths or exception conditions.

Presentation Options

In some cases, it is necessary to link sequence diagrams to each other; for example, it might not be possible to put all lifelines in one diagram, or a subsequence is included in several diagrams; hence, it is convenient to put the common subsequence in a separate diagram, which is referenced from the other diagrams. In these cases, the cut between the diagrams can be expressed in one of the diagrams with a dangling arrow leaving a lifeline but not arriving at another lifeline, and in the other diagram it is expressed with a dangling arrow arriving at a lifeline from nowhere. In both cases, it is recommended to attach a note stating which diagram the sequence originates from or continues in. This is purely notational. The different diagrams show different parts of the underlying interaction.

Activation is shown as a tall, thin rectangle, the top of which is aligned with its initiation time and bottom of which is aligned with its completion time. The procedure being performed may be labeled in text next to the activation symbol or in the left margin, depending on style. Alternately, the incoming arrow may indicate the procedure, in which case it may be omitted on the activation itself. In procedural flow of control, the top of the activation symbol is at the tip of an incoming arrow (the one that initiates the procedure), and the base of the symbol is at the tail of a return arrow.

Statechart Diagram

The statechart diagram models the different states that a class can be in and how that class transitions from state to state. Statechart diagrams are used to model the dynamic aspects of a system. These dynamic aspects may include event-ordered behavior of any kind of object including classes, interfaces, components, and nodes.

Objects have behaviors and states. The state of an object depends on its current activity or condition. A statechart diagram shows the possible states of the object and the transitions that cause a change in state. A statechart diagram can be used to describe the behavior of instances of a model element such as an object or an interaction. Specifically, it describes possible sequences of states and actions through which the element instances can proceed during its lifetime as a result of reacting to discrete events (e.g., signals, operation invocations).

Semantics

Statechart diagrams represent the behavior of entities capable of dynamic behavior by specifying its response to the receipt of event instances. Typically, it is used for describing the behavior of class instances, but statecharts may also describe the behavior of other entities such as use cases, actors, subsystems, operations, or methods.

Notation

A statechart diagram is a graph that represents a state machine. States and various other types of vertices (pseudostates) in the state machine graph are rendered by appropriate state and pseudostate symbols, whereas directed arcs that interconnect them generally render transitions. States may also contain subdiagrams by physical containment or tiling. Note that every state machine has a top state that contains all the other elements of the entire state machine. The graphical rendering of this top state is optional.

States

A state is a condition during the life of an object or an interaction during which it satisfies some condition, performs some action, or waits for some event. A composite state is a state that, in contrast to a simple state, has a graphical decomposition. Conceptually, an object remains in a state for an interval of time. However, the semantics allow for modeling flow-through states that are instantaneous, as well as transitions that are not instantaneous. A state may be used to model an ongoing activity. Such an activity is specified either by a nested state machine or by a computational expression.

Notation

A state is shown as a rectangle with rounded corners. Optionally, it may have an attached name tab. The name tab is a rectangle, usually resting on the outside of the topside of a state and it contains the name of that state. It is normally used to keep the name of a composite state that has concurrent regions, but may be used in other cases as well. A state may be optionally subdivided into multiple compartments separated from each other by a horizontal line. They are as follows:

- Name compartment — This compartment holds the (optional) name of the state as a string. States without names are anonymous and are all distinct. It is undesirable to show the same named state twice in the same diagram, as confusion may ensue. Name compartments should not be used if a name tab is used and vice versa.
- Internal transitions compartment — This compartment holds a list of internal actions or activities that are performed while the element is in the state. The action label identifies the circumstances under which the action specified by the action expression will be invoked. The action expression may use any attributes and links that are in the scope of the owning entity. For list items where the action expression is empty, the backslash separator is optional. A number of action labels are reserved for various special purposes and, therefore, cannot be used as event names. The following are the reserved action labels and their meanings.
  - Entry — This label identifies an action specified by the corresponding action expression that is performed on entry to the state (entry action).
  - Exit — This label identifies an action, specified by the corresponding action expression that is performed on exit from the state (exit action).
  - Do — This label identifies an ongoing activity ("do activity") that is performed as long as the modeled element is in the state or until the computation specified by the action expression is completed (the latter may result in a completion event being generated).
  - Include — This label is used to identify a submachine invocation. The action expression contains the name of the submachine that is to be invoked. In all other cases, the action label identifies the event that triggers the corresponding action expression.

These events are called internal transitions and are semantically equivalent to self-transitions except that the state is not exited or reentered. This

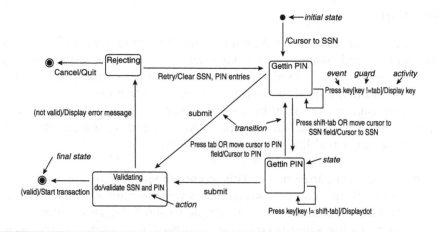

Figure 10.8   Statechart Diagram

means that the corresponding exit and entry actions are not performed. The general format for the list item of an internal transition is event-name `('`comma-separated-parameter-list`')' '['`guard-condi- tion`]' '/'` action-expression. Each event name may appear more than once per state if the guard conditions are different. The event parameters and the guard conditions are optional. If the event has param- eters, they can be used in the action expression through the current event variable (see Figure 10.8).

Collaboration Diagram

Collaboration diagrams are also interaction diagrams. They convey the same information as sequence diagrams, but they focus on object roles instead of the times that messages are sent. In a sequence diagram, object roles are the vertices and messages are the connecting links. It does not show time as a separate dimension, so the sequence of communications and the concurrent threads must be determined using sequence numbers.

Semantics

Collaboration diagrams are a collection of instances that exchange stimuli within an overall interaction. This interaction accomplishes the task of implementing certain behavior. To understand the mechanisms used in a design, it is important to see only those instances and their cooperation involved in accomplishing a purpose or a related set of purposes, projected from the larger system of which they are part. Such a static construct is called collaboration.

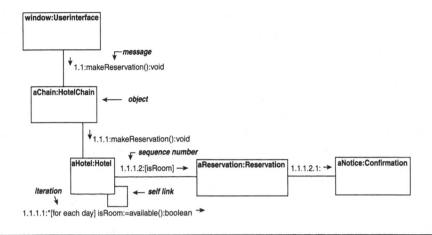

Figure 10.9   Collaboration Diagram

Collaboration includes an ensemble of classifier roles and association roles that define the participants needed for a given set of purposes. Instances conforming to the classifier roles play the roles defined by the classifier roles, and links between the instances conform to association roles of the collaboration. Classifier roles and association roles define a usage of instances and links, and the classifiers and associations declare all required properties of these instances and links (see Figure 10.9).

An interaction is defined in the context of collaboration. It specifies the communication patterns between the roles in the collaboration. More precisely, it contains a set of partially ordered messages, each specifying one communication, for example, what signal to be sent or what operation to be invoked, as well as the roles to be played by the sender and the receiver, respectively.

A `CollaborationInstanceSet` references an ensemble of instances that jointly perform the task specified by the `Collaboration-InstanceSet`'s collaboration. These instances play the roles defined by the classifier roles of the collaboration; that is, the instances have all the properties declared by the classifier roles (the instances are said to conform to the classifier roles). The stimuli sent between the instances when performing the task are participating in the `InteractionInstanceSet` of the `CollaborationInstanceSet`. These stimuli conform to the messages in one of the interactions of the collaboration. Because an instance can participate in several `CollaborationInstanceSets` at the same time, only one `InteractionInstanceSet` does not necessarily reference all its communications. They can be interleaved.

A collaboration may be attached to an operation or a classifier, like a use case, to describe the context in which their behavior occurs; that is, what roles instances play to perform the behavior specified by the operation or the use case. Collaboration is used for describing the realization of an operation or a classifier. A collaboration that describes a classifier, such as a use case, references classifiers and associations in general, while a collaboration describing an operation includes the arguments and local variables of the operation, as well as ordinary associations attached to the classifier owning the operation.

The interactions defined within the collaboration specify the communication pattern between the instances when they perform the behavior specified in the operation or the use case. These patterns are presented in sequence diagrams or collaboration diagrams. Collaboration may also be attached to a class to define the static structure of the class; that is, how attributes, parameters, etc., cooperate with each other. A parameterized collaboration represents a design construct that can be used repeatedly in different designs.

The participants in the collaboration, including the classifiers and relationships, can be parameters of the generic collaboration. The parameters are bound to particular model elements in each instantiation of the generic collaboration. Such a parameterized collaboration can capture the structure of a design pattern (note that a design pattern involves more than structural aspects). Whereas most collaborations can be anonymous because they are attached to a named model element, collaboration patterns are free-standing design constructs that must have names. Collaboration may be expressed at different levels of granularity. A coarse-grained collaboration may be refined to produce another collaboration that has a finer granularity.

The object-role rectangles are labeled with either class or object names (or both). Class names are preceded by colons (:). Each message in a collaboration diagram has a sequence number. The top-level message is numbered 1. Messages at the same level (sent during the same call) have the same decimal prefix but suffixes of 1, 2, etc., according to when they occur.

Class Diagram

A class diagram is a diagram that shows a set of classes, interfaces, collaborations, and their relationships (dependency, generalization, and association). Each class is depicted by a rectangle with three sections. The first section represents the class name; the middle section represents the attributes of the class. The third section represents the operations that can be performed on the class (see Class Example). Each class can have public (assessable by other class operations) and private (not available to other class operations) attributes and operations (see Figure 10.10). You typically

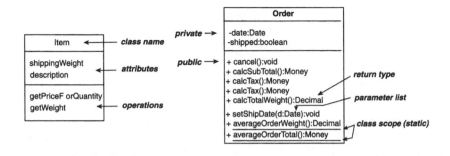

Figure 10.10 Classes

use class diagrams to model the static design view of a system. This view primarily supports the functional requirements of a system (i.e., the services the system should provide to its end users).

The class diagram shows how the different entities (people, things, and data) relate to each other; in other words, it shows the static structures of the system. A class diagram can be used to display logical classes, which are typically the kinds of things the business people in an organization talk about loans, home mortgages, and interest rates. Class diagrams can also be used to show implementation classes, which are the things that programmers typically deal with.

Class diagrams show the static structure of the model, in particular, the things that exist (such as classes and types), their internal structure, and their relationships to other things. Class diagrams do not show temporal information, although they may contain reified occurrences of things that have or things that describe temporal behavior.

A class diagram is a graph of classifier elements connected by their various static relationships. Note that a class diagram may also contain interfaces, packages, relationships, and even instances, such as objects and links. Perhaps a better name would be "static structural diagram" but "class diagram" is shorter and well established (see Figure 10.11).

Semantics

A class diagram is a graphic view of the static structural model. The individual class diagrams do not represent divisions in the underlying model.

Notation

A class diagram is a collection of static declarative model elements, such as classes, interfaces, and their relationships, connected as a graph to each

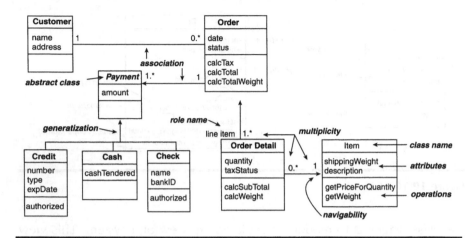

Figure 10.11   Class Diagram

other and to their contents. Class diagrams may be organized into packages either with their underlying models or as separate packages that build upon the underlying model packages.

Mapping

A class diagram does not necessarily match a single semantic entity. One or more class diagrams may represent a package within the static structural model. The division of the presentation into separate diagrams is for graphical convenience and does not imply a partitioning of the model itself. If a diagram is part of a package, then its contents map into elements in the same package (including possible references to elements accessed or imported from other packages).

Object Diagram

Object diagrams model the instances of things contained in the class diagram. Object diagrams are used to model the static design view or static process view of the system. It specifically is capturing a "snapshot" of the system at a moment in time through the visualization of a set of objects, states, and their relationships. An object diagram contains objects and links (see Figure 10.12).

An object diagram shows a set of objects and their relationships at a point in time. It is essentially an instance of a class diagram or the static part of an interaction diagram. An object diagram expresses the static parts of an interaction, consisting of the objects that collaborate, excluding any

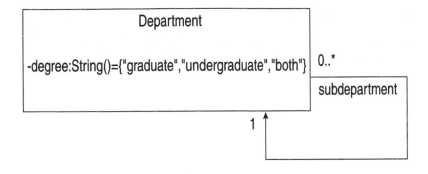

Figure 10.12   Object Diagram: University Department

of the messages that are passed among them. An object diagram is a collection of objects and links.

Object diagrams are special kinds of class diagrams, showing instances instead of classes. They are useful for explaining small pieces with complicated relationships, especially recursive relationships. This class diagram shows that a university department can contain lots of other departments.

The object diagram in Figure 10.13 instantiates the class diagram, replacing it by a concrete example. Each rectangle in the diagram corresponds to a single instance. Instance names are underlined in UML diagrams. Class or instance names may be omitted from object diagrams as long as the diagram meaning is still clear (see Figure 10.13).

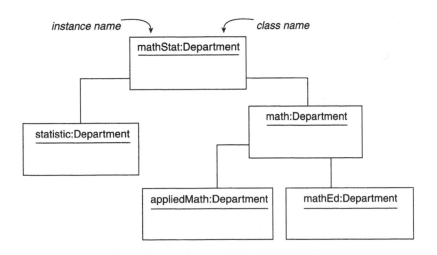

Figure 10.13   Object Diagram: Department

When modeling objects, it is not always possible to completely specify the object structure of a system, because for an individual class there may be several possible instances. Because of this, object diagrams should be used to expose meaningful or significant objects possible relating to a prototype.

Chapter 11

Knowledge Modeling with UML

Knowledge modeling is the visualization of knowledge patterns. These patterns are discovered through knowledge acquisition. During the knowledge acquisition process, the knowledge engineer works with the domain experts to uncover and document the results of their meetings. To elicit feedback from the domain experts, the knowledge engineer will develop certain knowledge models to visualize what has been learned from the domain experts.

As we learned from our chapter on knowledge modeling, our focus has been on five major representations of knowledge. These representations include ladders, network diagrams, tables, grids, decision trees, and CBR. This chapter examines the knowledge modeling and UML concepts learned in previous chapters and combines the two concepts. We will specifically examine building UML knowledge models for the following — ladders, network diagrams, and decision trees. UML will be used as the notation or language to construct these types of models. To begin, we will first determine if the domain is appropriate to knowledge acquisition and knowledge modeling.

The following represents an approach to domain analysis and knowledge acquisition. Although there may be several approaches that may be applicable, based on research conducted through the National Science Foundation (NSF) the following method is more likely to be successful[1]:

1. Domain analysis has two components — appropriateness and probability of success. This ontology should drive the choice of questions to be asked by the knowledge engineer. The ontology should be extensible, either generally or as customized by specific end users. Probability of success will be driven by rules or similarity to a case from a case base (see Chapter 7).

2. Appropriateness and probability of success related to ROI, the issue of "what counts as a domain" is both interesting and important. Some problems may be too general, some too specific. Granularity may have to be taken into account during appropriateness evaluation. A domain may become inappropriate if its scope is changed during specification.

3. Given the reality of today's business climate, and the foreseeable future, a domain may be deemed appropriate if its knowledge-based implementation helps reduce labor needs within an organization (see Chapter 2).

4. Implement the Kline and Dolins architecture questions to help determine appropriate approach. These categories include:
   a. Is deep reasoning or shallow reasoning needed to solve problems within the domain?
   b. What are the key problem characteristics within the domain?
   c. What are characteristics of typical input provided during problem solution?
   d. What are the aspects of knowledge representation?
   e. What knowledge (if any) can we bring to bear to solve problems within the domain?
   f. What are the details of the problem-solving process?
   g. What are the solution characteristics?
   h. How will end users interact with the program?

The guidelines contained within Kline and Dolins also can be used to detect suboptimal use of techniques or the need to redesign an application to make it more amenable to a particular technique, should a favored one surface.

Once the appropriateness of the domain has been determined, knowledge acquisition and knowledge modeling techniques can be applied. We will now examine how to apply UML to knowledge modeling.

UML Applied to Knowledge Models

UML will be used as the central modeling notation to capture knowledge from a specific domain. The knowledge that will be captured via UML will typically be tacit or explicit in nature. The UML will be adopted to construct several types of knowledge modeling constructs. These constructs include:

- Laddering, which is a treelike structure that is used to capture concepts, complex entities (machines, organizations, and documents), decisions, and properties associated with concepts and processes.
- Network diagrams, which include:
  - Concept maps — A concept map is a type of diagram that shows knowledge objects as nodes and the relationships between them as links (usually labeled arrows).
  - Process maps — This type of diagram shows the inputs, outputs, resources, roles, and decisions associated with each process or task in a domain. The process map is an excellent way of representing information of how and when processes, tasks, and activities are performed.
  - State transition networks — A transition network is a set of states and the transitions between them. As noted above, they are good at capturing the notion of process. For example:
    - Control processes such as those in a digitally controlled heating system.
    - Processes controlling manufacture or design.
    - Workflow processes such as those found in product data management software.
- Decision trees (also a treelike structure) — Decision trees classify instances by sorting them down the tree from the root node to some leaf node, which provides the classification of the instance. Each node in the tree specifies a test of some attribute of the instance, and each branch descending from that node corresponds to one of the possible values for this attribute. This type of construct is an excellent way to represent tacit knowledge as a set of rules for implementation into a rules-based system.

The first step to knowledge modeling is to capture the knowledge of the domain. To do so we must construct use cases, specifically knowledge use cases. When constructing knowledge use cases, we will produce both a visual model with a Knowledge Use Case Model as well as the textual version in the form of a knowledge use case specification.

Knowledge Use Case Model

The knowledge use case model will consist of the same widgets as a traditional use case model. However, the traditional stick figure representing an actor will also represent the human agent (see Figure 11.1).

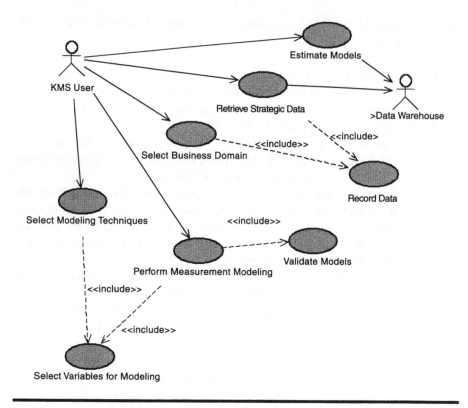

Figure 11.1   Knowledge Use Case Model

Knowledge Use Case Specification

Use case specifications describe the behavior of the system under development (see Chapter 10). What makes a knowledge use case specification (KUCS) different from other use cases that describe the system is that a KUCS describes the knowledge process of the system (see Table 11.1). As discussed in Chapter 10, a use case defines a set of sequences of actions or scenarios that the system is to perform. These set of actions have an observable benefit to the actors. The relationship between business process and use cases shows that when an IT application is viewed functionally, it is viewed as performing a set of use cases supporting various tasks within the system under development. In a KMS, the use cases will support knowledge production process, which includes knowledge validation. In a KMS, it will also support the various activities in the KM process. The KUCS that are developed will support the human agents, which interact with the KMS (see Figure 11.2).

Table 11.1   Knowledge Use Case Specification Sample

Knowledge Use Case Specification Sample
The following template is provided for a KUCS, which contains the textual properties of the use case. The Knowledge Use Case Model can be developed in a visual modeling tool, such as Rational Rose. And directly corresponds to KUCS.

1.0   **Use Case Name**
   1.1   Brief description
         The description briefly conveys the role and purpose of the use case. A single paragraph will suffice for this description.

2.0   **Information Acquisition**
   2.1   Basic flow
         This use case starts when the human agent or actor does something. The human agent always initiates the knowledge use case.
   2.2   Alternative flows
         2.2.1   <First alternative flow>
         Alternate flows will describe actions or events that are beyond the normal events that will happen during the execution of the knowledge use case. There can be several alternate flows.
         2.2.2   <Second alternative flow>

3.0   **Knowledge Claim Formulation**
   3.1   Basic flow
         This use case starts when the human agent or actor does something. The human agent always initiates the knowledge use case.
   3.2   Alternative flows
         3.2.1   <First alternative flow>
         Alternate flows will describe actions or events that are beyond the normal events that will happen during the execution of the knowledge use case. There can be several alternate flows.
         3.2.2   <Second alternative flow>

4.0   **Knowledge Claim Validation**
   4.1   Basic flow
         This use case starts when the human agent or actor does something. The human agent always initiates the knowledge use case.
   4.2   Alternative flows
         4.2.1   <First alternative flow>
         Alternate flows will describe actions or events that are beyond the normal events that will happen during the execution of the knowledge use case. There can be several alternate flows.
         4.2.2   <Second alternative flow>

Table 11.1 (continued)   Knowledge Use Case Specification Sample

5.0 **Preconditions** A precondition of a use case is the state of the system that must be present prior to a use case being performed. 5.1 <Precondition one> 6.0 **Postconditions** A postcondition of a use case is a list of possible states the system can be in immediately after a use case has finished. 6.1 <Postcondition one> 7.0 **Extension Points** Extension points of the use case.

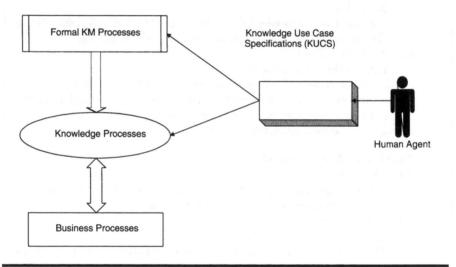

Figure 11.2   Knowledge Process and Knowledge Use Case Specification

The knowledge use case may be described at various levels of abstraction or concreteness. To develop an overall understanding of KMS, we must first focus on the high-level use cases. These are the use cases that describe the KMS functionality at an abstract or "20,000 foot level."

An example of a high-level use case would be to "perform knowledge discovery in a database." The following is a set of tasks that the use case will perform:

- Retrieve and display strategic, tactical goals and objectives, and results of knowledge discovery
- Select entity objects representing business domains to be mined for new knowledge

- Explore data and clean for modeling
- Record and transform data
- Reduce data
- Select variables for modeling
- Transform variables
- Perform measurement modeling
- Select modeling techniques
- Estimate models
- Validate models

Each task in the "perform knowledge discovery in a database" use case could itself be a use case. Only through further analysis would we know for sure. However, because this is a high-level abstraction, we can conclude that the more abstract use case will decompose into more concrete use cases. Further, we can classify use cases in KMS by whether they support knowledge production (KP), knowledge integration (KI), or KM and even further whether they support the various subprocesses and activities in the KP, KI, or KM processes. The following are examples of KUCS classified as KP, KI, or KM.[2]

Knowledge Production Use Cases

The following sections are examples of KUCS classified as KP.

Information Acquisition

- Performing cataloging and tracking of previously acquired enterprise data, information, and knowledge bases related to business processes.
- Perform cataloging and tracking of external data, information, and knowledge bases related to enterprise business processes.
- Order data, information, or external claimed knowledge and have it shipped from an external source.
- Purchase data, information, or external knowledge claims.
- Extract, reformat, scrub, transform, stage, and load, data, information, and knowledge claims acquired from external sources.

Knowledge Claim Formulation

- Prepare data, information, and knowledge for analysis and analytical modeling.
- Update all data, information, and knowledge stores to maintain consistency with changes introduced into KMS.

- Perform analysis and modeling, including revising, reformulating, and formulating models and knowledge discovery in databases with respect to:
  - Planning and planning models
  - Descriptions and descriptive models
  - Measurement modeling
  - Cause-effect analyzing and modeling
  - Predictive and time-series forecasting and modeling
  - Assessment modeling

Knowledge Claim Validation

- Test competing knowledge models and claims using appropriate analytical techniques, data, and validation criteria.
- Assess test results and compare competing knowledge models and claims.
- Store outcomes of information acquisition, individual and group learning, knowledge claim formulation, and other knowledge claim validation activities into data, information, or knowledge store accessible through electronic queries.
- Load into data, information, or knowledge and updates into enterprise stores and provide access to enterprise query and reporting tools.

Knowledge Integration Use Cases

The following sections are examples of KUCS classified as KI. They involve storing the outcomes of knowledge integration activities into an accessible data, information, or knowledge store.

Searching and Retrieving Stored Data, Information, or Knowledge

- Receiving transmitted into data, information, or knowledge through e-mail, automated alerts, and data, information, and knowledge base updates.
- Retrieving through computer-based querying data, information, and knowledge of the following types:
  - Planning
  - Descriptive
  - Cause and effect
  - Predictive and time-series forecasting
  - Assessment

- Search and retrieve from enterprise stores through computer-based querying, data, information, and knowledge of the following types:
  - Planning
  - Descriptive
  - Cause and effect
  - Predictive and time-series forecasting
  - Assessment
- Using e-mail to request assistance from personal networks

Broadcasting

- Publish and disseminate data, information, and knowledge using the enterprise intranet.
- Present knowledge using KMS.

Sharing

- Use e-mail to request assistance from personal networks.
- Share data, information, and knowledge through collaboration spaces.

Teaching

Present e-learning or CBT modules to knowledge workers, delivered through the KMS (see Chapter 2).

Knowledge Management Use Cases

The following sections are examples of KUCS classified as KM.

Leadership

- Identify KM responsibilities based on segmentation or decomposition of the KM process.
- Retrieve available qualification information on KM candidates for appointment.
- Evaluate available candidates according to rules relating qualifications to predicted performance.
- Communicate appointments to KM constituency.
- Plan and schedule motivational events.

Building External Relationships

Communicate with external individuals through e-mail and online conferencing technology.

Knowledge Management Knowledge Production

- All knowledge production and knowledge integration use cases specified for knowledge processing.
- Specify and compare alternative KM options in terms of anticipated costs and benefits.

Knowledge Management Knowledge Integration

- Querying and reporting using data, information, and knowledge about KM staff plans, KM staff performance description, KM staff performance cause-effect analysis, and KM staff performance prediction and forecasting.
- Querying and reporting using data, information, and knowledge about accessing KM staff performance in terms of costs and benefits.

Crisis Handling

- Search and retrieve from enterprise stores through querying and reporting, data, information, and knowledge of the following types about crisis potential:
  - Planning
  - Descriptive
  - Cause and effect
  - Predictive and time-series forecasting
  - Assessment

Changing Knowledge-Processing Rules

- Search and retrieve from enterprise stores through computer-based querying data, information, and knowledge of the following types about knowledge process rules:
  - Planning
  - Descriptive
  - Cause and effect
  - Predictive and time-series forecasting
  - Assessment
- Communicate rule-changing directives through e-mail

Allocating Resources

- Select training programs.
- Purchase training vehicles and materials.

The above listing only provides a more concrete idea of the nature of the KMS use cases that relate to knowledge acquisition. To gain an understanding of the magnitude of use cases that are needed to cover all aspects of a KMS further analysis is needed. Such an analysis should center on the KMS components detailed in Chapter 2 (i.e., workflow, e-learning, knowledge acquisition, CRM, collaboration, and document management).

UML to Create Knowledge Models

The following describes the relationship between traditional knowledge modeling techniques described in Chapter 9 with their UML counterpart.

Concept Ladder

A concept ladder shows classes of concepts and their subtypes (see Chapter 9). All relationships in a concept ladder take the form of an IS A relationship. For example, a whale is a mammal. The following represents an example of a concept ladder constructed in UML (see Figure 11.3).

This UML diagram utilizes the class diagram construct. Each IS A relationship is associated with a generalization as a stereotype pointing back to the parent class.

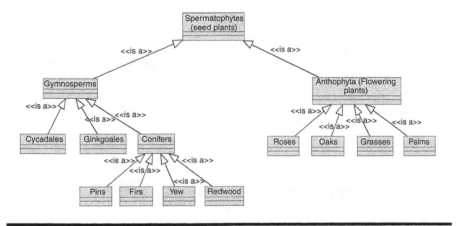

Figure 11.3   Concept Ladder

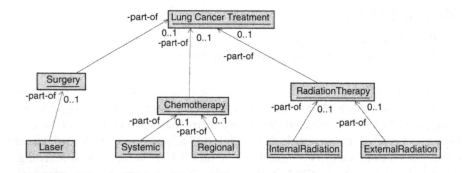

Figure 11.4   Composition Ladder

Composition Ladder

A composition ladder shows the way a knowledge object is composed of its constituent parts (see Chapter 9). Figure 11.4 is an example of a composition ladder constructed in UML.

Decision Ladder

A decision ladder shows the alternative courses of action for a particular decision (see Chapter 9). Figure 11.5 is an example of a decision ladder constructed in UML.

Attribute Ladder

An attribute ladder shows attributes and values. All the adjectival values relevant to an attribute are shown as subnodes, but numerical values are

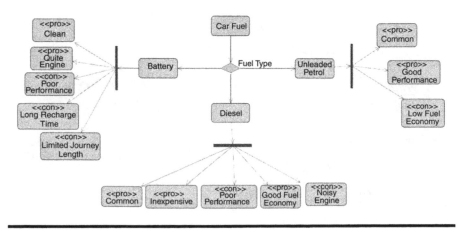

Figure 11.5   Decision Ladder

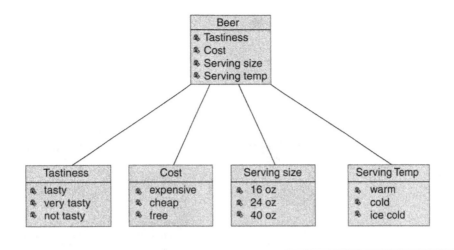

Figure 11.6   Attribute Ladder

not usually shown (see Chapter 9). Figure 11.6 is an example of a concept ladder constructed in UML.

Process Ladder

This ladder shows processes (i.e., tasks, activities) and the subprocesses (i.e., subtasks, subactivities) of which they are composed. All relationships are the part of relationship (see Chapter 9). Figure 11.7 is an example of a concept ladder constructed in UML.

Network Diagrams

Network diagrams show nodes connected by arrows. Depending on the type of network diagram, the nodes might represent any type of concept, attribute, value, or task, and the arrows between the nodes any type of relationship (see Chapter 9).

Concept Map

A concept map is a type of diagram that shows knowledge objects as nodes and the relationships between them as links (usually labeled arrows). The knowledge objects (concepts) are usually enclosed in circles or boxes of some type, and relationships between concepts or propositions indicated by a connecting line between two concepts (see Chapter 9). Figure 11.8 is an example of a concept map constructed in UML.

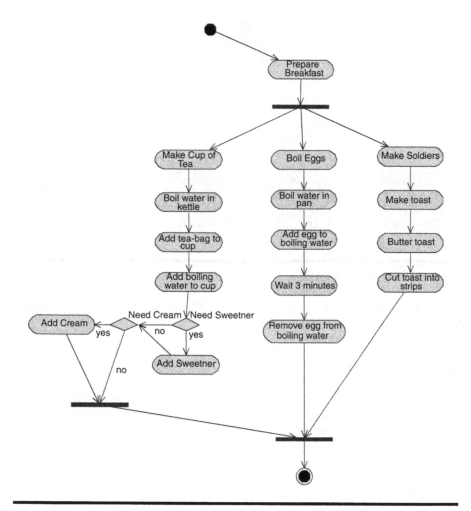

Figure 11.7 Process Ladder

The concept map shown in Figure 11.8 uses UML objects to represent knowledge objects.

Process Map

A process map shows the inputs, outputs, resources, roles, and decisions associated with each process or task in a domain (see Figure 11.9). Process maps represent information of how and when process tasks and activities are performed (see Chapter 9).

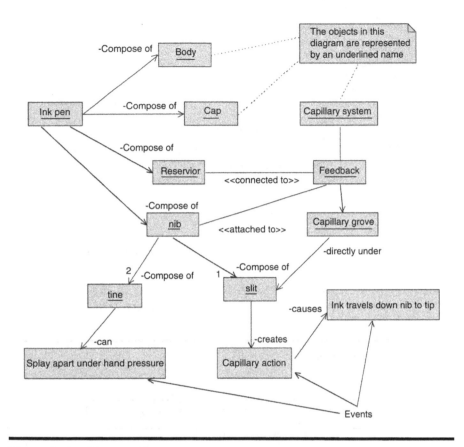

Figure 11.8 Concept Map

State Transition Network

A state transition network diagram comprises two elements:

1. Nodes that represent the states that a concept can be in.
2. Arrows between the nodes showing all the events and processes or tasks that can cause transitions from one state to another (see Figure 11.10).

As stated in Chapter 9, a transition network is a set of states and the transitions between them. State transition networks are good at capturing the notion of process. For example:

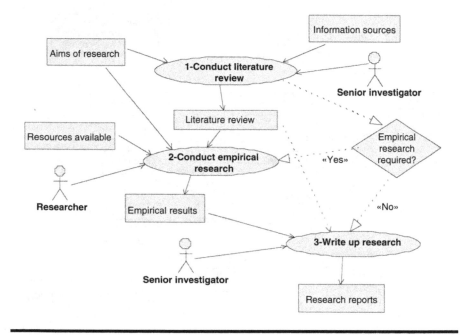

Figure 11.9   Process Map

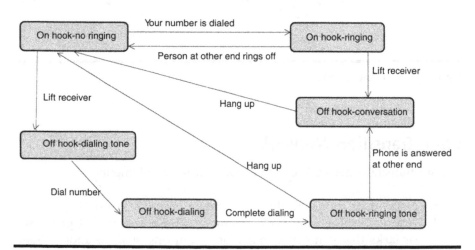

Figure 11.10   State Transition Network

- Control processes such as those in a digitally controlled heating system.
- Processes controlling manufacture or design.
- Workflow processes such as those found in product data management software.

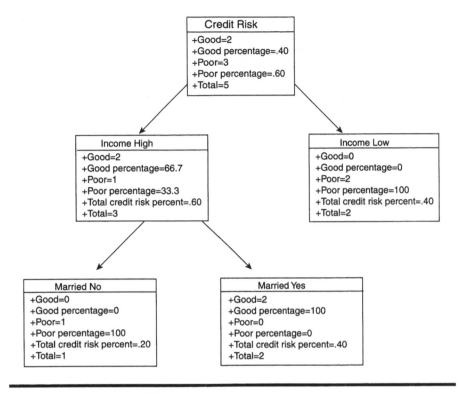

Figure 11.11   UML Decision Tree

Decision Trees

Decision trees classify instances by sorting them down the tree from the root node to some leaf node, which provides the classification of the instance. Each node in the tree specifies a test of some attribute of the instance, and each branch descending from that node corresponds to one of the possible values for this attribute (see Chapter 9).

An instance is classified by starting at the root node of the decision tree, testing the attribute specified by this node, then moving down the tree branch corresponding to the value of the attribute. This process is then repeated at the node on this branch and so on until a leaf node is reached.

In UML, the decision tree will be constructed using the class diagram paradigm (see Figure 11.11).

Notes

1. A.J. Rhem & Associates, Inc. UML Based Framework for Knowledge Acquisition. NSF-sponsored project, 2004.
2. Firestone, J.M. *Enterprise Information Portals and Knowledge Management* (Oxford: Butterworth-Heinemann, 2003), pp. 204–205.

Chapter 12

Defining a Knowledge Acquisition Framework

In defining a knowledge acquisition framework, it should encompass the following capabilities:

- Determine the domain area — Talk to the domain expert and find out what problems or aspects of the problem-solving process may be amenable to automation. Perform evaluation analysis to determine if the domain area is likely to use a knowledge base system.
- Decompose the knowledge — Identify the type of knowledge being gathered (i.e., tacit, explicit, declarative, procedural). Break the domain into smaller subtasks. If the knowledge is contained in a database, apply data mining techniques to extract the knowledge.
- Determine interdependencies — Analyze how individual components of knowledge are related and integrated when they are used to solve a task. Point out missing pieces of knowledge. Determine what pieces of knowledge are related and how. Detect inconsistencies among the various aspects of the knowledge.
- Recognize knowledge patterns — Identify patterns within the various types of knowledge gathered. Apply the knowledge gathered to similar situations that the domain expert may have encountered or to similar cases (CBR) that may have been solved previously.
- Determine judgments in knowledge — Determine if the knowledge being captured is judgmental (uncertain or "fuzzy") in nature. A determination must be made if there are conflicts between rules.

- Perform conflict resolution — If the knowledge being captured has uncertainty or is fuzzy in nature, the first step in resolving this uncertainty is to specify preconditions in the contexts of one or more of the conflicting rules to prevent them from being considered.
- Guide knowledge engineer in constructing the knowledge base — Perform knowledge modeling of the domain utilizing one or more of the techniques mentioned in the previous concepts.

The knowledge acquisition task should focus on a representation of expertise that is natural to domain experts, so that they can think about their expertise rather than how to represent it in a computer. For a framework to assist the knowledge engineer, an underlying workflow component should be implemented. This component will guide the knowledge engineer in modeling specific domain knowledge.

Knowledge Acquisition Workflow

When it has been determined that a knowledge base system will be developed as part of the overall KMS effort, the knowledge engineer's attention must focus on capturing the variety of knowledge within the organization.

Within the knowledge acquisition framework, the knowledge acquisition workflow (KA workflow) module works as a result of constructing the knowledge base (see Table 12.1). Once the type of knowledge to be captured has been determined (tacit, explicit, declarative, procedural, etc.), the KA workflow helps the user understand the general nature of the knowledge-oriented task and guides the knowledge modeling effort using UML to illustrate the knowledge.

To understand the framework that encompass knowledge acquisition some help comes from the European CommonKADS initiative.[1] In this initiative, tasks are primarily defined in one of three types:

1. System modification (the task is to modify an existing system) (see Figure 12.1)
2. System analysis (see Figure 12.2)
3. System synthesis (see Figure 12.3)

During the CommonKADS, the first question ask to the user is "Does the task (application) involve" one of the three following situations:

1. Establishing unknown properties of behavior of domain objects
2. Composing a new structural description of a possible domain object
3. A combination of the above

Table 12.1   Knowledge Acquisition Framework Grid

Concept	Task	Problem-Solving Method	Result
Determine domain area	Talk to the domain expert and find out what problems or aspects of the problem-solving process may be amenable to automation. Perform evaluation analysis to determine if the domain area is likely to use a knowledge base system.	Perform evaluation analysis using the checklist approach.	Qualified domain areas for the construction of a knowledge base system.
Decompose the knowledge	Identify the type of knowledge being gathered (i.e., tacit, explicit, declarative, procedural). Break the domain into smaller subtasks. If the knowledge is contained in a database, apply data mining techniques to extract the knowledge.	Several methods can be used here. To gather tacit knowledge the use of decision trees is recommended. To obtain knowledge from databases, the use of data mining techniques are highly desirable. Each method will facilitate the knowledge being broken into smaller, more manageable subtasks.	The knowledge of the domain area is broken into smaller subtasks.
Determine interdependencies	Analyze how individual components of knowledge are related and integrated when they are used to solve a task. Point out missing pieces	Incorporate the use of Interdependency Models (IMs). Tools such as EMeD (Expert Method Developer) allows users to specify problem-solving	Missing pieces of data are filled in, inconsistencies are corrected, and a more complete view on how

Table 12.1 (continued) Knowledge Acquisition Framework Grid

Concept	Task	Problem-Solving Method	Result
	of knowledge. Determine what pieces of knowledge are related and how. Detect inconsistencies among the various aspects of the knowledge.	knowledge and identifies the interdependencies between the various aspects of the knowledge.	the knowledge components are related is established.
Recognize knowledge patterns	Identify patterns within the various types of knowledge gathered. Apply the knowledge gathered to similar situations that the domain expert may have encountered or to similar cases (CBR) that may have been solved previously.	Using CBR, developing decision trees, or data mining techniques to discover patterns is the recommended approach.	The knowledge becomes more consistent and the knowledge base is able to be constructed more efficiently.
Determine judgments in knowledge	Determine if the knowledge being captured is judgmental (uncertain or fuzzy) in nature. A determination must be made if there are conflicts between rules.	If we have conflicts between rules, we should ask the expert for an explicit, relative judgment between the active rules in that context.	Conflicting rules are identified or conflicting knowledge about an area of a domain is identified.
Perform conflict resolution	If the knowledge being captured has uncertainty or is fuzzy in nature, the first step in resolving this uncertainty is to	The effect of this is to add expertise, restricting the number of situations in which the rules are applicable.	Conflicts between rules or conflicts between knowledge are resolved.

Table 12.1 (continued)   Knowledge Acquisition Framework Grid

Concept	Task	Problem-Solving Method	Result
	specify preconditions in the contexts of one or more of the conflicting rules to prevent them from being considered.		
Construct knowledge base	Perform knowledge modeling of the domain utilizing one or more of the techniques mentioned in the previous concepts.	Construct knowledge models utilizing UML.	Knowledge-based system o KMS is constructed for the domain areas under consideration.

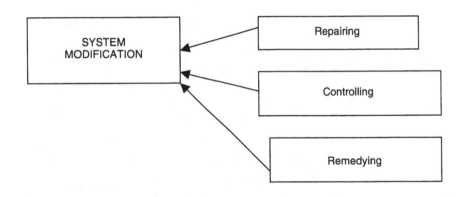

Figure 12.1   System Modification

System analysis goes with situation 1, system synthesis with situation 2, and system modification with situation 3. The full decision tree of tasks is depicted in Figure 12.1.

It is also possible to further refine the diagnosis task under "system analysis" (e.g., single-fault diagnosis vs. multiple fault diagnosis).

Now we will examine the architecture design within the knowledge acquisition framework and understand the determination of the knowledge structures involved in knowledge acquisition.

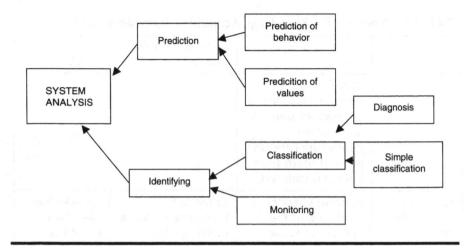

Figure 12.2   System Analysis

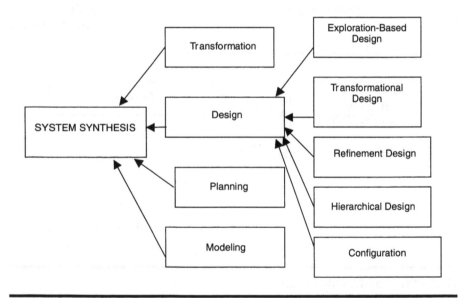

Figure 12.3   System Synthesis

Architecture Design

Guidelines for the production of an architectural design to knowledge acquisition have been provided by Kline and Dolins (1989) and modified by others. These guidelines exists as "probing questions" and are of the form:

IF a certain feature exists in the analyzed knowledge of a domain, THEN consider using a particular knowledge representation or implementation technique.

Or:

IF a certain feature is true of desired (or requisite) interaction between the end user and the application, THEN consider using a particular knowledge representation or implementation technique.

The categories of the design features are as follows:

- Depth of reasoning and architecture:
  - Shallow, model-based, blackboard
- Knowledge representation structures:
  - Rules, frames, object-oriented programming, networks, ...
- Inference types:
  - Goal-driven, data-driven
- Control of flow of inference:
  - Search strategy, constraints on search, metacontrol
- Handling of uncertainty, incompleteness or inaccuracy of data
- User interface
- Knowledge acquisition

Notional Output to User

Answering the probing questions (given below) provides evidence for various design features. Evidence strength is calculated via logic that combines the weights associated with answers to the questions. Table 12.2 is a sample of what the output to the user might look like.

Probing Questions

The probing questions in Appendix A are taken from work done by Kline and Dolins (1985, 1989).[2] In fact, the questions below are from their 1985 tech report. However, not all questions from their 1985 report are included.

Here is a sample question. The weighting at the end of each conclusion is a sort of confidence factor (CF), but can be implemented as a weight much as the information in the domain analysis portion of the framework.

Table 12.2 Notional Output to User after Answering the Probing Questions

Design Feature	Implementation Recommendation
Shallow reasoning	Strong
Rules	Strong
Goal-driven reasoning	Moderate
Depth-first search	Moderate
Truth maintenance	Moderate
Certainty factors	Moderate
"Canned" text for explanations	Moderate
Data-driven reasoning	Weak
Model-based reasoning	Strong negative

Sample probing questions:

IF the application is such that a preenumerated set of solutions can be established (as distinct from constructing solutions as a result of constraint satisfaction), THEN use goal-driven reasoning WEIGHT: 1, ELSE use data-driven reasoning WEIGHT: 5.

Knowledge Acquisition Framework

Determine Domain Area

Now that a basis of understanding has been established for the knowledge acquisition framework, it is time to detail the major aspects of the framework mentioned at the beginning of the chapter. The first step in the knowledge acquisition process is to know what domain area will be the focus of knowledge elicitation. To determine the domain area, a good approach to use is the checklist framework.

The checklist framework addresses technical issues, but equally emphasizes the practical aspects of evaluating a potential knowledge base system application. The checklist framework incorporates six categories. The categories, which comprise the checklist framework and their relative weights are task (25), payoff (20), customer management (20), system designer (15), domain expert (10), and user (10). For an application to be considered promising, it must score at least 50 percent in the task category (13 points) and payoff category (10 points). If either scores less than 50 percent, the knowledge engineer should choose another task. An application must also score at least 50 percent overall (50 points) to qualify; scores below 50 percent in any of the later four categories indicates potential difficulties. Once a domain area qualifies, it is time to move on to the knowledge acquisition process for that domain.

Desirable Task

The nature of the task is the most critical category for assessing the value of applying expert system technology. Not only must the task be technically feasible, but use of expert systems must also be necessary and appropriate. The task should involve significant symbolic processing, complexity, judgment, and uncertainty, and it should not be solvable using conventional programming methods or be too difficult, therefore requiring AI applied research (see Table 12.3). If the proposed application scores less than 50 percent in the task category, either the task can be solved using conventional programming techniques, or the task is inappropriate or too difficult for expert system technology.

Payoff

The need for the system must be translatable into benefits relevant to user management. Expert systems can provide several benefits that include reduced costs, improved quality, increased revenues, captured expertise, easily distributed expertise, raised barriers to market entry, and a training effect on users. Compared to conventional data processing systems, expert systems often incur additional expenses, the extent of which depends on the complexity of the proposed application. These additional expenses include additional hardware, software, development cost of eliciting knowledge from domain experts, and system maintenance costs.

If score for the payoff category is less than 50 percent (10 points), another task should probably be chosen. If the benefits are too low (criteria 1–7), the task probably does not provide sufficient value to the user organization. If the system costs too much to deliver (criteria 8–11), either the system needs to be developed in a simpler shell, custom coded in a language such as C, or reduced in functionality (see Table 12.4).

Customer Management

In most checklists, the management category has often been overlooked. This checklist addresses the issues for lower- and upper-level executives.

Table 12.3   Desirable Task

(2)   1. Task is primarily cognitive, requiring analysis, synthesis, or decision making rather than perception or action.

(2)   2. Involves primarily symbolic knowledge and reasoning.

(2)   3. Is complex, involving many parameters.

(1)   4. Involves chains of reasoning on multiple levels of knowledge.

(2)   5. Uses heuristics or rules of thumb and requires judgment or reasoning about subjective factors.

(1)   6. Cannot be solved using conventional computing methods.

(2)   7. Often must be solved with incomplete or inaccurate data.

(2)   8. Often requires explanation, justification of results, or reasoning.

(1)   9. Is at an intermediate stage of knowledge formalization that uses heuristics and classification rather than search or algorithms.

(1) 10. Task knowledge is confined to a narrow domain.

(1) 11. Task knowledge is stable.

(1) 12. Incremental progress is possible; task can be subdivided.

(1) 13. Does not require reasoning about time or space.

(1) 14. Is not natural-language intensive.

(1) 15. Requires little or no common sense or general-world knowledge.

(1) 16. Does not require the system to learn from experience.

(1) 17. Is similar to one in an existing expert system.

(1) 18. Data and case studies are available.

(1) 19. System performance can be accurately and easily measured.

_____ = Points Earned = _____ score

25 Points Possible

I have found, from speaking with management at several major corporations, that lower-level managers have been willing to support expert system projects by supplying domain experts, serving as test sites for expert system prototypes, and by preparing test cases and transcribing data needed for system testing. However, without the support of upper-level executives, expert system applications face an uphill battle for

Table 12.4 Payoff

(4) 1. Senior management is willing to commit significant funding.

(2) 2. Willing to commit significant staffing resources to develop and deploy the system.

(1) 3. Supportive, enthusiastic, and has appointed a project coordinator.

(1) 4. Receptive to innovation and new technologies.

(3) 5. Site management has committed staffing resources for acquiring knowledge, preparing test cases, and validating the system.

(1) 6. Is supportive, enthusiastic, and has appointed a project contact from management.

(2) 7. Management accepts primary responsibility for maintaining the installed system.

(1) 8. Use of the system will not be politically sensitive.

(1) 9. Either system requires minimal changes to existing procedures, or if it requires substantial changes, management agrees to changes and recognizes the need for user training on the system.

(2) 10. Management understands that estimates for resources and deadlines are difficult to estimate and probably will not be met.

(2) 11. Management realizes the system will make mistakes and may perform no better than a moderately proficient user.

____ = Points earned = ____ score

20 Points possible

implementation. Although technical feasibility may have been demonstrated for many expert system projects, funding of hardware purchases for deployment has been difficult to obtain. Thus, further development and deployment of some applications have been delayed significantly or suspended indefinitely (see Table 12.5).

System Designer

One aspect of project selection that has been ignored is desirable traits for the system designer. The knowledge engineers or AI consultants may also be considered as system designers. The technical success of the system depends chiefly on the designer and secondarily on the domain

Table 12.5 Customer Management

(2)	1.	System would significantly increase revenues.
(2)	2.	Reduce costs.
(2)	3.	Improves quality.
(2)	4.	Capture undocumented expertise or expertise that is perishable or in short supply.
(1)	5.	Distribute accessible expertise to novice users.
(1)	6.	Provide training effect on users through usage.
(1)	7.	Raise barriers to future market entrants.
(1)	8.	Require no or minimal more data entry than current system.
(2)	9.	Be developed using commercial shells; little customized coding needed. Will become quite costly if customization is needed.
(1)	10.	System maintenance would be low.
(2)	11.	System would be delivered on an affordable desktop computer or workstation or using existing hardware and platforms.
(1)	12.	Could be phased in; partial completion would still be useful.
(2)	13.	Would result in benefit-cost ratio of at least 10:1 — Ideal.

_____ = Points earned = _____ score

20 Points possible

expert. If the designer has an insufficient background in AI or lacks familiarity with the expert system software that will be used in developing the application, the project may fail. Major project delays and revisions often result from low scores in this category. Although not as critical as the task, payoff, or management categories, a score of less than 50 percent (7 points) can pinpoint potential problems (see Table 12.6).

Domain (Business) Expert

The system must be constructed from a source of expertise, which could consist of formal, written knowledge or informal heuristics (such as rules of thumb) not documented elsewhere. Interviewing domain experts or observing their actions must obtain heuristics. If substantial domain knowledge is lacking, methods other than expert systems, such as a more

Table 12.6   System Designer

(2)   1. Designer has experience in designing and developing expert systems.

(1)   2. Knows how to use a development tool appropriate for the system and has used the chosen tool or shell.

(1)   3. Is experienced in acquiring and eliciting knowledge from written sources and domain experts.

(2)   4. Has AI background to recognize which techniques will be useful in developing the system.

(1)   5. Understands cognitive psychology.

(2)   6. Has managed and developed more traditional computing applications. Able to understand the impact the expert system will have on the overall environment.

(2)   7. Is knowledgeable or an expert in the domain. Knows the business problem to be solved.

(1)   8. Has hardware and software available for development.

(2)   9. Can commit at least six months of full-time effort for developing testing and implementing the system.

_____ = Points earned = _____ score

15 Points possible

conventional framework will be appropriate. Therefore, heuristic expertise is crucial to the success of expert systems (see Table 12.7).

User

Considering the needs and preferences of users is essential to system success. Users should feel a strong need for assistance, yet feel comfortable with the system. Thus, the role played by the expert system is crucial to user acceptance. Most often, systems should be designed as assistants so the user remains in control of the task. If the system automates the task, it is essential that users have other more desirable tasks to replace the automated task. Users and experts will resist all proposed expert system applications if users are displaced, replaced, or lose prestige.

The user category represents 10 out of the 100 points possible on all the checklist categories combined. Although not as critical as the other

Table 12.7 Domain (Business) Expert

(2)   1. Recognized experts exist.

(1)   2. Expert performance is probably better than that of amateurs.

(1)   3. Task is routinely taught to beginners.

(1)   4. Experts are accessible for extended periods of time.

(1)   5. Are cooperative.

(1)   6. Communicate well.

(2)   7. Available to develop test cases and help evaluate the system.

___ = Points earned = ____ score

10 Points possible

Table 12.8 User

(2)   1. Users feel a strong need for the system.

(2)   2. Will not be deskilled or unfavorably displaced as a result of implementing the system.

(1)   3. Want to be involved in the system's development.

(2)   4. Does not have unrealistically high expectations.

(3)   5. Have roughly the same level of expertise.

___ = Points earned = _____ score

10 Points possible

categories, a score of less than 50 percent (5 points) can foreshadow difficulties during and after implementation (see Table 12.8).

The greatest advantage of the checklist is that applications can be evaluated without expending resources. Another advantage is eliminating tasks from consideration that are inappropriate due to their intrinsic nature, lack of benefits, unfavorable organizational characteristics, weak system designer skills, or other negatives.

This checklist also focuses attention on potential problem areas within specific categories, even when those categories receive overall passing scores. Furthermore, it can assist in identifying and validating promising slices of domain knowledge and can assist in identifying software tools and hardware platforms likely to work best for system implementation.

Decomposing the Knowledge Acquisition Task

When attempting to solve any large-scale problem, knowledge engineers would typically break the job into a number of smaller tasks; to help a domain expert build a knowledge base, the knowledge engineer should similarly break the job of knowledge acquisition into a number of smaller tasks. By breaking the task into subtasks, knowledge engineers recognize that the knowledge and reasoning inherent in well-developed skills are complex and that they must help to manage the expert's focus of attention in building a knowledge base if they are to achieve a reliable and accurate result.

Structuring the task of building a knowledge-based application into a number of distinct substeps will ease the expert into the task of building a knowledge base gradually. This will also enable the expert to maintain a global perspective that prevents confusion when detailed knowledge is specified. Such decomposition of the knowledge acquisition task also helps the experts to focus their attention on one aspect of expertise at a time, increasing the availability of pertinent information in a timely fashion.

Determine Interdependencies

Interdependency is when two or more things depend on one another equally. One component depends on another. Finding the interdependencies between different pieces of knowledge will guide the domain expert in completing the knowledge acquisition task. Tasks are specified as goal hierarchies, where a goal is broken down into smaller goals or subgoals all the way down to the primitive or basic tasks. Determining the interdependencies between these tasks will facilitate identifying the missing pieces of knowledge, determine what pieces of knowledge are related, and determine any inconsistencies with the knowledge gathered for that domain.

Focus on Pattern Recognition as the Basis of Expertise

When experts solve most of their problems, they are not problem solving per se as much as they are recognizing aspects of similar problems they have encountered in the past and building a composite solution. Problem solving by novices frequently involves many trips down the garden path and back until a correct solution is found. When experts are applying their well-known expertise, they proceed inexorably toward problem solution, never wavering. Therefore, when representing expertise, a pattern-recognition paradigm would best facilitate the expert's problem-solving capabilities. Also, expertise should be represented as patterns that might form a recognizable aspect of a problem, rather than force the expert to recall aspects of situations that may match conditions in production rules.

Qualitative Reasoning about Uncertainty and Fuzzy Logic

It is known that people are notoriously poor at making absolute numerical judgments, but they are great at making relative judgments. For example, should two planes fly by, most people would make inaccurate estimates about the speed of each plane, but most would correctly judge which was the faster of the two aircraft. If there are conflicts between rules, knowledge engineers should ask the expert for an explicit, relative judgment between the active rules in that context rather than trying to assign certainty factors or other numerical representations of belief that are combined in some arbitrary fashion to make a judgment (e.g., one never has a COLD .67 or CHOLERA .33; one either has a cold in that context, or one does not).

People often deal with numbers but they seldom use the numerical value of the number in their manipulations. The number usually means something specific — for example, a temperature of 67 could be cool, normal, hot, dangerously low, or normal depending on the application — and that is what the expert considers. This framework must permit the expert to attach numerical ranges to symbolic meanings, if desired.

Many people confuse the above example of uncertain reasoning with fuzzy reasoning. Probabilistic reasoning is concerned with the uncertain reasoning about well-defined events or concepts such as symptom A and illness X. On the other hand, fuzzy logic is concerned with the reasoning about fuzzy events or concepts. Examples of fuzzy concepts are "temperature is high" and "person is tall." When is a person tall? At 60, 63, or 65? If we define the threshold of tallness at 63, then the implication is that a person of 60 is not tall. When humans reason with terms such as "tall," they do not normally have a fixed threshold in mind, but a smooth fuzzy definition. Humans can reason effectively with such fuzzy definitions, therefore, to capture human fuzzy reasoning we need fuzzy logic. An example of a fuzzy rule, which involves a fuzzy condition and a fuzzy conclusion, is:

IF salary is high, THEN credit risk is low. This is explicit conflict resolution.

When legitimate conflicts exist between rules, the clashes must be resolved. Conflicts exist when several rules attempt to set the same right-hand side object to different values. The conflicts are legitimate if the expert does not have the knowledge necessary to prevent the clash, but may possess the expertise to sort out the conflicting rules. When a clash between rules is identified, the expert should first determine that each conflicting rule has been correctly specified and then take steps to explicitly remove or deal with the conflict.

There is a tendency to resolve conflicts using preferences because it is easier to indicate which rules are preferred in a particular conflict than it is to specify contexts to prevent clashes from occurring in the first place. This inclination should be avoided because the best expertise is that which avoids conflicts between knowledge sources completely, and this expertise may be revealed with a little thoughtful consideration. A plethora of preferences in a knowledge base reflects poorly developed or poorly specified expertise. Therefore, the first step in resolving a legitimate clash should be to specify preconditions in the contexts of one or more of the conflicting rules to prevent them from being considered. The effect of this is to add expertise, restricting the number of situations in which the rules are applicable.

There are situations in which sufficient expertise to avoid conflicts is unavailable, but there are many instances where expertise has been developed to resolve conflicts that have arisen. One might, for example, not be able to specify why advice from one advisor is preferable to the opinions of another, but the disposition is known. This is the type of situation in which preferences should be used to resolve conflicts: where the knowledge in one rule is known to be superior to the knowledge in another, but the reason for the choice is unknown or too difficult to specify.

Finally, there are situations in which sufficient expertise to even choose between knowledge sources does not exist. For example, in the case of conflict, set the value to the lowest one to be "conservative" or resolve the conflict randomly. In the latter case, perhaps either settings from the conflicting rules is equally valid and there is no reason to consistently set one over the other. Because the bias method of resolving conflicts does not even consider the source of the knowledge, it is the least preferred method.

The concepts discussed here are important to knowledge acquisition from human experts, because they involve basic human characteristics. In defining a knowledge acquisition framework, the knowledge engineer may incorporate one or several of the methods for knowledge acquisition mentioned earlier. Whether they implement the framework using the Interdependency Model paradigm or decision trees, by incorporating the knowledge acquisition framework detailed here, the framework will encompass many of the best practices used in knowledge acquisition.

This knowledge acquisition framework is organized into seven groups of activities, with the corresponding task, problem-solving method, and result used to facilitate each concept.

Notes

1. Schreiber, A., et al. CommonKADS: A Comprehensive Methodology for KBS Development, in *IEEE Expert: Intelligent Systems and Their Applications* 9 (6), 1994, pp. 28–37.
2. Kline, P.J., and Dolins, S.B. *Designing Expert Systems: A Guide to Selecting Implementation Techniques* (New York: John Wiley & Sons, 1989).

Chapter 13

Business Case: Department of Motor Vehicles Reporting System

This business case is intended to address the needs of the Department of Motor Vehicles (DMV) reporting system. This business case includes information about processing errors received from states, verification of data, and notification to the broker or agent, state, and insurance carrier, and applying the rules associated with the error correction process.

This business case also addresses the gathering of policy information, insured, and vehicle data from multiple sources; ensuring integrity of the data; and applying rules, on a state-by-state basis, to determine what should be reported to the state.

The DMV reporting system will provide the following:

- Single data repository for error information and processing.
- State-specific reporting rules to ensure reduction in errors caused by timing and reporting of ineligible information.
- Automated responses to the state, broker or agent, and insurance carrier for matched information requests, such as verifications.

DMV Reporting System Overview

The state DMV requires all vehicles to be registered and insured. Commercial insurance companies doing business within the state are require to report new insurers within 30 days of issuing a policy. Failure to meet this objective will result in fines. At the same time, the state is sending out Mandatory Verification of Insurance Forms (MVF) to the insurance companies to verify insurance information. The state utilizes the information given during registration, and sends out for a response from the insurance company. The insurance company is required to send a response within three days. Failure to meet this objective will result in fines. This is totally separate from the requirement of sending in the new record. The state requires commercial insurance companies to report at three levels, policy, insurer, and vehicle.

Business Scenarios

The following represents several business scenarios that the DMV reporting system must provide for.

Policy Level Insurance Reporting

At the *policy level*, the insurance company is required to report type of policy (corporation or for-hire). Corporation covers fleet cars and other general information regarding the insurance company. The for-hire policies are for 1099 drivers (taxi cabs, limos).

Each individual must register the vehicle within the state the vehicle is operated in. The problem occurs when the state has to verify that the individual registrant has insurance on the vehicle. Because the insurance company tracks the vehicle's insurance information by the policy and the state will track the vehicle's insurance information by the individual registrant, it is difficult for the state to verify that the registrant has insurance on the vehicle that is owned by the company.

Insurer Level Insurance Reporting

At the *insurer level*, the company is required to report type of insurer, individual or company. Companies that use sale representatives or non-profit organizations that pay for all employee expenses, like churches, allow their employee to register the vehicles. This would require the insurance company to report at the insurer level as an individual. Companies like Coca-Cola or Pillsbury use trucks to distribute their goods. These vehicles are at the insurer level and would be reported as a company type. The most important part of the insurer level is that the insurance company for the insurer or registrant reports the name to the state. This is the first check performed by the state on new records. If the record does not pass this check, the record is errored out and returned on the error file within two days. The insurance company is still required to report within 30 days or get fined. For errors like these, the state will do a VIN match and return on the error file what they believe the name should be. Until an insured passes this check, the insured's record is not counted as being reported and could be incurring fines. Once an error record is sent out, the state uses an error tracking number to keep track of the issues. This tracking number must accompany the updated record sent back to the state. Multiple errors can be fixed on one return.

Vehicle Level Insurance Reporting

At the *vehicle level*, all the vehicles for that insurer must be listed that are covered by the insurance company. The most important item at this level is the VIN. Vehicles made after 1980 are required to pass an 18-digit VIN check and must match what was reported to the state during the registration process.

Insurance companies do business based on policies, but the state information is based on vehicle information. Commercial insurance may from time to time move insurers from one policy to another. This change must be reported to the state within 30 days or be fined. This means cancellation records for the old policy must be sent in and a new record for the new policy regarding the insurer and vehicles submitted.

An insurance company will be fined on mistakes as well, like canceling a policy or insurer incorrectly, and are required to send in a special record known as a reinstate.

Also, it is important that term dates of the policy match what was reported to the state DMV. This is another issues area. The state does not want any lapse in coverage.

The states require that for-hire vehicle report cancellation of insurance 45 days prior to term end date. This was a required field at the insurer level. Failure to report this within 45 days results in fines.

The for-hire vehicle must not have an effective date greater than 45 days from the submission or create date. This record will not be processed by state.

There are additional required fields of information needed when a policy is coded; for an individual some are date of birth, gender, zip code. These missing fields would cause the record to error out, bringing the possibility of additional fines.

Insurance companies sometimes make mistakes on cancellation of policies. When this happens, a company can send a REC (rescinded cancellation). The states must keep track of their for-hire vehicles. Errors and fines will come from incorrect reporting of these vehicles. Like reporting a cancellation for a vehicle as an individual, but in fact it is a for-hire vehicle, and vice versa.

Auto Fix Errors

A state sends daily error files to each company with clients residing in their state. The majority of errors that are reported are on the insurer name. The state expects to receive the name as it appears on the registration. The state also sends back with this error the way the vehicle insurer name appears within their database. The insurance company must update their database with what the state sent back on the error file and resend the correction with the error record number to the state. Also, agents and policy information must be updated.

The following indicates the fines, errors, and business rules associated with this system.

Fines:

- Past 30 day for new policy insurance for corporations.
- Past three days for response to MVF by insurance companies.
- Change of insurance policy not reported to the state within 30 days.
- Canceling a policy or insurer incorrectly.

Errors:

- Term dates of the policy match what was reported to the state DMV.
- The name of the insurer or registrant is incorrect for the associated VIN.
- VIN does not match what was reported to the state during the registration process.
- Tax ID or driver's license number invalid — individual policies only.
- Invalid date of birth (DOB) format.
- Date format invalid.
- Invalid or missing zip code.
- Insurance company or sender unknown.
- Name not provided by organization.
- Future effective or termination date for not-for-hire vehicles not allowed.

- Transactions for for-hire vehicles future effective date greater than 45 days after current date.
- Transactions for for-hire vehicles future cancellation date less than 45 days prior to current date.
- Registrant DOB missing — individual policies only.
- Registrant gender missing — individual policies only.
- DOB missing — individual policies only.

Business rules:

- Insurance company is required to report new insurer within 30 days of issuing policy.
- A change to an insurance policy must be reported to the state within 30 days.
- If an insurance company cancels a policy or insurer incorrectly, a reinstate of policy must be issued.
- The insurance company is required to send a response to a MVF within in three days.
- The state requires commercial insurance company to report at three levels — policy, insurer, and vehicle.
- At the policy level, the insurance company is required to report type of policy.
- At the insurer level, the company is required to report type of insurer individual or company.
- Cannot future date transactions for not-for-hire vehicles.
- At the vehicle level, all the vehicles for that insurer must be listed that are covered by the insurance company.
- Vehicles made after 1980 are required to pass an 18-digit VIN check and must match what was reported to the state during the registration process.
- Transactions for for-hire vehicles cannot be sent more than 45 days prior to effective date.
- Transactions for for-hire vehicles future cancellation date must be reported at least 45 days prior to cancellation.
- You cannot have two for-hire vehicle transactions with the same effective date.

Approach

The approach to this system in applying the knowledge acquisition framework and subsequent UML modeling techniques to model the rules identified in this business case should take on the following aspects:

- Understanding of the business needs.
- What the system would do and how it would be done.
- Collaborative sessions to create knowledge use cases and knowledge models.
- Conducting knowledge use case and knowledge model walkthrough to ensure all team members had same understanding.
- Understanding of the steps involved in the knowledge acquisition framework and producing the required artifacts.

Chapter 14

Applying Your Knowledge Framework

In previous chapters, we have learned how to apply a standard notation (UML) to knowledge modeling and have defined a framework for capturing knowledge (knowledge acquisition) to produce the knowledge that will be the cornerstone of our KMS. Now we must take the next step, apply our UML-based framework and develop a KMS. As stated in earlier in this book (Chapter 2), knowledge acquisition is just one piece of the KMS architecture pie. Albeit an important part of the overall KMS, it has been a challenge to effectively build this into our KMS.

To begin this process we will adopt the framework established in Chapter 12. We will officially call this framework the Rhem Knowledge Acquisition Framework or Rhem-KAF. To recap, this framework is organized into seven groups of activities. These activities are as follows:

1. Determine domain area.
2. Decompose the knowledge.
3. Determine interdependencies.
4. Recognize knowledge patterns.
5. Determine judgments in knowledge.
6. Perform conflict resolution.
7. Construct knowledge base (KMS).

We will apply our framework to develop the KMS to support our business case stated in Chapter 13, the DMV reporting system. Our KMS will focus on supporting the decisions that must be made by the DMV.

Determine Domain Area

The first step in applying our framework will be to determine the domain area. In determining the domain area for this system, it is recommended that the knowledge engineer developing the system speak to the domain experts to find out what aspects of the problem or problem solving should be automated and included in our KMS. By applying the checklist approach (Chapter 12) to perform evaluation analysis, which includes analyzing the task, payoff, customer management, system designer, domain expert, and user, we will be able to determine what areas if any should be developed.

After reviewing the business case for the DMV reporting system, the following is determined to be the problem-solving processes amenable to automation and should be included in our KMS:

- Specific rules regarding fines
- Specific rules regarding the processing or handling of errors
- State-specific reporting rules

Decompose the Knowledge

The next step now that we have determined what problem-solving processes to implement will be to decompose the knowledge. In decomposing the knowledge, we must first identify the types of knowledge being gathered. The knowledge being gathered can fall into one or more categories (i.e., tacit, explicit, declarative, and procedural). Once we have determined the types of knowledge, we should decompose the domain into several smaller subtasks. This will allow the knowledge engineer and the SME to focus on more concrete definable pieces of work and facilitate a more accurate depiction of the knowledge.

In our business case, this task has been identified for us clearly. For most domains, we may not be as fortunate. In identifying the knowledge, the business case indicates that each state has specific rules regarding errors, and these rules are data driven. Thus, the knowledge will be categorized as explicit. The business case also indicates that there is state-specific reporting rules and published fines that will be levied based on certain criteria. This knowledge is also classified as explicit.

Now that we have established the type of knowledge that has to be incorporated into our system, let us look at how we can break our task into manageable subtasks. Again, our business case outlines this for us effectively and in this instance corresponds to the problem areas that we identified earlier. These subtasks include determining fines, determining errors, and determining state-specific reporting rules.

Determine Interdependencies

In determining the interdependencies in our knowledge being gathered, we must analyze how individual components of knowledge are related and integrated when they are used to solve a task. In this area we need to point out missing pieces of knowledge and determine what pieces of knowledge are related and how. Also, if we detect inconsistencies among the various aspects of the knowledge being gathered, we must consult with the SMEs to work toward a consensus.

In our business case, each of our subtasks has interdependencies between them. If an insurance company fails to meet certain reporting rules, one of the fines is initiated. Having errors in information, thus failing one or more of the error rules when an insurance company reports to a state, may delay when that insurance company completes their required reporting. This also may initiate a fine. Our analysis here must focus on finding any inconsistencies between determining fines, determining errors, and determining state-specific reporting rules. Because we cannot directly speak to the SMEs, we must analyze the business scenarios supporting the business case.

Recognize Knowledge Patterns

To recognize knowledge patterns, we must identify patterns within the various types of knowledge being gathered. To facilitate this, we must apply the knowledge gathered to similar situations that the domain expert may have encountered or to similar cases (using CBR) that may have been solved previously.

When recognizing knowledge patterns, we must validate the knowledge captured by the knowledge engineer, cases both real and contrived, are executed or traversed through decision structures (decision trees, interdependency models, or data mining processes). This exercise is a method to verify that the conclusions arrived at by the knowledge-based system or knowledge acquisition processes are the same as those arrived at by the domain expert.

To accomplish this task, our business case provides us with several scenarios. These scenarios include policy level insurance reporting, insurer level insurance reporting, vehicle level insurance reporting, and auto fix error scenario. By analyzing these scenarios, it will aid our recognition in identifying knowledge patterns and applying these patterns to address similar scenarios that the SMEs need to solve. Besides CBR (see Chapter 8), constructing decision trees (see Chapter 9) is a method of visually modeling to discover patterns in knowledge.

Determine Judgments in Knowledge

When gathering knowledge we must determine if the knowledge being gathered is uncertain. This occurs when there are intuitive judgments being made. This in turn is difficult to capture and usually shows up when there is a conflict or contradiction between the knowledge being gathered. When this occurs, we should ask the SME for an explicit, relative judgment between the knowledge being gathered in the context of the domain.

Because of the nature of our business case, the explicit knowledge being presented does not have any conflicts or fuzzy judgment pieces of knowledge. Any perceived conflicts are resolved through the business scenarios detailed in the business case. However, if conflicts did exist we would have to consult with the SMEs to provide explicit knowledge in those cases where conflict has occurred.

Perform Conflict Resolution

When the knowledge being captured has uncertainty or is fuzzy in nature, we specify in the preconditions of KUCS restrictions when this knowledge can be used. The effect of this is to add expertise that will in essence reduce the number of situations when this knowledge is applicable. As a result, conflicts between knowledge and rules can be resolved. To review the structure and contents of a KUCS, refer to "Knowledge Use Case Specification" in Chapter 11.

Construct the Knowledge Management System

After completing the analysis involved in the previous six steps, you are now ready to produce your knowledge models. Following the KA workflow, perform knowledge modeling of the domain utilizing one or more of the modeling techniques described in Chapter 11. The result of this step will yield fully constructed models of the domain that will be used to develop the knowledge base in the KMS.

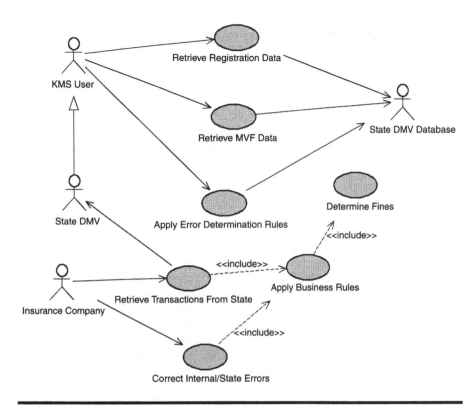

Figure 14.1   DMV Knowledge Use Case Model

The following artifacts details show the result of applying our knowledge framework including knowledge modeling techniques to construct the knowledge base for our KMS that will support the DMV business case.

Results of Business Case — DMV Reporting System

The following sections cover the knowledge management artifacts that will be developed as part of the DMV KMS (see Figure 14.1 and Table 14.1).

DMV Knowledge Models

Apply Error Determination Rules

The knowledge model applied here is the UML version of a process ladder. The process ladder is constructed using an activity flow diagram (see Figure 14.2). This process ladder illustrates the application of rules for determining or detecting errors in the DMV data.

Table 14.1   Use Case: Apply Error Determination Rules

1.0 Use Case Name: Apply Error Determination Rules

1.1   Brief description
This use case details the application of error rules to ensure the integrity of data being processed. This use case begins when the state DMV receives data from the insurance company. At the completion of this use case, when successful it will store the data into the enterprise knowledge or data repository.

2.0 Knowledge Claim Validation

2.1   Basic flow
    2.1.1   This use case begins when the state DMV receives data from the insurance company and accesses the state DMV database to check its validity. The validity checks are as follows.
    2.1.2   Term dates of the policy match what was reported to the state DMV — If this validation fails Alternate Flow 1 is initiated.
    2.1.3   The name of the insurer or register is incorrect for the associated VIN — If this validation fails Alternate Flow 1 is initiated.
    2.1.4   VIN does not match what was reported to the state during registration process — If this validation fails Alternate Flow 1 is initiated.
    2.1.5   Tax ID or driver's license number is invalid — individual policies only — If this validation fails Alternate Flow 1 is initiated.
    2.1.6   Invalid DOB format — If this validation fails Alternate Flow 1 is initiated.
    2.1.7   Date format invalid — If this validation fails Alternate Flow 1 is initiated.
    2.1.8   Invalid or missing zip code — If this validation fails Alternate Flow 1 is initiated.
    2.1.9   Insurance company or sender unknown — If this validation fails Alternate Flow 1 is initiated.
    2.1.10 Name not provided by organization — If this validation fails Alternate Flow 1 is initiated.
    2.1.11 Future effective or termination date for not-for-hire vehicles not allowed — If this validation fails Alternate Flow 1 is initiated.
    2.1.12 Transactions for for-hire vehicles future effective date greater than 45 days after current date — If this validation fails Alternate Flow 1 is initiated.
    2.1.13 Transactions for for-hire vehicles future cancelation date less than 45 days prior to current date — If this validation fails Alternate Flow 1 is initiated.

Table 14.1 (continued)   Use Case: Apply Error Determination Rules

> 2.1.14 Registrant DOB missing — individual policies only — If this validation fails Alternate Flow 1 is initiated.
>
> 2.1.15 Registrant gender missing — individual policies only — If this validation fails Alternate Flow 1 is initiated.
>
> 2.1.16 DOB missing — individual policies only — If this validation fails Alternate Flow 1 is initiated.
>
> 2.1.17 Knowledge validation ends.
>
> **3.0 Alternative Flows**
>
> 3.1   Alternate flow 1
>
> 3.1.1   An error is logged and the transaction is marked to be returned.
>
> **4.0 Preconditions**
>
> 4.1   The KMS user or state DMV has received insurance information from the insurance company.
>
> 4.2   The KMS user or state DMV has retrieved MVF data.
>
> 4.3   The KMS user or state DMV has retrieved registration data.
>
> **5.0 Postconditions**
>
> 5.1   Data is stored in the enterprise knowledge or data repository.

Table 14.2   Use Case: Determine Fines

> **1.0 Use Case Name: Determine Fines**
>
> 1.1   Brief description
> This use case details the application of rules to levy fines against the insurance company. This use case begins when the state DMV receives data from the insurance company. At the completion of this use case, all fines if any would have been levied against the insurance company.
>
> **2.0 Evaluate MVF Data Determining Fines — Knowledge Management**
>
> 2.1   Basic flow
>
> 2.1.1   This use case starts when the state DMV receives MVF data from the insurance company.
>
> 2.1.2   Once MVF data has been received, it is analyzed for possible fines by applying to the following rules.
>
> 2.1.3   Past 30 days for new policy insurance — For corporations, if violated a $1000 per insurer fine is levied otherwise no fine is levied (Alternate Flow 1).

Table 14.2 (continued)   Use Case: Determine Fines

2.1.4 Past three days for response to MVF by insurance companies — If violated a $1500 per insurer fine is levied otherwise no fine is levied (Alternate Flow 1).
 	
    2.1.5 Change of insurance policy not reported to the state within 30 days — If violated a $2000 per insurer fine is levied, otherwise no fine is levied (Alternate Flow 1).
 	
    2.1.6 Canceling a policy or insurer incorrectly — If violated a $2500 per insurer fine is levied, otherwise no fine is levied (Alternate Flow 1).
 	
    2.1.7 Determine fines ends.
 	
3.0 Alternative Flows
 	
3.1   Alternate flow 1 — No fine is levied — Determine fines ends.
 	
4.0 Preconditions
 	
4.1   Insurer information has been received by the state from the insurance company.
 	
5.0 Postconditions
 	
5.1   Fines are levied against the insurance company.

Table 14.3   Use Case: Apply Business Rules

1.0 Use Case Name: Apply Business Rules
 	
1.1   Brief description
This use case details the application of the business rules associated when the insurance company reports motor vehicle information to the state DMV.
 	
2.0 Information Acquisition
 	
2.1   Basic flow
    2.1.1 This use case starts when the KMS user has initiated the apply error determination knowledge use case or when the insurance company has initiated the verify insurance information knowledge use case to discover knowledge of the insurer and policy.
 	
    2.1.2 Insurance company is required to report new insurer within 30 days of issuing policy. If not reported, see Alternate Flow 1.

Table 14.3 (continued) **Use Case: Apply Business Rules**

2.1.3	When a change to an insurance policy occurs, it must be reported to the state within 30 days. If not reported, see Alternate Flow 1.
2.1.4	If an insurance company cancels a policy or insurer incorrectly, a reinstate of policy must be issued.
2.1.5	The insurance company is required to send a response to the MVF within three days. If not completed, see Alternate Flow 1.
2.1.6	The state requires commercial insurance company to report at three levels — policy, insurer, and vehicle.
2.1.7	At the policy level, the insurance company is require to report type of policy.
2.1.8	At the insurer level, the company is required to report type of insurer individual or company.
2.1.9	At the vehicle level, the insurance company cannot future date transactions for not-for-hire vehicles.
2.1.10	At the vehicle level, all the vehicles for that insurer must be listed that are covered by the insurance company.
2.1.11	Vehicles made after 1980 are required to pass an 18-digit VIN check and must match what was reported to the state during the registration process.
2.1.12	Transactions for for-hire vehicles cannot be sent more than 45 days prior to effective date.
2.1.13	Transactions for for-hire vehicles future cancelation date must be reported at least 45 days prior to cancelation.
2.1.14	Cannot have two for-hire vehicle transactions with the same effective date.
2.1.15	Knowledge discover ends.

3.0 Alternative Flows

3.1 Alternate flow 1
    3.1.1 Determine fines use case is initiated.

4.0 Preconditions

4.1 The insurance company has received registration data.

5.0 Postconditions

5.1 Insurer and policy rules have been applied.

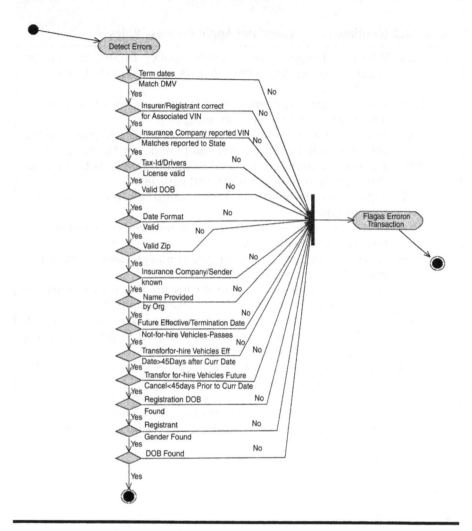

Figure 14.2 Activity Flow Diagram

Determine Fines

The knowledge model constructed for determining fines reflects the UML version of a decision tree (see Figure 14.3). The decision tree is constructed using a class diagram. When determining fines there are several paths that can be taken. When a new policy is issued, the fine is determined by comparing the issue date with the date reported to state. If there is a 30-day or more gap, a specific fine amount is issued. Following the path for response to MVF, if the date of receipt and the response date shows a three-day or more gap, a specific fine amount is issued. When we follow

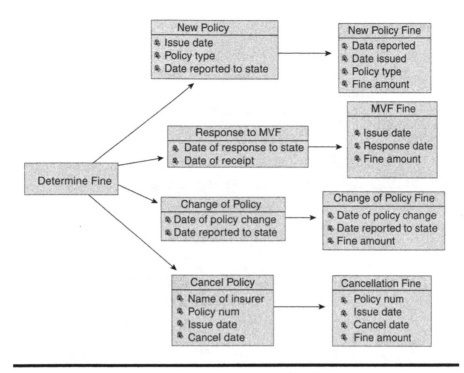

Figure 14.3   Decision Tree

the change of policy, we are comparing the date the policy changed with the date reported to the state. If there is a 30-day or more gap, a specific fine amount is issued. Finally, when canceling a policy, name of insurer, policy number, issue date, and cancel date must be reported correctly otherwise a specific fine amount is issued.

Apply Business Rules

The knowledge model applied here is the UML version of a process ladder (Figure 14.4). The process ladder is constructed using an activity flow diagram. This process ladder illustrates the business rules applied to processing an insurer. Also, the parameters involved in commercial insurance company reporting are illustrated. Although we have combined both the processing of an insurer and the parameters for a commercial insurance company reporting, we could have easily produced separate diagrams for both.

Table 14.2, Table 14.3, Figure 14.5, and Figure 14.6 are other pertinent use cases that are a part of the DMV KMS.

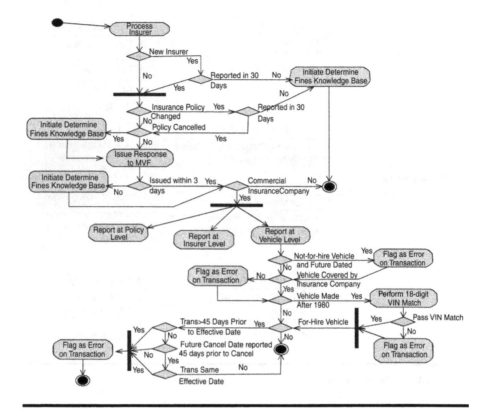

Figure 14.4   Process Ladder

Table 14.4   Receive Transactions from State

Use Case Description	This use case describes how the insurance company, from the state, receives transactions and indicates the rules (knowledge) that are applied.
Goal	Process transactions from the state.
Primary User(s)	Insurance company employees with read and write access.
Secondary User(s)	None.
Use Case Trigger	User reviews error reports from state or internal report.
Special Requirements	None.
Post Condition/State	Transactions are successfully processed.

Table 14.4 (continued)   Receive Transactions from State

Main Flow

1.0 The system performs a match to vehicle.

1.1   If a match to vehicle is found:
    1.1.1   The vehicle information is added to the database.
    1.1.2   If verification data is received from the state.
        1.1.2.1   Execute process — Received from state verification (apply business rules)
        1.1.2.2   Send e-mail notification to agent or broker.
        1.1.2.3   Send e-mail notification to insurance company's central office.
        1.1.2.4   Use case ends.
    1.1.3   Otherwise there is an error.
        1.1.3.1   System will check if error is internal or state.
        1.1.3.2   If error is internal or state:
            1.1.3.2.1   Execute error correction — Internal or state (apply error correction internal or state rules)
            1.1.3.2.2   Send e-mail notification to agent or broker.
            1.1.3.2.3   Send e-mail notification to insurance company's central office.
            1.1.3.2.4   Use case ends.
        1.1.3.3   Otherwise system will check if error is with the system.
        1.1.3.4   If system error:
            1.1.3.4.1   Execute error correction — system (apply system error correction rules).
            1.1.3.4.2   Send e-mail notification to agent or broker.
            1.1.3.4.3   Send e-mail notification to insurance company's central office.
            1.1.3.4.4   Use case ends.
        1.1.3.5   Otherwise execute error correction — Auto fix.
        1.1.3.6   Apply auto fix rules.
        1.1.3.7   Send e-mail notification to agent or broker.
        1.1.3.8   Send e-mail notification to insurance company's central office.
        1.1.3.9   Use case ends.

Alternate Flow 1 — Vehicle Match Not Found

1.0   Save orphan vehicle record.

2.0   Send e-mail to error correction specialist.

3.0   If error is corrected:
    3.1   Go to 1.1.1 of main flow.

Table 14.4 (continued)   Receive Transactions from State

4.0   Otherwise:
4.1   Execute — Produce error report.
4.2   Send e-mail to management with error report attachment.
4.3   Use case ends.

Table 14.5   Correct Internal or State Errors

Use Case Description	This use case describes how to perform error correction.
Goal	Correct error (internal or state) and to set status code.
Success Condition	Error is corrected in DMV and status code of error is changed.
Primary User(s)	Insurance company employees with read and write access.
Secondary User(s)	None.
Special Requirements	None.
Post Condition/State	Error corrections are recorded in DMV, error status is changed to a value that maps to "closed," and error activity is recorded.

Main Flow

1.0   The system determines that the error is attached to a vehicle.
    1.1   Otherwise, see Alternate Flow 1

2.0   The system applies error correction rules.

3.0   The system decides to correct error in source system by changing the status code on the error to one of the resolved status codes.

4.0   The information is recorded into DMV and the user is notified of the successful action.

5.0   Use case ends.

Table 14.5 (continued)   Correct Internal or State Errors

Alternate Flow 1 — Refers to Step 1 in Main Flow — System Determines Error Is Not Attached to Vehicle

1.0   The system determines that the error is not attached to a vehicle.

2.0   The system determines the vehicle in which the error came from.

3.0   The system finds the vehicle.

4.0   System attaches the error to the corresponding vehicle.

5.0   Continue with Step 2 in the main flow.

Alternate Flow 2 — Refers to Step 4 in Alternate Flow 1 — System Cannot Find a Vehicle for the Error

1.0   System does not find a vehicle in which to attach the error.

2.0   Insurance company does insure the insured or registrant that is on the error.

3.0   User returns to DMV to build the vehicle.

4.0   Continue with Step 5 in Alternate Flow 1.

Alternate Flow 3 — Refers to Step 5 in Alternate Flow 2 — Insurance Company Does Not Insure the Insured or Registrant

1.0   Insurance company does not insure the insured or registrant that is on the error.

2.0   System updates error status to "dead."

3.0   Continue with Step 4.0 in main flow.

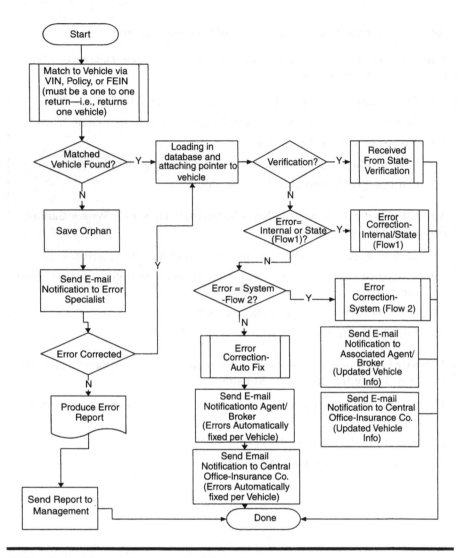

Figure 14.5   Transactions Received from State

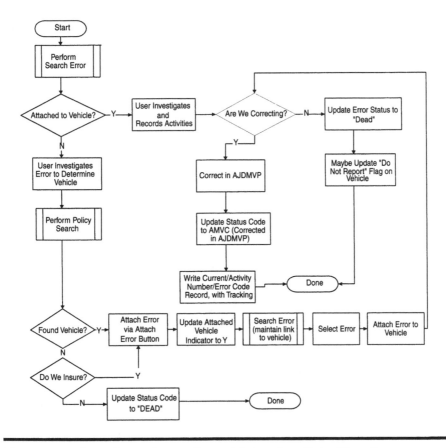

Figure 14.6   Error Correction — Correct Internal or State (Flow 1)

Chapter 15

Summary

In recent years, the demand for KMSs has increased dramatically. They are used in applications ranging from medicine to engineering and aerospace to finance. As KMSs are being called on to provide automation in increasingly complex domains, the complexity and difficulty of building a KMS increases dramatically.

Knowledge acquisition, in particular, is one of the most difficult and error-prone tasks in building these types of systems. Knowledge acquisition involves identifying the relevant technical knowledge, recording it, and getting it into computable form so the problem-solving engine of the expert system can apply it. Knowledge acquisition is a form of requirements analysis, which plays a critical role in building quality software. Requirements analysis in general is the process of identifying a user's needs and determining what to build in a system. It has been shown that defects injected into software during requirements analysis are costlier to correct than those injected during subsequent phases of the development life cycle. Research has also shown that many system failures can be attributed to the lack of clear and specific requirements analysis. The financial consequence of poor requirements analysis has long been understood. In fact, knowledge acquisition is the most difficult and expensive part of building and maintaining expert systems.

To elicit knowledge from an expert, the traditional approach to knowledge acquisition is that, regardless of the variation used, it is costly because at least two (typically) expensive people are involved (i.e., the domain expert and the knowledge engineer).

The second thing to note is that the methods are error prone. Surprisingly, people cannot easily say what it is that they do in a manner that can be understood by others. This is mostly because skills are usually learned through apprentice-style learning, and the small, faltering steps required by the expert during initial learning have long since become embedded in longer phases of automated behavior, and the constituent steps are no longer readily accessible. Therefore, interpretations of what the expert does are often faulty and incomplete, sometimes based on rationalizations by the expert of what they think they are doing rather than what they actually are doing. These misinterpretations are often easily committed by well-trained knowledge engineers, let alone less well-trained practitioners.

The third thing to note about the traditional approach to knowledge acquisition is that it is time consuming because errors, gaps, and inconsistencies may be difficult to discover, requiring many interactions between experts and knowledge engineers to debug a field-ready application.

As knowledge acquisition continues to be one of the most difficult and error-prone tasks that a knowledge engineer does when building a knowledge-based system, the cost and performance of the application depends directly on the quality of the knowledge acquired. During this process, the knowledge engineer must determine where in the organization the knowledge exists, how to capture it, and how to disseminate this knowledge throughout the enterprise. As discussed in this book, an important method to capturing or modeling knowledge is to incorporate UML. Using UML for knowledge acquisition will allow for a consistent method for capturing the knowledge of a particular enterprise, organization, or human (domain) expert.

Establish Your Framework

Although there is a vast amount of literature available on KM, there is not much written on how to build and implement a KMS. Therefore, in this book I have established a framework for knowledge engineers to follow. The Rhem-KAF was originally established in 1998 and since then has been incorporated in a software product "Knowledge Acquisition Facility." This product has been developed in part due to a grant from the NSF. This grant issued through the NSF's Small Business Innovation Research Program was awarded to my firm, A. J. Rhem & Associates, Inc., in 2004. A demo of this product can be accessed at www.ajrhem.com/method.html.

This framework addresses specific needs of the knowledge engineer during the knowledge acquisition process. These needs include the capability to decompose the knowledge acquisition task into manageable subtasks, focus on a representation of expertise that is natural to domain experts, to recognize the patterns in knowledge, and to resolve conflict when aspects of knowledge of a particular domain become uncertain.

In any KMS there are three main activities — knowledge generation, knowledge sharing, and knowledge codification. Our framework addresses knowledge codification. Nonaka (1994) explains these activities in a comprehensive theory about organizational knowledge creation based on interactions between tacit and explicit knowledge. The process begins with the enhancement of an individual's tacit knowledge through hands on experience, supporting the generation of knowledge. Socialization then follows, involving the transfer and sharing of tacit knowledge between individuals. Dialogues allow the conceptualization of the tacit knowledge and trigger externalization — the transformation of knowledge from tacit to explicit. Finally, the knowledge is combined with existing knowledge and codified.

Knowledge Modeling

UML is a notation that can be extrapolated to include the development of knowledge models (see Chapter 11). Because this is a widely used notation, the knowledge engineer can easily use it to successfully capture, apply, and validate knowledge. The use of UML has an ancillary benefit in training knowledge engineers. There are many techniques and methodologies to help the knowledge engineer, and related to each of them there are various sets of skills that are required by the knowledge engineer. These may include exhibiting the skills of a cognitive psychologist, a communication expert, a programmer, and a domain expert. There could be situations in which the knowledge engineer may be required to play more than just one of these roles. By moving to standard representations, we can eliminate much of the special training required by the knowledge engineer.

Models are used to capture the essential features of real systems by breaking them down into more manageable parts that are easy to understand and to manipulate, as indicated in our framework (Rhem-KAF). Models are associated with the domain they represent. According to Booch, "A model is a simplification of reality." Real systems are large entities consisting of interrelated components working together in a complex manner. Models help people to appreciate and understand such complexity by enabling them to look at each particular area of the system in turn.

Models are used in systems development activities to draw the blueprints of the system and to facilitate communication between different people on the team at different levels of abstraction. People have different views of the system and models can help them understand these views in a unified manner.

The modeling process constructs conceptual models of knowledge-intensive activities. According to our framework, during the knowledge acquisition stage, most of the knowledge is unstructured and often in tacit form, although it can take on other forms such as procedural, declarative, and explicit. The knowledge engineer will try to understand the various types of knowledge and then use simple visual diagrams (constructed in UML) to stimulate discussion among users and knowledge experts. This discussion process generates ideas and insights as to how the knowledge is used, how decisions are made, the factors that motivate, and so on. The knowledge engineer then has to construct the conceptual model from what has been discussed during the knowledge acquisition stage. This communicates the knowledge to the knowledge engineer, where the knowledge base can be designed, constructed, and implemented.

Many authors of KMSs have discussed the importance of knowledge modeling in KM. The argument is that models are important for understanding the working mechanisms within a knowledge-based system, such as the tasks, methods, how knowledge is inferred, the domain knowledge, and its schemas. Conceptual modeling is central to knowledge engineering. Modeling contributes to the understanding of the source of knowledge, the inputs and outputs, the flow of knowledge, and the identification of other variables such as the impact that management action has on the organizational knowledge.

Benefits

We anticipate incorporating UML in the development of KMSs will generate widespread benefits. This will result in the development of KMSs with reduced costs, less errors, and less development time. Furthermore, these systems will be more effective at automating knowledge-based tasks. This has the potential to advance the state of the art in the knowledge engineering field.

Current Environment

Several methods exist for capturing knowledge. Most methods are expensive, error prone, and time consuming. However, the following represent some of the more viable current tools on the market today.

Knowledge Acquisition Tools

Acquire

This knowledge-based authoring tool and expert system shell provides a step-by-step method for acquiring and structuring knowledge without the use of programming. Acquire® software, provided by Acquired Intelligence in Canada, is a knowledge acquisition system and expert system shell. It is a complete development environment for building and maintaining knowledge-based applications. It provides a step-by-step method for knowledge engineering that allows the domain experts themselves to be directly involved in structuring and encoding the knowledge. (The direct involvement of the domain expert improves the quality, completeness, and accuracy of acquired knowledge, lowers development and maintenance costs, and increases control over the form of the software application.) Features include a structured approach to knowledge acquisition; a model of knowledge acquisition based on pattern recognition; knowledge represented as objects, production rules, and decision tables; handling uncertainty by qualitative, nonnumerical procedures; extremely thorough knowledge bases; sophisticated report-writing facilities; and self-documenting knowledge bases in a hypertext environment.

CommonKADS

CommonKADS is a leading approach to support structured knowledge engineering. It has been gradually developed and has been validated by many companies and universities in the context of the European ESPRIT IT Programme. It now is the European *de facto* standard for knowledge analysis and knowledge-intensive system development, and it has been adopted as a whole or has been partly incorporated in existing methods by many major companies in Europe, as well as in the United States and Japan. CommonKADS enables developers to spot the opportunities and bottlenecks in how organizations develop, distribute, and apply their knowledge resources, and so gives tools for corporate KM. CommonKADS also provides the methods to perform a detailed analysis of knowledge-intensive tasks and processes.

The core of CommonKADS is formed by its knowledge analysis framework. CommonKADS provides all the tools required to analyze knowledge-intensive tasks at different grain-size levels. The analyst is supported in the modeling process by powerful templates, which constitute predefined reusable knowledge models that have been proven to work in the past. The templates enable a top-down approach and provide handles for quality control and feasibility assessment. The results of knowledge analysis are documented in the knowledge model. It contains a specification of the information and knowledge structures involved in a knowledge-intensive task. The knowledge model plays a key role in both KM work and in consecutive system-development activities.

ModelDraw is a drawing tool that can be used to create four UML diagrams — use case diagrams, activity diagrams, class diagrams, and state diagrams. The tool also supports the construction of CommonKADS knowledge modeling diagrams. The tool can generate diagrams in both Windows® WMF/EMF, and eps formats for inclusion in Word and other documents.

KADS22 is an interactive interface for the CML2 (Conceptual Modeling Language) knowledge modeling language. KADS22 provides an interactive graphical interface (much like the familiar Windows programs) with the following functionality: parsing CML2 files, pretty-printing, hypertext browsing, generation of the graphical notation, search, glossary generation, and HTML (Hypertext Markup Language) generation.

CML2 is the CommonKADS knowledge modeling language. The syntax description and the parser correspond to the draft CommonKADS book as submitted to the publisher.

The CML2 parser is a standalone executable. The parser can be used to check a file containing CML2 for syntactical correctness.

Epistemics

Epistemics designs, writes, and markets a number of software toolkits. These toolkits aid knowledge engineers and those working in KM when performing a number of key tasks associated with knowledge acquisition, analysis, modeling, validation, publishing, and implementation. Products include the following: PCPACK4, SOPHx-PACK PC, PACK 2, MetaPACK.

Expect — An Integrated Environment for Knowledge Acquisition

This integrated acquisition interface includes several techniques previously developed to support users in various ways as they add new knowledge to an intelligent system. As a result of this integration, the individual techniques can take better advantage of the context in which they are invoked and provide stronger guidance to users. The Expect project has focused on acquiring problem-solving knowledge for users for the last decade, using an expressive language that is open to inspection. The aim has been to alleviate the bottleneck in creating knowledge-based systems by providing support for both knowledge engineers and end users to specify problem-solving knowledge. See http://www.isi.edu/expect.

Protégé-2000

The original Protégé was developed for domain-specific applications.[1] Now in its latest version, Protégé 2000 is a modeling technique developed by Musen and colleagues from Stanford Medical Informatics. The Protégé 2000 knowledge modeling environment is a frame-based ontology editing tool with knowledge acquisition tools that are widely used for domain modeling.[2] The frames are the main building blocks for a knowledge base.[2] The Protégé ontology (that models the domain) has classes, slots, facets, and axioms.

Classes are abstract representations of domain concepts. "Classes in Protégé 2000 constitute a taxonomic hierarchy and are templates for individual instance frames."[2] A subclass can have all the instances of the class. Protégé 2000 allows multiple inheritance: a class can have two or more superclasses; it also supports a metaclass concept. Slots are properties or attributes of classes. There are two forms of slot. "Own slots define intrinsic properties of class or individual instance frames. Template slots are attached to class frames to define attributes of their instances, which in turn define specific values for slots."[3]

Slots are first-class objects in Protégé 2000; they can be used globally or locally. Facets are properties or attributes of a slot and are used to specify constraints on slot values. The constraints include slot cardinality (i.e., it specifies the number of values the slot can have), value type for the slot (such as integer, string), and minimum and maximum values for a numeric slot. Axioms define additional constraints on frames; these may link values together or exploit knowledge interchange format (KIF)–based predicate logic.

Instances information is acquired using online forms. They are composed of a set graphical entry fields and provide an easy-to-use user interface — an important feature of Protégé 2000. It automatically provides a form to acquire instances of a class when the user defines a class and attaches a template slot to it. The user can customize the form by changing the layout or changing the form's field labels and can choose different ways of displaying and acquiring slot values.[2] The knowledge acquisition process in Protégé 2000 consists of three steps: First, a class and its template slot have to be defined. Second, the form to acquire the instances of the class has to be laid out. Third, the class instances are acquired.

Notes

1. Grosso, W.E., Eriksson, H., Fergerson, H., Gennari, S.W., Tu, S.W., and Musen, M.A. Knowledge Modeling at the Millennium. *The Design and Evolution of Protégé—2000*, 1999.
2. Noy, N.F., Grosso, W.E., and Musen, M.A. Knowledge-Acquisition Interfaces for Domain Experts: An Empirical Evaluation of Protégé—2000. *Twelfth International Conference on Software Engineering and Knowledge Engineering (SEKE2000)*, Chicago, IL, 2000.
3. Schreiber, A., et al. *Knowledge Engineering and Management: The CommonKADS Methodology* (Cambridge, MA: MIT Press, 2000).

Appendix A

Probing Questions[1]

Note: In this appendix, an arrow (→) means "implies."

A. Depth of Reasoning and Architecture (aka "Problem Characteristics")

A1 If the program will be solving a diagnosis problem then

Can evidence be found that confirms some of the intermediate steps along a causal path connecting ultimate causes to symptoms?

Or:

Can the intervening steps only be determined after we have discovered the correct diagnosis from evidence linking symptoms directly with sets of bottom-line conclusions?

Confirm intermediate steps	"Deep" reasoning, implemented with causal models or reasoning from first principles (expensive to implement).
Infer intermediate steps	"Shallow" reasoning also called heuristic associations, usually implemented with rules.

A2 If the program will be solving a diagnosis problem then

Will it be necessary to diagnose novel faults that human experts have never seen before?

Or:

Are the faults of interest limited and predictable?

Novel faults	"Deep" reasoning, implemented with causal models or reasoning from first principles (expensive to implement).
Predictable faults	"Shallow" reasoning also called heuristic associations, usually implemented with rules.

A3 Is it necessary to find values for a number of variables where the variables can take on numeric or boolean values?

And:

Are there constraints among the variables that make it possible to use the known values of some of the variables to solve for other variables?

And:

Does the identity of the variables whose values are known at the outset differ from problem to problem?

Yes, differ from problem to problem	Constraint propagation Weight 7
No, same variables known at outset	Forward chaining rules Weight 8

A4 Will it be necessary to weigh evidence consisting of separate beliefs or implications to determine their joint effects?

Yes	Then use scoring functions such as EMYCIN certainty factors, fuzzy set theory, Bayesian updating, or Dempster-Shafer belief revision.

A5 Which of the following best describes the problem you want to pose to your expert system?

(a) The user will provide a candidate solution and expects the program to evaluate the strength of the evidence for and against that candidate.

(b) The user expects the program to independently evaluate the evidence for and against each of the candidate solutions, and then either identify the most likely candidates or rank the candidates according to the support each receives.

(c) Rather than considering candidates independently, the user expects the program to look for evidence that discriminates between likely solutions, so that the program can rank the support for the candidates relative to each other rather than in absolute terms only.

(d) The user expects the program to rank candidates according to their ability to provide a coherent and comprehensive explanation of the findings. The emphasis is less on selecting from a set of alternatives, than it is on constructing an explanation that shows how one or more candidates combine to produce a satisfactory account of the findings.

(a) Scoring functions

(b) Sequence of Yes-No decisions

(c) The use of group and differentiate

(d) Use of causal models

A6 Is the clinching evidence for conclusions sometimes unavailable?

And:

In these cases, is it possible to be confident that the correct conclusion is one of a small number of possibilities?

Yes   Use of confirmation by exclusion

A7 Is this a diagnosis problem?

And:

Would it be unwise to assume that there is only a single underlying fault because multiple faults are either too common or too serious to run the risk of a misdiagnosis?

Yes   Use of subtractive method

B. Knowledge Representation Structures

B1 What is the appropriate characterization of the knowledge available in this domain?

(a) There is a poorly structured collection of many isolated facts. It is unclear what kinds of distinctions between facts are the important ones.

(b) There is a complex, highly structured collection of facts and relationships. There is a rich and fairly well established set of distinctions made between different kinds of information.

(c) There is a concise, unified theory.

    (a) Use of rules or assertions to represent the knowledge

    (b) Use of frames or semantic networks to represent the knowledge

    (c) Use of mathematics or algorithms to represent the knowledge

B2 Will the program often have incomplete knowledge of the facts of the problem? That is, does the input data constrain the facts of the problem to a range of possibilities without saying specifically which of the possibilities is actually the case?

And:

Is there limited access to information in this domain, so that these uncertainties about the facts of the case cannot be resolved simply by asking for the information?

And:

Is it important to achieve as complete and understanding of the actual facts of the case as is possible?

Yes   Adopt or develop methods for representing and reasoning with incomplete knowledge. For example, you could represent the information in first-order logic (aka predicate calculus) and use resolution to generate inferences (expensive).

No   Use inference mechanisms that achieve computational efficiency by sacrificing the ability to represent and reason with incomplete knowledge. For example, represent the knowledge using Horn clauses and use Prolog to derive inferences. Other common representational schemes (rules, frames, semantic nets, etc.) usually have minimal ability to represent and reason with incomplete knowledge.

B3 Do the facts needed to solve problems in this domain consist of a large, fixed set of statements involving few kinds of semantic relationships?

And:

Does the reasoning required to solve this problem depend on the patterns defined by these relationships?

    Yes   Represent the facts with semantic networks

B4 Does solving a problem in this domain require a chain of reasoning involving subdomains that are understood in quite different degrees of detail?

Or:

Is there great variability in the amount of detail that is provided by different pieces of evidence?

        Yes, subdomains of different detail or evidence of variable detail Break the knowledge base into several different levels of description and describe the relations between the levels (expensive to implement).

B5 On the average, do we know five or more new facts about a domain object simply by being told that it is of type x?

Or:

Are there new facts not known with certainty, but assumed unless there is evidence to the contrary?

    Yes   Place the object in a data structure (e.g., frames, semantic nets, objects) whose inheritance mechanisms will provide the facts when needed, and whose default values will be assumed unless an exception is explicitly asserted.

    Neither   Assert the new facts explicitly (cheap to implement).

B6 In any one problem will it be necessary to reason about a number of different instances of the same kind of objects?

And:

Will it be necessary to be aware of important differences between instances despite their commonalities?

Yes   Use frames, objects, or contexts to represent the instances.

B7 Will the program need to represent the capabilities and behaviors of a number of Objects?

And:

Are there significant commonalties among the capabilities and behaviors of different objects?

Yes   Define new objects, use inheritance and inheritance overriding.

B8 Can all of the possible solutions that the program needs to consider be listed in advance?

And:

Is there heuristic knowledge available that tells us what sorts of findings implicate each of these solutions?

Preenumerated solutions   Use rules to encode the heuristic knowledge. In some cases, simple data structures such as variables, assertions, or attribute-object-value triples may be sufficient for knowledge representation.

Constructed solutions   Use more elaborate data structures and inference processes to support the assembly, modification, and refinement of tentative solutions.

B9 Is it frequently the case that a particular piece of evidence restricts the solution to a range of possibilities without saying much about which of those possibilities is actually the right one?

Yes   Associate manifestations with sets of possible conclusions, these sets usually take the form of a stored hierarchy of hypotheses.

No   Associate manifestations with individual conclusions.

B10 Will the program be solving a diagnosis problem?

And:

Is it important to accurately assess causal relationships in this domain so that predisposing factors are recognized as such and treated differently from findings actually caused by the underlying conditions?

Or:

Do the findings observed depend strongly on the severity of the underlying condition or the degree of its progression?

Or:

Are there sets of correlated findings that tend to occur together under several different diagnostic outcomes?

Yes, to any of them   The use of intermediate hypotheses

C. Handling of Uncertainty, Incompleteness, or Inaccuracy of Data (aka "Input Characteristics")

C1 If the evidence is unreliable or there is ambiguity about the interpretation of evidence, then the following considerations are relevant:

(a) Can we anticipate the major areas of uncertainty and unreliability ahead of time when we design the program?

(b) Is it important to accurately assess the amount of uncertainty to be attached to the program's conclusions for a particular problem?

(c) Will the program need to take active measures to reduce or discount the particular uncertainties encountered when working on a problem?
   (a) The need to build in redundancy in those areas where uncertainty is anticipated.
   (b) Use of scoring functions (e.g., Bayes rule, Dempster-Shafter, fuzzy set theory, EMYCIN certainty factors).
   (c) Explicit use of rules for deciding what evidence to believe (or keeping track of reasons for believing evidence).

C2 Will the program be performing a monitoring task so that several measurements are made of the same quantity over time? If so, what is required to make the proper interpretation of these measurements?

(a) The proper interpretation of a measurement depends only on the current value of that measurement.
(b) The proper interpretation of a measurement depends on the time course of that measurement.
(c) The proper interpretation of a measurement depends on knowing which of several states the system under analysis is in when the measurement is made.
(d) The proper interpretation of a measurement requires having followed this particular case over time so that a customized set of expectations is developed. These expectations provide an understanding of the significance of this measurement for this particular case.
   (a) Associate interpretations directly with measurements (cheap to implement).
   (b) Develop primitives for querying and asserting parameters whose values vary over time.
   (c) Associate interpretations with pairings of states and measurement ranges.
   (d) Develop a customized set of expectations adapted to the case at hand (expensive to implement).

C3 Will the program be working with input data that have been entered at a variety of different times?

And:

In the course of solving the problem, do events occur that are certain to invalidate old information?

Or:

Is new information just generally more trustworthy than old information?

Invalidating events	Reason explicitly about time or use a truth maintenance system (expensive to implement).
Decay in trustworthiness	Use recenctness of data in conflict resolution or attach "expiration dates" on information.

C4 Will the program be solving a signal-interpretation problem?

And:

Would the data be best described as having a low or high signal-to-noise ratio?

Low S/N ratio	Model-driven reasoning
High S/N ratio	Data-driven reasoning

C5 Is there a series of data-gathering opportunities for each problem?

And:

Does the correct solution remain the same, or change only slightly, between data-gathering opportunities?

And:

Are the data that are available for a problem generally sufficient to uniquely determine the correct solution?

Yes	Maintain only a single, "best" hypothesis between data-gathering sessions.
No	Maintain several candidate hypotheses.

C6 Are there certain data items you do not want to ask for until you have considered other data items? (They might be irrelevant, not crucial, or too expensive to attain.)

Or:

Would it be possible to ask for the same data items for every problem?

Gathering information in stages is important	Explicitly represent dependencies between hypotheses or use "screening clauses" in rules.
Always the same set of items	Questionnaire (cheap to implement).

D. Control of Flow of Inference (aka "What Knowledge Can We Bring to Bear to Solve this Problem?")

D1 Does solving the problem involve transformations between several different levels of descriptions?

Or:

Are several diverse knowledge sources available?

Yes to either	Use a blackboard data structure to record hypotheses.

D2 What kinds of knowledge do we have?

(a) Heuristic rules of thumb.
(b) Constraints that describe or specify an acceptable solution.
(c) Example of problems and their solutions.
(d) Models that describe structure and function.
  (a) Rules whose left-hand sides describe findings of some sort and whose right-hand sides propose solutions.
  (b) The use of constraint propagation or use a theorem prover to prove that a candidate solution satisfies the constraints.
  (c) The use of partial matching.
  (d) The use of causal models.

D3 Is the system solving a diagnosis problem?

And:

Does the system being diagnosed undergo frequent design changes?

Yes   Rely on information about the correct behavior of the system being diagnosed.

No   Rely on information about the incorrect behavior of the system being diagnosed.

E. Inference Types (aka "Details of the Problem-Solving Process")

E1 Do experts typically make an initial guess at one solution, which they then go on to confirm or disconfirm?

Or:

Do they generate several candidate hypotheses and then discriminate between them?

Initial guess at one   Model-driven reasoning

Several hypotheses   Group and differentiate

E2 Will the program be solving a signal-interpretation problem?

And:

Do the human experts look for parts of the data whose interpretation is unambiguous, and having found them, use them to guide the interpretation of adjacent regions where there is more ambiguity?

Yes   Opportunistic search

E3 Does making progress on problems in this domain typically require making assumptions?

And:

Is it possible that the assumptions will only be discovered to be false after many other conclusions have been derived on the basis of these assumptions?

And:

Is there no way to establish a "time limit," such that if an assumption is really false, it will be discovered by then?

Unclear when assumptions will be falsified	Use a truth maintenance system to record dependencies between assumptions and conclusions.
Assumptions revocable only during a well-defined period	Chronological backtracking.

E4 When evidence is obtained that strongly suggests a particular hypothesis, will it be important for the system to immediately recognize the implications of this evidence?

Or:

Will it be acceptable for the system to continue pursuing hypotheses in an order that it had originally scheduled?

Immediately recognize the implications of evidence	Event-driven reasoning (i.e., forward-chaining)
Pursue one hypothesis at a time	Goal-driven reasoning (i.e., backward-chaining)

E5 Is it generally the case that it is relatively easy to guess that a certain crucial step will be required to solve a problem in this domain? (One way to tell that a step is crucial is to ask if you are willing to temporarily increase the distance to your final goal to achieve it.)

Yes   Use means-ends analysis.

E6 Does solving this problem involve a complex looping or branching process, or interacting subgoals?

Yes   Do not use rules, use a procedural language.

E7 Are all the kinds of relationships the program will have to reason about known in advance?

Or:

Will the program need to create new kinds of relationships in the process of solving a problem?

Yes   Use metalevel reasoning to generate new relationships.

F Solution Characteristics

F1 Are all plausible solutions required? (Perhaps because overlooking a possible solution or accepting a less-than-optimal solution leads to costly or dangerous situations.)

Or:

Is just one solution required?

F2 Is it possible to construct a test that can be applied to each candidate solution, such that passing the test is proof that the candidate is a genuine solution?

Or:

Is it possible to construct a test so that failing that test is proof that the candidate is not a genuine solution?

Or:

Is there only a large "gray area" of better and worse candidates to choose from?

Rule candidates in	Use generate and test (if there is an efficient generator).
Rule candidates out	Generate and test, pruning, or confirmation by exclusion.
Gray area	Scoring functions, group and differentiate, or opportunistic search.

G User Interface

G1 Should the explanations that the expert system provides concentrate on accounting for details of the situation under analysis?

Or:

Is it sufficient to get explanations that tell how the program arrived at its answer?

Explain the situation	Causal models or blackboards
Explain the program	Rules (and see question G2)

G2 Which of the following ways of explaining how the program arrived at its answer will be required?

Or:

Rely on the system's metaknowledge about its own reasoning processes to provide an explanation that specifically addresses the case under discussion (expensive).

Or:

Use an automatic programmer to derive a set of rules from a deep model of the domain (expensive).

Or:

Place the information in the knowledge base by hand.

(a) Users will want to know what knowledge was used to reach this conclusion.

(b) Users will want to know why that knowledge was used instead of some other knowledge.

(c) Users will want a justification or explanation of the knowledge itself.

    (a) Backtracing capability.

    (b) Use "canned" descriptions of the reasoning processes (cheap to implement).

    (c) Store and retrieve a text string of justifying documentation (cheap).

G3 Is it feasible for users to request all the available information that is relevant?

Or:

Is it important to make the best use of the limited information that has been provided?

Or:

Is it necessary to weight the potential benefits and costs of requesting particular items of information?

G4 Will the program gather its information from users?

And:

Are there strong expectations on the part of the users that questions will be asked in a particular order?

Request whatever data are available	Goal-driven reasoning (i.e., backward-chaining).
More important to make the best use of limited data	Data-driven reasoning (i.e., forward-chaining).
Weigh benefits and costs	Choose questions according to the impact they are likely to have given the particular reasoning method.

Yes	Separate the questioning strategy from the reasoning strategy.
No	Gather information in whatever order is most convenient for the reasoning strategy.

G5 Will the program's input data come from interaction with users?

And:

Are the inputs that the program requires best communicated by menu selections or short natural-language inputs from the user in response to questions from the program?

And:

Would it be reasonable to expect users to volunteer all the required input data by filling in forms or templates with whatever information they have access to or think is relevant?

Respond to system questions	Goal-driven reasoning
User volunteered	Data-driven reasoning
Mixed initiative	Combine goal-driven and data-driven reasoning

Note

1. Kline, P.J., and Dolins, S.B. *Designing Expert Systems: A Guide to Selecting Implementation Techniques* (New York: John Wiley & Sons, 1989), 219.

Appendix B

Glossary

Acquisition: Accessing one or more remote sites and retrieving digital content.

Activity diagram: A behavior diagram that illustrates the flows among activities and actions associated with a particular object or set of objects.

Actor: A coherent set of roles that an entity (human or nonhuman) outside of the system being modeled plays when interacting with one or more use cases.

Agent: A system that searches for available information and filters incoming information based on specified characteristics.

Artifact: Within the UML, an artifact is a classifier that represents a physical piece of information, such as a model, a file, or a table, used or produced by a software development process. An artifact can also contain other artifacts as part of a composition relationship. An artifact represents the manifestation of one or more packageable elements.

Artificial intelligence (AI): The use of computer algorithms, models, and systems to emulate human perception, cognition, and reasoning.

Association: An association is a static (structural) relationship among two or more classifiers (typically classes). An association contains an ordered list of association ends. An association can have a name that describes the nature of the relationship. A link is an instance of an association. The UML defines two kinds of associations — binary associations and n-ary associations.

Case based reasoning (CBR): A branch of AI that attempts to combine the power of narrative with the codification of knowledge on computers.

Involves extraction of knowledge from a series of narratives, or cases, about the problem.

Class: A class is a named description of a set of objects that share the same attributes, operations, relationships, and semantics. These objects can represent real-world things or conceptual things. A class may realize one or more interfaces. A class can be either an active class or a passive class.

Class diagram: A class diagram is a structure diagram that shows a set of classes, interfaces, or collaborations and the relationships among these elements.

Collaborative tools: Tools such as groupware that enable both structured and free-flow sharing of knowledge and best practices. An example is Lotus Notes® software.

Collaboration: The term collaboration refers to a description of a structure of collaborating classifiers, instances of which each performs a specialized function (in other words, serve some role) that collectively accomplishes some desired functionality.

Communities of Practice: Aka affinity groups. (A) Informal networks and forums, where tips are exchanged and ideas generated. (B) A group of professionals informally bound to one another through exposure to a common class of problems, common pursuit of solutions, and thereby themselves embodying a store of knowledge.

Data: (A) Set of discrete, objective facts about events. Data is transformed into information by adding value through context, categorization, calculations, corrections, and condensation. (B) Facts and figures, without context and interpretation.

Data acquisition: Accessing one or more general databases and transferring data into a problem-specific database.

Data mining: (Also known as knowledge discovery in databases — KDD.) Extraction of implicit, previously unknown, and potentially useful information from databases. The process uses machine learning, statistical correlations, statistical analysis, and sophisticated search strategies to extract data in such a way that the information is easily comprehensible. Then the human can decide how to turn this information into knowledge. The source databases are usually already owned by the organization. Marketing departments frequently used data mining to learn more about customers and how to better market products and services. The skilled knowledge manager will help create database search strategies that enable successful data mining. However, in some ways data mining is the antithesis of what a knowledge manager is trying to accomplish in an organization. A knowledge manager sets up systems to store and retrieve information on a timely basis; a data miner seeks information in databases that was previously underutilized.

Domain: A field or area requiring expertise (e.g., physics, design, or manufacturing). It is often used to refer to the area of knowledge that is the focus of a particular knowledge acquisition project. A knowledge base will usually represent the knowledge in a domain or subdomain.

Experience: Refers to what we have done and what has happened to us in the past.

Expert system (ES): An information system that uses codified tacit knowledge in a knowledge base and an inference engine to solve problems that normally require significant human expertise.

Explicit knowledge: Formal or codified, comes in the form of books, documents, white papers, databases, and policy manuals.

Human capital: The capabilities of the individuals required to provide solutions to customers.

Inference engine: Rule-based algorithms that interact with a knowledge base to draw conclusions about a set of inputs.

Information: (A) A message, usually in the form of a document or an audible or visible communication … meant to change the way the receiver perceives something, to have an impact on his judgment and behavior … it is data that makes a difference. (B) Patterns in the data.

Intellectual capital: Refers to the commercial value of trademarks, licenses, brand names, formulations, and patents.

Intellectual property: Refers to the intangible or intellectual nature of works or creations and the body of laws governing such property; there are six areas of intellectual property: patents, trademarks, industrial designs, confidential information, copyright, and integrated circuit topography protection.

Intelligence: An ability to learn and understand new knowledge or reason in new situations.

IS A: Relation that denotes what class an object is a member of. For example, "Car—is a—vehicle" and "chicken—is a—bird." It can be thought of as being a shorthand for "is a type of."

Knowledge: (A) A fluid mix of framed experience, values, contextual information, and expert insight that provides a framework for evaluating and incorporating new experiences and information. It originates and is applied in the minds of knowers. In organizations, it often becomes embedded not only in documents or repositories but also in organizational routines, processes, practices, and norms. Key concepts of knowledge are experience, truth, judgment, and rules of thumb. (B) Actionable information. (C) A defined body of information … depending on the definition, the body of information might consist of facts, opinions, ideas, theories, principles, and models (or other frameworks) … also refers to a person's state of being with respect to some body of information. These states include ignorance, awareness, familiarity, understanding, facility, and so on. (D) The integration of ideas, experience, intuition, skill, and lessons learned that has the potential to create value for a business, its employees, its products and services, its customers, and ultimately its shareholders by informing decisions and improving actions.

Knowledge acquisition: Eliciting and formally coding tacit knowledge into facts and rules and entering them in a knowledge base.

Knowledge architect: The staff member who oversees the definitions of knowledge and intellectual processes and then identifies the technological and human resources required creating, capturing, organizing, accessing, and using knowledge assets. Architecture is the technology and human infrastructure to support the organization's KM initiatives. It includes physical (e.g., hardware and tools) and logical (e.g., knowledge policies) dimensions.

Knowledge assets: Also called intellectual capital, are the human, structural and recorded resources available to the organization. Assets reside within the minds of members, customers, and colleagues, and also include physical structures and recorded media.

Knowledge audit: The formal process to determination and evaluation of how and where information knowledge is used within the organization. The audit examines policies, forms, procedures, storage, and any other ways that knowledge is collected, stored, and cataloged.

Knowledge base: A database containing tacit knowledge in the form of formally coded facts and if-then-else decision rules.

Knowledge-based economy: An economy in which value is added to products primarily by increasing embedded knowledge content and in which the content value evolves to exceed the material value.

Knowledge bridge: The connection that a KM expert builds between the business processes and the technological-, sociological-, personal-, financial-, sales-, creative-, and customer-oriented functions of the organization. Building a knowledge bridge is the "glue" to make the long-term connections between the functions that sometimes are in competition for resources.

Knowledge content: The meaning that underlies data, information, knowledge, or wisdom.

Knowledge creation: The process that results in new knowledge or organizes current knowledge in new ways to make techniques to use existing knowledge. Once knowledge is created, the organization has a knowledge flow.

Knowledge flow: The way knowledge travels, grows, and is stored. Knowledge flows (A) up and down from management; (B) within circles of sharing (such as shared interests between staff performing similar or complementary roles); (C) through planning, investigation, and training; or (D) through common sources such as books, reports, databases, or knowledge bases.

Knowledge facilitators: Help harness the wealth of knowledge in the organization. Facilitators engender a sense of ownership by those involved, by helping them arrive at a jointly developed solution.

Know-how: The technical expression of knowledge. Examples are the manual and mental skills of a master craftsman or tradesman.

Knowledge interrogators: Aka corporate librarian and knowledge integrator. The person responsible for managing the content of organizational knowledge as well as its technology. They keep the database orderly, categorize and format documents and chucking the obsolete, and connect the users with the information they seek.

Knowledge management: (A) Make an organization's knowledge stores more accessible and useful. (B) A business activity with two primary aspects: (1) treating the knowledge component of business activities as an explicit concern of business reflected in strategy, policy, and practice at all levels of the organization, and (2) making a direct connection between an organization's intellectual assets — both explicit [recorded] and tacit [personal know how] — and positive business results. (C) Conscious strategy of getting the right knowledge to the right people at the right time and helping people share and put information into action in ways that strive to improve organizational performance.

Knowledge map (K-Map): A tangible representation or catalog of the concepts and relationships of knowledge. The catalog is a navigational aid that enables a user to find the desired concept and then retrieve relevant knowledge sources.

Knowledge source: The person, document, nonprint source, or place that is the origin or prime cause of knowledge.

Knowledge object: A physical object used to support knowledge synthesis (e.g., a plant, insect, or rock collection).

Knowledge owner: The person or people responsible for knowledge, a knowledge domain, or set of documents. The knowledge owner is responsible for keeping the knowledge and information current, relevant, and complete. The knowledge owner usually acts at a local or decentralized level. The knowledge owner may or may not be the author or creator of the specific content. The owner may be the expert in the subject area or a skilled editor.

Knowledge processes: Organizational context, human activities, content value, information systems, and IT that are used to add value to content by increasing the amount of underlying processing and depth and breadth of meaning.

Knowledge product: Knowledge that has been adapted to the needs of specific users.

Knowledge production: Acquiring content, transforming it into a higher order of meaning and value, and disseminating it as knowledge products.

Knowledge use: The effective integration of knowledge by people or organizations. It is the result of understanding and application of knowledge and the knowledge gathering process. It is hard to define because it is the result and application of all the terms defined on this page.

Knowledge worker: A member of the organization who uses knowledge to be a more productive worker. These workers use all varieties of knowledge in the performance of their regular business activities. Everyone who uses any form of recorded knowledge could be considered a knowledge worker. Alternative job titles for person in charge of knowledge management: Director of knowledge mobilization, Director of global knowledge exchange, and Senior Vice President of Strategic Knowledge Capabilities.

Ladder: A hierarchical (treelike) network diagram. A ladder can comprise a single type of relationship throughout or have multiple relationships. Some types of ladders include concept ladder, which uses the IS-A relationship and a composition ladder that uses the PART OF relationship.

Laddering: A knowledge acquisition technique that involves the construction, modification, and validation of ladders. It is a valuable method for acquiring knowledge of concepts.

Node: A term used in a ladder or diagram to refer to an element that is not a link (i.e., is a rectangular or other shaped element). Each node can represent a knowledge object in a knowledge base.

PART OF: A well-used relation in knowledge engineering to show the certain knowledge objects (parts) compose a "larger" knowledge object. For example, "Engine—part of—car," "Piston—part of—Engine." In modeling the composition of an object, a "decomposition" ladder (tree, hierarchy) is often used. This uses the PART-OF relation throughout, which acts in a direction from the child objects to the parents.

Relationship: An instantiated relation (i.e., a relation that connects two specific knowledge objects).

Sharing: The human behavior that describes the exchange of knowledge. Sharing and learning are social activities and may occur in face-to-face meetings or via written or visual stimuli. At least two people are required for sharing. Sharing knowledge is a positive activity in an organization. Coveting knowledge is the opposite of sharing.

State: A named condition or situation in the life of an object that lasts for some finite amount of time, during which the object satisfies some condition, performs some activities or actions, or waits for some event.

Swimlane: A pair of parallel vertical or horizontal lines on an activity diagram used to delineate a partition.

Tacit knowledge: Information and skills that are not easily communicated and documented (e.g., expertise, gut feel). An expert may not even be aware they use certain tacit knowledge when performing particular tasks.

Tacit knowledge: (A) Knowledge developed and internalized by the knower over a long period of time ... incorporates so much accrued and embedded learning that its rules may be impossible to separate from how an individual acts. (B) Informal or uncodified ... found in the heads of employees, the experience of customers, the memories of past vendors ... highly experiential, difficult to document in any detail, ephemeral, and transitory.

Use case specification: Defines a sequence of actions performed by one or more actors and the system, which results in an observable result of value to one or more actors. A use case specification always has one main flow of events (also known as a basic course of action and will generally have at least one exceptional flow of events (or alternate course of action).

Use case diagram: A use case diagram is a behavior diagram that shows a set of use cases and actors and the relationships among them.

Value proposition: The logical link between action and payoff that KM must create to be effective. Customer intimacy, product-to-market excellence, and operational excellence are examples.

Appendix C

References

Aamodt, A., and Plaza, E. *AICom — Artificial Intelligence Communications* 7, Sec. 1, 1994, pp. 39–59.

Atherton, J.S. 2003. Learning and Teaching: Tacit Knowledge and Implicit Learning. Available online: http://www.dmu.ac.uk/~jamesa/learning/tacit.htm (Accessed July 5, 2004).

Barbiero, D. 2004. Tacit Knowledge, Philosophy of Mind. Available online: http://www.artsci.wustl.edu/~philos/MindDict/tacitknowledge.html#belief (Accessed July 5, 2004).

Bellinger, G. The Way of Systems. OutSights, Inc., 2004.

Booch, G., Rumbaugh, James, and Jacobson, Ivar. *The Unified Modeling Language User Guide.* (Reading, MA: Addison Wesley, 1999).

Capturing Undocumented Industry Personnel. *EPRI Journal Online*, 2002. Available online: www.epri.com/journal/details.asp?doctype=features&id=389.

Clare, M. Solving The Knowledge-Value Equation (Part One), *Knowledge Management Review* 5 (2), May/June 2002, p. 16.

Davenport, T.H., and Prusak, Laurence. *Working Knowledge* (Watertown, MA: Harvard Business School Press, 1998).

Epistemics. Information on knowledge acquisition. Available online: http://www.epistemics.co.uk/Notes/63-0-0.htm (Accessed November 2002).

Firestone, J. M. *Enterprise Information Portals and Knowledge Management* (Oxford: Butterworth-Heinemann, 2003), pp.204–205.

Fuller, S. *Philosophy of Science and Its Discontents* (New York: Guilford Press, 1993).

Grosso, W.E., Eriksson, H., Fergerson, H., Gennari, S.W., Tu, S.W., and Musen, M.A. Knowledge Modeling at the Millennium. *The Design and Evolution of Protégé—2000*, 1999.

Kline, P.J., and Dolins, S.B. *Designing Expert Systems: A Guide to Selecting Implementation Techniques* (New York: John Wiley & Sons, 1989).

The Knowledge in Knowledge Management. Available online: http://home.att.net/~nickols/knowledge_in_KM.htm.

Leffingwell, D., and Widrig, D., *Managing Software Requirements — A Use Case Approach*, 2nd ed. (Reading, MA: Addison Wesley, 2003).

Merill, M. Knowledge Objects. Utah State University, *CBT Solutions*, March–April 1998, pp. 1–11.

Mitchell, T. Decision Tree Learning, in *Machine Learning.* ed. T. Mitchell (New York: McGraw-Hill, 1997), pp. 52–78.

Nickols, F. The Knowledge in Knowledge Management. *Distance Consulting*, 2003. Available online: http://home.att.net/~nickols/articles.htm.

Novak, J. Applying Learning Psychology and Philosophy to Biology Teaching. *The American Biology Teacher* 43(1), 1981, pp. 12–20.

Novak, J. *The Theory Underlying Concept Maps and How to Construct Them* (Ithaca, NY: Cornell University Press, 1988). Available online: http://cmap.coginst.uwf.edu/info/printer.html.

Novak, J., and Gowin, D. *Learning How to Learn* (New York: Cambridge University Press, 1984).

Noy, N.F., Grosso, W.E., and Musen, M.A. Knowledge-Acquisition Interfaces for Domain Experts: An Empirical Evaluation of Protégé—2000. *Twelfth International Conference on Software Engineering and Knowledge Engineering (SEKE2000)*, Chicago, IL, 2000.

Pitelis, C. *The Growth of the Firm: The Legacy of Edith Penrose* (Oxford: Oxford University Press, 2001).

Rhem, A.J. Evaluating Potential Expert System Applications, *The Professional,* August 1992.

Rhem, A.J. Getting Started in Artificial Intelligence. [revised], IEEE/ACM International Conference on Developing and Managing Intelligent System Projects, April 1993.

Rhen, A.J., & Associates, Inc. Available online: http://www.ajrhem.com/training.html.

Rhen, A.J., & Associates, Inc. UML Based Framework for Knowledge Acquisition. NSF sponsored project, 2004.

Schreiber, A., et al. CommonKADS: A Comprehensive Methodology for KBS Development, in *IEEE Expert: Intelligent Systems and Their Applications* 9 (6), 1994, pp. 28–37.

Schreiber, A., et al. *Knowledge Engineering and Management: The CommonKADS Methodology* (Cambridge, MA: MIT Press, 2000).

Tyler, S.A. *Cognitive Anthropology* (New York: Holt, Rinehart, and Winston, 1969).

Winston, P. "Learning by Building Identification Trees," in *Artificial Intelligence*, ed. P. Winston (Reading, MA: Addison-Wesley, 1992), pp. 423–442.

Index